RICHTER · RON VANDER KELEN · STU VO

MATT VANDENBOOM · DARRYL SIMS · AL TOON ·

S · LAMARK SHACKERFORD · JOE RUDOLPH · TAREK SALE

N STEMKE · JAMAR FLETCHER · WENDELL BRYANT · BROO

ARD · BRANDON WILLIAMS · JOHN STOCCO · JOE THOMA

· SCOTT TOLZIEN · BRET BIELEMA · SIDNEY WILLIAMS · D

R KELEN · STU VOIGT · LARRY MIALIK · DENNIS LICK · E

ARRYL SIMS · AL TOON · JOE ARMENTROUT · PAUL GRUB

RUDOLPH · TAREK SALEH · CECIL MARTIN · MIKE SAMU

DELL BRYANT · BROOKS BOLLINGER · LEE EVANS · ANTHO

TOCCO · JOE THOMAS · TAYLOR MEHLHAFF · TRAVIS BECK

SIDNEY WILLIAMS · DALE HACKBART · DAN LANPHEAR ·

LIK · DENNIS LICK · BILL MAREK · DAVE CROSSEN · DAV

NTROUT · PAUL GRUBER · DON DAVEY · TROY VINCENT ·

MARTIN · MIKE SAMUEL · RON DAYNE · CHRIS MCINTOS

GER · LEE EVANS · ANTHONY DAVIS · DAN BUENNING · J

R MEHLHAFF · TRAVIS BECKUM · LANCE KENDRICKS · JO

KBART · DAN LANPHEAR · JIM BAKKEN · PAT RICHTER · R

DAVE CROSSEN · DAVID GREENWOOD · MATT VANDENBO

WHAT IT MEANS TO BE A BADGER

WHAT IT MEANS TO BE A
BADGER

BARRY ALVAREZ
AND WISCONSIN'S GREATEST PLAYERS

JUSTIN DOHERTY

TRIUMPH
B O O K S

Library of Congress Cataloging-in-Publication Data

Doherty, Justin.
    What it means to be a Badger : Barry Alvarez and Wisconsin's greatest players / Justin Doherty.
        p. cm.
    ISBN 978-1-60078-373-9 (alk. paper)
 1. University of Wisconsin—Madison—Football—History. 2. Wisconsin Badgers (Football team)—History. 3. College football players—Wisconsin—Madison—History. I. Title.
    GV958.U5867D64 2011
    796.332'630977583—dc23

                                              2011017780

This book is available in quantity at special discounts for your group or organization. For further information, contact:

Triumph Books
542 South Dearborn Street
Suite 750
Chicago, Illinois 60605
(312) 939-3330
Fax (312) 663-3557
www.triumphbooks.com

Printed in U.S.A.
ISBN: 978-1-60078-373-9
Design by Nick Panos
Editorial production and layout by Prologue Publishing Services, LLC
All photos courtesy of the University of Wisconsin

To Badgers fans everywhere

CONTENTS

FOREWORD

What It Means to Be a Badger

Anyone who has ever been to Madison for a football game will tell you there is nothing like spending a Saturday at Camp Randall Stadium. The smells and sights and sounds of Badgers fans enjoying their tailgate parties. Everybody dressed in red and white from head to toe. A cool, crisp autumn day in the heart of Big Ten football country. It is flat-out special, and it has been this way at Wisconsin for decades.

Like any college football program, ours has journeyed through periods of triumph as well as adversity. The great 1942 team knocked off top-ranked Ohio State only to see several of the young men on its roster eventually head off to war, some never to return. There was the introduction in 1948 of Paul Bunyan's Axe, to be awarded each year to the winner of our annual game with Minnesota. The "Hard Rocks" defense led the nation by allowing only 5.9 points per game in 1951. Alan Ameche became our first Heisman Trophy winner in 1954. There were Rose Bowl appearances in 1953, 1960, and 1963, the latter, of course, still being remembered as one of the great games of all-time with Ron Vander Kelen and Pat Richter starring in the Badgers' near comeback victory over No. 1–ranked USC.

The program struggled for a number of years in the 1960s, but things slowly began to turn around. Running backs like Rufus Ferguson and Billy Marek, and offensive linemen like Dennis Lick and Mike Webster helped to reestablish the great ground game that has become a signature of our program. Dave McClain took over as coach in the late 1970s and, eventually, guided Wisconsin to its first bowl appearances in some 20 years, with players like David Greenwood, Tim Krumrie, Al Toon, Matt VandenBoom, and many others. Coach McClain then passed away suddenly in 1986, and the program struggled once again.

I was hired by athletics director Pat Richter in 1990. In spite of the program's downturn in recent years, I felt Wisconsin football had potential, and I came in with a plan. I had been fortunate enough to play in a winning program at Nebraska and coach in winning programs at Iowa and Notre Dame. I knew it wasn't going to be easy, but I felt we could have success if we stuck with the plan I had and got the players to buy in. About 50 players left the program in my first year, but we were changing the culture. I wanted tough kids in the program, kids who were passionate and wanted to work hard and believed in what we were trying to accomplish. One of the guys in the program when I got to Wisconsin was Don Davey, a defensive lineman. Don was a senior in 1990, but he was someone I could hold up as an example to the younger players. He was tough, smart, and talented, and he could have started in any program in the country. I thought we'd be all right if we could find some more Don Daveys. Eventually, we did.

Joe Panos, who transferred to Madison from UW-Whitewater, was tough as nails and as good a leader as I've ever been around. He came to typify our program by the time we won the 1993 Big Ten title and the 1994 Rose Bowl. So did Ron Dayne, who came to us as a heralded freshman in 1996. Other schools thought he was too big to be a tailback. Four years, 7,125 yards, and a Heisman Trophy later, he proved himself to be the perfect size for a tailback— a Wisconsin tailback. Our Big Ten and Rose Bowl championship teams of the late 1990s were loaded with toughness, talent, and character. That's a pretty tough combination to beat. Chris McIntosh, Mike Samuel, Donnel Thompson, Chris Ghidorzi, Jamar Fletcher—I could go on and on. Those teams were blessed with great leadership and focus.

We didn't win another conference championship during my time as head coach, but we sure had some great moments and victories and players. I think back to Brooks Bollinger leading us to an upset overtime win against Colorado in the 2002 Alamo Bowl; Lee Evans' comeback from his knee injury to catch the winning touchdown pass against Ohio State in 2003; the great walk-on-to-All-American story of Jim Leonhard; the late fourth-quarter wins at Purdue in 2004 and Minnesota in 2005. And then, to top it all off and end my coaching career with the win over No. 7 Auburn in the Capital One Bowl on New Year's Day in 2006, well, I couldn't have drawn it up any better.

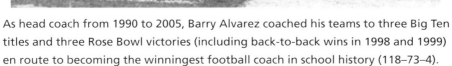

As head coach from 1990 to 2005, Barry Alvarez coached his teams to three Big Ten titles and three Rose Bowl victories (including back-to-back wins in 1998 and 1999) en route to becoming the winningest football coach in school history (118–73–4).

I've spent the past five years as an athletics director watching a young coach navigate his way through the rigors of college football in the Big Ten. Bret Bielema has proven himself to be one of the top coaches in the college game. In just five seasons, he has been a Big Ten Coach of the Year, coached a Big Ten championship team to the Rose Bowl, and accumulated a 49–16 record. I'd also add that Bret's team last season had the highest fall grade-point average on record for a Badgers football squad. Last season was a memorable one in Wisconsin football history, and Bret has the program right where we all want it to be.

As I look at the history of the program and, in particular, the past 20 years that I've been in Madison, something rings true to me. You can't run a successful football program or business or venture of any kind without quality people. They have to have talent, of course, but they also have to have character, passion, and a strong work ethic. Growing up in western Pennsylvania, we were taught to play physical, hard-nosed football. Field position and time of possession were important. That's the way we played at Nebraska, as well. It's a recipe for success that I think has been a perfect fit at Wisconsin because work ethic and physical football are central to the type of game that is played around our state.

You'll notice something as you read the stories in this book. Regardless of when these former Badgers played—50 years ago or last season—there are some common threads running through all of them. First, they love the University of Wisconsin. They met lifelong friends in Madison, on and off the field, and many of them will tell you their college years were the best of their lives. They also, to a man, loved the fans at Wisconsin. They appreciated your support. They also appreciated the opportunity to have been student-athletes at one of the world's great universities and in the nation's best conference.

Wisconsin has been a special place for my family and me. Most of the players I've mentioned here have a good story to tell, and I know you'll enjoy reading them in the following pages because Wisconsin has been a special place to so many former Badgers, as well.

—Barry Alvarez

The FIFTIES

SIDNEY WILLIAMS

QUARTERBACK

1956–1958

I WAS AN ONLY CHILD AND HAD AN UNCLE who was about four years older than I am who used to buy lots of sports magazines. We would sit down and read through them together. I just sort of became a sports junkie. From that, I started playing football out in the streets. The streets were not paved where I lived, so we started there, then we'd go down to a college field about two blocks from where I lived and started playing tackle football. I think around the sixth grade I organized a team called the West End Rinkidinks. We played the South End Bulldogs, the East End Eagles, the Gibbs Wildcats, and the Park Street Alleycats. No equipment or anything, but we scheduled games and we played.

A good friend of mine did have all the football equipment. He had helmets, he had footballs, he had his little football pants, so he started off as the quarterback. I can't remember exactly what position I was playing, but, at some point, it ended up that I became the quarterback. So I continued to play sandlot ball like that until about the ninth grade, and then our team organized a junior high school team, and I started playing there. So there was always that interest in football, basketball, and track. That's really how it all got started. This was all in Little Rock, Arkansas. I started again reading various sports magazines, and, at that time, the Big Ten Conference was without a doubt the most powerful conference in the country, so I decided that I wanted to play in the Big Ten. I did fairly well in high school and ended up getting a scholarship.

I would've been in about 11th grade when I became a starting quarterback, was the leading scorer on the basketball team, and half-mile champion, and I thought at that time I could play in the Big Ten. So I made the choice between going to one of the historically black schools and going to the Big Ten. I had something like 18 scholarship offers. The interesting thing at that time, of course, being in Little Rock, like other athletes of color down South, we couldn't go to any of the major state universities. So the guy I think I can credit with making it possible for big-time and full-time recruiting in the Big Ten was a halfback named J.C. Caroline. He was from Columbia, South Carolina, and he was recruited by the University of Illinois. He had a dynamite game as a sophomore against Michigan. Well, after that, coaches in the Big Ten started going south and recruiting, and some of the Big Ten coaches in their coaching camps included some of the coaches from the historically black schools to come in and serve on their coaching teams. There were a lot of connections made there with the Big Ten—I remember Iowa was one, Michigan State, Michigan. So a lot of those summer camps where some of the black coaches were allowed to participate opened things up for coming to the Big Ten. I think I actually wrote to the University of Wisconsin and just sort of gave an outline of what I'd done in high school. And based upon that, I got a letter inviting me to come up, and that was how I ended up in Madison.

The first summer I went up to Wisconsin I got a construction job, and on that construction team was a guy named Alan Ameche. I had a chance to work with him and, anecdotally, I just remember that Alan couldn't get any construction work done because the kids were all around him asking him this and that. And the construction boss would say, "Well, Alan, you can't be leaning on the shovel all day." I think they eventually let him go, but I think the next day he was working for another construction company. So that was one impression. I had a lot of new opportunities there—being close to Lake Mendota, which is absolutely beautiful. I'd never been out on a dock before, so just going out there and going swimming was new for me. Going out and seeing the football stadium and having a brat for the first time was great. I actually had a steak for the first time—I never had steak before, not a grilled steak. The coaching staff was very nice. Being able to go down, seeing the difference in the way things were integrated there—that made a big impression. It was a beautiful campus, and I met a lot of nice friends. I had some friends of my mother's over in Milwaukee, so I had a chance to go down there and visit them, too. But it was just the enormous size of the campus and all that, that made such an impression. I'd never been on an institutional grounds that large.

I came in as a quarterback. They had three or four on the freshman team, so I played quarterback my freshman year and was actually switched to end the next year. Playing end my second year, I got hurt. I was rushing the passer, and one of the backs threw out an elbow right across my upper arm. It created a calcium deposit there, so they redshirted me after that. Before my second year had started, I set out to do something. When we came back for fall practice that second year, one of the things we had to do is complete the mile run. I won that, and the first notice of me was made in the papers, a small line indicating I had won that. So I got hurt and came back during the spring and continued playing end. I played end through spring practice, came back for fall practice, and was still playing end.

I don't believe we had one quarterback who was over 5′9″ or maybe 5′10″, and, of course, you had to play both ways in those days. One of the things I did was make a very good showing at end on defense. Guards would pull out and come around, I'd go across and sort of knock them back into the ball carrier. One of our coaches felt that none of our quarterbacks were physically able to do a good job at safety, so he convinced the coaching staff to switch me to safety, and that's how I got my start. I started doing very well in that fall practice and easily made the team. Then, of course, later on in that year—it was '56—I became a starting quarterback the last two games. The last two years primarily were split. I had a big battle with Dale Hackbart—we split the time [as starting quarterback] during my senior year.

Back home, at the time, I knew most of the Little Rock Nine. And as a matter of fact, I went back for the 50th celebration of that in Little Rock and saw them all. I don't think they'll mind me telling this, but the Little Rock Nine name is trademarked, and I did the trademark work for them. I heard about all what was going on back there while I was in Wisconsin—it was troubling because I could sit down and visualize it. I can remember when I used to walk to my high school, we walked right past Central High School. As a matter of fact, in grade school, I walked past the all-white grade school, so when I moved on to high school, I walked past Little Rock Central. Those kids really went through a lot of hell. It's just surprising to see some of the reaction that happened there. Central had some good football teams, and a few guys were really good players. It was disappointing to see some of them out there with that rowdy crowd.

The first African American starting quarterback in Big Ten history, Sidney Williams was selected by the New York Giants in the 1958 NFL Draft.

Being the first African American starting quarterback in the Big Ten is something I am very proud of. I'm very proud of the job that I was able to help the team do during that time. I think it was certainly a start to what we're seeing today. It's almost getting to the point where it's not a subject of discussion these days, particularly in the college ranks, and it's even getting better in the pro ranks. It was a great feeling. One thing I can say, truly, during all that turmoil and all the things that were happening, and the fact that I was playing quarterback, I do not recall one racial incident or one racial slur while I was playing. I know that has occurred in other situations, but it never even occurred from our opponents. Even when we played down in Florida (against Miami) and West Virginia. One of the things that really made me feel good was when I went up to Wisconsin during the summer before my freshman year. I went over to the barber shop that generally cut African Americans' hair, and there was a guy there—he was a white man, but he was generally friendly with the guys in the barber shop. We were talking, and I walked in there, and, of course, the guy asked what position I played. I said I played quarterback. This guy told me I would never play quarterback at Wisconsin. So I told him to just wait and see. I never saw him again, at least I never recognized him. I just wonder what his take would have been on that. That was the type of thing that drove me to success, comments like that. Also the fact that I did not want to get cut from the squad and have to go back to Little Rock and tell everyone what happened back in Wisconsin. There were a lot of things that inspired me to do what I did. And, of course, the engineering education was great. It was helpful to me in getting my first job after college and it was helpful in practicing in the area of law that I practiced in.

I do have a real appreciation for the opportunity I had because, after two tries at pro football and getting hurt both times, it was nice to have something to fall back on. After I was hurt in Canada in '59, I was able to get on the phone and call one of the alumni who worked in an engineering company in Chicago. He was able to set up an interview for me, so I didn't have to sit around long after I left the football camp. I had a job and was able to start law school in Chicago, so I can't say enough about the education I had. The professors I had did not allow me to do less than I had to do. They were very helpful to me and somewhat sympathetic to the football schedule.

From the football standpoint, I played with a group of guys who were tough. They were tough-minded, good on defense, very good and very loyal to the team, and never said quit. I think back to our '58 season, that could and probably should've been a Rose Bowl trip. We fought, but, hey, we gave it our best. In terms of the school, you couldn't have asked for more of an academic foundation. The courses were rigid, the professors were very good. You knew that once you came off the football field and once you got out of the classroom, you'd been subjected to the best type of training and school that you could get. That's what I take out of it.

Sidney Williams was the first African American starting quarterback in Big Ten history. He won UW's Ivan Williamson Scholastic Award in 1958. He was selected by the New York Giants in the 1958 NFL Draft. Williams, who lives in Kalamazoo, Michigan, was a highly respected patent lawyer for the Upjohn company. He was appointed executive director of trademarks and domestic patents for the company in 1990. He retired in 1995.

DALE HACKBART

QUARTERBACK

1957–1959

GROWING UP ON THE EAST SIDE OF MADISON, there was a park that all the kids from the east side kind of hung out at, called Ethan Park. I can remember as a seventh or eighth grader, we used to go down there and have pickup baseball and football games. It would be like touch football, only we really played tackle. All my buddies went out for ninth-grade football at Madison East High, so I just kind of joined in. That's basically how I got my start.

I remember the first maybe week or so of practice, I was going to be an offensive end—that's the position I went out for. Claude Hungerford was the coach, and he'd line guys up, and you'd run down the field, and he had a couple of quarterbacks that he had picked out, throwing balls. I'd catch 'em and run back, and in the interim I'd throw the ball back to the center. Then, of course, he'd snap the ball and I'd get in line, get a run, catch a ball and run—for two or three days. Hungerford called me over and said, "How would you like to play quarterback?" He kind of took me back a little bit, but I said, "Sure." So he had me line up underneath center and take a few snaps and get in the rhythm of throwing to my other buddies who were going out for offensive end. He just actually picked me out of the crowd and said, "You're going to be my quarterback in ninth grade." And that was it. That was my start.

My sophomore year in high school, I didn't play at all because we were on the JV squad. My junior year, I played a little bit; I didn't start at all and just was on the team. My senior year was when I really kind of blossomed as a quarterback. After the season was over with, I made the all-city football team, which was a big honor for me. It was Madison East, Madison West, and Wisconsin High. I was selected to the all-area team, which was kind of like southern Wisconsin, including Milwaukee, and then, lo and behold, they picked me as all-state quarterback. Actually, I didn't really have intentions of going on to college. As a matter of fact, with all my high school buddies [doing things together], there were probably six or seven of us who decided we were going to join the Marine Corps. It was during my senior year that Milt Bruhn, the Wisconsin head coach, contacted me and started talking to me a little bit about going to the University of Wisconsin.

I go back to my high school days, my old east-side buddies, we used to sneak into games at Wisconsin and watch them. Minnesota really heavily recruited me, probably more so at the time than Wisconsin did. I went up there probably three or four times; I traveled with my parents and gave them what you would call a verbal commitment—there was no signing, it was a verbal commitment that I'd attend the University of Minnesota. Then my parents got involved. My mom and dad said, "Do you really want to go to Minnesota? Wouldn't you rather stay here in Wisconsin?" Basically, long story short, they convinced me that Madison was the place to be. And actually Milt found out that I was interested in going to Minnesota, and he called me up one day and said, "You need to come down to the university here—we need to talk to you." He got me into his office, locked the door, and said, "I'm not going to let you out of here until you commit because you're going to go to the University of Wisconsin." And that was it. Between Milt and my mom and dad, all three of them convinced me that Wisconsin was the place to be.

I didn't play as a sophomore at Wisconsin—this was when you had to play both ways. I didn't really play a whole lot my sophomore year until basically the last three games of the season. Perry Moss came to me—Perry was the offensive coordinator—and he just said, "I'm going to give you an opportunity to play and start a game." It was against Northwestern. Anyway, I started those three games as a sophomore. We won—we beat Northwestern, we beat Illinois, and we beat Minnesota in the last game. And I think that was kind of the takeoff for my career at Wisconsin. I played in all the games both my junior and senior years. I think that was a real highlight, having an opportunity to play as a sophomore. Looking beyond those years, we actually finished 7–1–1 overall my junior year, but we lost to Iowa, and they went to the Rose Bowl. The other highlight would've been the challenge of coming back the next year in that we had a great opportunity and we won an undisputed Big Ten championship and went to the Rose Bowl.

The 1959 championship team was a strong group of seniors who were really determined to make their mark, having felt as though we basically cheated ourselves the year before. There were a lot of characters on the team. I think everybody really dedicated themselves that year. When you look back at that Big Ten season and the teams in the Big Ten, there weren't any pushovers whatsoever. It was a real battle to go through a full season, especially our senior year, and have to really battle to win every game. And I just think the guys on the team, including the juniors and sophomores who took the lead of the seniors, were all pretty persistent about winning the Big Ten and winning the Rose Bowl.

There were two games that stand out, in particular. The game that really sticks out in my mind is the Ohio State game. We had played Ohio State the year before and tied them. In looking at the films, we had third-and-one and fourth-and-one to go, and Milt decided to go for it both times and both times we scored, but the officials didn't give us a touchdown. It clearly showed on the films that we had scored, and eventually we tied Ohio State 7–7, so when they came into Madison the next year, Milt was really fired up about the whole thing. He worked our tails off and gave us a couple days off—like Thursday afternoon and Friday to get our legs back. That was a real turning point, when we took Ohio State on and beat them in Madison 12–3.

10

Leading up to the Rose Bowl, we had to beat Minnesota in order to be in contention to go to the Rose Bowl, and we did. It was really a neat thing for all of us to get together, for the team, that was our goal, to go out to California and play on national television. There were only four bowl games— the Rose Bowl, the Sugar Bowl, the Orange Bowl, and the Cotton Bowl. The Rose Bowl was the granddaddy of them all. I know, as a kid just watching television with my parents, when the Rose Bowl came on, you watched the Rose Bowl parade and then you watched the game. I remember doing that when the '52 Badgers played in the Rose Bowl and we lost to Southern Cal. So it was an honor for us to represent the Big Ten and go out there and play. Unfortunately, that was probably the worst game we had played in three years.

I also played one year of basketball my junior year when Bud Foster was the coach. I was going to play again my senior year because the new coach, John Erickson, asked me to come back and play, but Dynie Mansfield, my

Quarterback Dale Hackbart led his 1959 team to a Big Ten championship and a Rose Bowl appearance.

baseball coach, wouldn't let me go back and play my senior year. He said I needed to play baseball, so I got two solid years of baseball in also.

I truly made the right decision to go to Wisconsin. Having grown up in Madison, watching the Badgers play and then having the opportunity of having the coaching staff come to you and say, "We'd like to have you play at Wisconsin," it was a great opportunity for me—other than going into the Marine Corps. Wisconsin is a great educational school, and you have to throw in my four years of having a really sound education along with having the opportunity to go out and play. It's a real honor to play at the University of Wisconsin, and I would encourage a lot of young kids who are coming up in high school to stay in state and attend the University of Wisconsin if they have the opportunity to do that.

Growing up in Madison and watching the Badgers play, I think it's a tradition. Being a Badger is a lot of tough work, going to class, participating in athletics, and then participating in your education—it's a big challenge. But it's a challenge that I accepted and I endured, so to speak. It's something you never forget. My heart has always been back in Madison, Wisconsin; I've always been a Badger.

Dale Hackbart quarterbacked the Badgers to the 1959 Big Ten title and the 1960 Rose Bowl. He was selected by both Green Bay and Minnesota in the 1960 NFL and AFL Drafts, respectively. He went on to play professionally for five different teams over a 10-season career. Hackbart, a Madison, Wisconsin, native, currently lives in Lafayette, Colorado, where he continues his long career in sales and engineering with the Bridgestone/Firestone Tire Company.

DAN LANPHEAR
OFFENSIVE LINE
1957–1959

M Y FATHER WAS A COACH IN THE 1940S, moved to Madison in 1948, and became the freshman football coach at Wisconsin, so I had that influence in my life. Also, I don't know if it still exists with the coaching staff, but he had tickets to everything. There were two coupon books that were kept on the desk by the stairway in our house. I had two brothers, so the three of us could go whenever and to whatever event—boxing, football, they didn't have hockey in those days, as I remember. So we got interested because we saw a lot of it. Also, the coaches lived in a neighborhood near Blessed Sacrament grade school and West High School. George Fox was a coach for the Badgers football team, and they had seven children. On Saturdays we used to go to a vacant lot before the game and play touch football. So that's kind of how I started. And then we went to Blessed Sacrament grade school and played touch football there and then on to Madison West.

I played football for four years and track for a couple years at Madison West. Even though my father worked for the University of Wisconsin, he actually thought I should go to Michigan. But there was a cost issue [that kept me from going there]. The University of Wisconsin, in those days, was a wonderful school, and I'm sure it still is, and you could do it for $90 a semester. I have two daughters who went to the university, and it was much more! Today, I don't know how people afford it. But I could work construction in the summertime and make enough money to last me all year in school and pay the tuition. And I worked every vacation doing something. There wasn't much of a choice. I mean, Wisconsin was the pretty clear choice for us because I could live at home and walk to the campus or take a bus for a nickel.

I was a freshman at Wisconsin in 1956. There were 10 tackles on that team, all of whom I thought were better than I was. We wore green leather helmets for the freshmen—that sounds ridiculous today—without a face mask; in order to get a face mask, you had to get hurt. They didn't figure out until later that maybe it could prevent people from getting hurt. So if you broke your nose, you got a face mask. My father was the freshman football coach, so I took a lot of ribbing for that. I was worried about just making the team. Then my sophomore year, Wisconsin started off with a bunch of seniors. Milt Bruhn was the coach, and he didn't like the seniors because they were too self-confident and weren't working hard enough. So he started a bunch of us sophomores. I think he did it to punish the seniors, thinking they would play better next time, but we won the games, we had a winning season, so they just let us play. I didn't think I'd make the team. I played tackle at 222, which in those days was all right, but by today's standards…

14

My junior year I got hurt, so that was pretty much a wash. I got hurt in the Purdue game and didn't play the rest of the year. They didn't know what was wrong, but I think I tore my Achilles tendon. I just couldn't play on it and it finally healed up. My senior year, we were pretty talented. We had Jim Bakken and Dale Hackbart. Hackbart is one of those guys who's never found a sport he's not good at it. Maybe golf. He could play basketball, baseball, and football. He was a quarterback and played offense and defense. He was a tough quarterback. It was hard to tackle him, and he was tall. And, of course, we learned later on that a tall quarterback is good to have because they can throw over the linemen. And Bakken could kick; both those guys had very long careers in sports.

We had a good team. There were four tackles: Jim Heineke, myself, Karl Holzwarth was another West High guy—he was also a kicker—and Lowell Jenkins. In my view, we were all about the same ability. Some of us had different things we could do better, but we were pretty similar. Jim Heineke and I were first-team. The way they played in those days, using substitutions was completely different. We would be in on every play, and I think once a quarter you could change the lineup. I played almost the whole game against Northwestern. I think I was out maybe two plays—every kickoff, every punt

Offensive lineman Dan Lanphear rebounded from an injury his junior year to become a force on the 1959 Big Ten title team.

return. The reason it was that way is because there was a shortage of players brought on by the Korean War. So they had people playing both ways because they didn't have enough players. You had to be in very good physical condition because you couldn't just play a few plays. You'd have people like Hackbart, he could kick, he could punt, he could pass.

The key game in 1959 was the Ohio State game. Ohio State had two running backs. One of them was a fullback named Bob White, and Bob later played for the Houston Oilers, whom I played for, but he was one of those big, tough Ohio State fullbacks. I tackled him, I believe, in the first or second quarter, and he never returned to the game. I'm not sure I know what happened. I've got a film of that game, but it's very hard to tell because of the technology of the day. Then there was another guy—a running back by the name of [Bob] Ferguson who was receiving a punt, and I was the first one down the field. I was going full blast. He probably could've gone one way or the other and I would've flown through the air, but he bobbled the ball a little bit, and I hit him head on and he fell over—we actually both went down. He went back to the huddle and collapsed, and they hauled him off the field. I heard that he had lost some teeth in the crash. I also blocked a punt that was recovered in the end zone in that game. We held Ohio State to a field goal; we only had 12 points, but we beat Ohio State so infrequently at Wisconsin, I don't remember the last time we had. So that was a big deal.

If you watch a game today, with all the technology we have, instant replay and all of that, everyone knows with enormous detail what every player did. When I visited the Houston Oilers locker room, they had machines—computers—that they could look at any player, any play, any situation—it's all computerized technology. But in those days, they didn't have that. I think that was to my favor in that era. It was a rainy day at the Ohio State game, and the film that I have was shot in probably 16 mm by nobody from the football operation, but by the photography department with a single camera. If you had three good plays as a lineman, you were a hero in those days. The rest of them could be awful. People remembered the three plays from that game, and I think that's why I got recognition.

We flew from Madison, Wisconsin, to Pasadena, California, for the 1960 Rose Bowl—most of us had flown maybe two or three times in our lives—on the Purdue DC3s they used to fly us to games. We were the hicks from the country in the big city, and it was sort of overwhelming. The coaching staff was also overwhelmed being on TV shows. It was a disaster. We couldn't have played worse. I do remember the score of that game was 44–8. It was a horrible day. Washington had a quarterback by name of Bob Schloredt, and he was pretty good. Washington was a good team, but we didn't think they were that good. We fumbled and bumbled and made every mistake you could make. In fact, I think I've only watched that game film once. Everything went wrong. I don't remember having a particularly bad day that day, but we had a lot of fumbles. We were outclassed. The Big Ten has always been a little bit three-yards-and-a-cloud-of-dust. We were a three-yards-and-a-cloud-of-dust team like Ohio State.

I look back on my times at Wisconsin as being very lucky to live in them. I worked my way through school. I did not get a scholarship. There were very few scholarships in those days. Some of us had sponsors who would buy us a suit or something once in a while; there was no money in it. But you could get a first-class education for $90 a semester plus books. I thought it was a wonderful city to live in, too. Cities have their problems today, but in those days, man, it was a great place to live. I enjoyed it and have a business degree from the University of Wisconsin business school. I worked for an IBM subsidiary in a computer business my whole life. I took the first data-processing course Wisconsin offered in 1960. It was pretty elementary because the computer hardware in those days was pretty elementary. It was a wonderful experience. You could walk everywhere. The campus is a beautiful place.

I still keep in touch with some of the football players, they've become lifelong friends. I think, from a business standpoint, there are people in the business world who have graduated from the Wisconsin business school everywhere in the country. They have a huge placement of executives. But I think the other thing is, in any team sport, the camaraderie is a big deal. You hear these soldiers coming back from war talking about what happened. The reason they're so motivated is they're trying to save their buddies. I can recall playing on the field with those guys like Tom Wiesner, Dale, and others and thinking, *I'm sure glad I'm on their team.* They were tough people.

Dan Lanphear, a native of Madison, Wisconsin, was a consensus All-American in 1959 and helped lead the Badgers to the Big Ten title and an appearance in the Rose Bowl that season. Lanphear was drafted by the Pittsburgh Steelers in 1960 and went on to play two seasons for the Houston Oilers. He spent his post-football life working in computer services for an IBM subsidiary; the First National Bank of Chicago; and the Ceridian Corporation. He is retired and lives in Barrington, Illinois.

The
SIXTIES

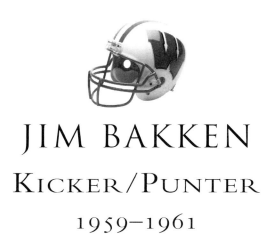

JIM BAKKEN

KICKER/PUNTER

1959–1961

F OR ME GROWING UP, it was the Badgers on Saturday and the Green Bay
Packers on Sunday, of course. Outside of knowing about the "Hard
Rocks," my first real Badgers experience was when our family drove up to
homecoming on whatever year it was—1946, '47, '48 (I was eight years old or
so)—and we saw "Goodbye Harry" signs. I didn't know what that meant, but
it stuck in my memory. Later on I found out it was [then Wisconsin football
coach] Harry Stuhldreher being vilified, if you will. Then the "Hard Rocks"
caught my attention, and the Badgers went to the Rose Bowl in 1953, and
that was when we bought our first TV. Our family bought the first TV so we
could watch the Rose Bowl. Without the Rose Bowl, maybe we wouldn't
have had a TV for a couple years. Beyond that, it was the game against Indiana in the snowstorm, in the early 1950s, where we sat in the south end zone
at Camp Randall and you could barely see the game. Wisconsin had red uniforms on; otherwise, you really couldn't see the players because the snow was
so deep and blinding.

I had a friend when I was in ninth or 10th grade, and we used to sneak into
the games when John Coatta and Jim Haluska were playing. We would wait
for the band, which was practicing in the north practice field, and the band
would then march in, and we would kind of maneuver ourselves in among
the band members. And of course the students would say, "Yeah, come on in
here," and that's how we would sneak into the games. But my interest in

football was really kept high by the Green Bay Packers. The Packers had a fullback named Fred Cone, who was also the place-kicker, and they had a quarterback by the name of Tobin Rote. I always wanted to go to a Packers game down in Milwaukee.

My first experience playing football was in the ninth grade at West High in Madison. Fred Jacoby had taken over as the head coach at West from Willis Jones, and I think he recognized that I had some skills because he put me on the varsity squad as a sophomore, and it was really a senior-dominated team. There were three of us who, as sophomores, got a chance to play. He put me down as the holder for place-kicks, and Karl Holzwarth, who went on to play for Wisconsin, was at West. He was two years older, and he was the place-kicker, so I was the holder on place-kicks and also played in the defensive secondary. I earned a letter as a sophomore. As a junior, I was selected as the quarterback; we all played all the positions. As a senior, our team was really good. They didn't have a state tournament then, but we were undefeated. So we were probably listed as the top team in the state. My first contact with the Wisconsin coaches was between my junior and senior years when Milt Bruhn and Deral Teteak took me out to lunch. They said they had been interested in me and so forth. There was always this notion that if I played football, it would be at Wisconsin. I only grew up a mile from Camp Randall and had a nice side yard near Monroe Street and on Saturday would see the cars going to the game, so it was just one of those natural things. I had a chance to maybe go to other schools, they contacted me my senior year, but it was basically Wisconsin, that's for sure.

21

Our system in high school was kind of a roll-out belly series, which was the precursor to the three backs and the option offense. It wasn't a dropback passing thing, but Dale Hackbart was the senior quarterback when I was a sophomore at Wisconsin. The rules were so goofy then, it was two-platoon football, you had to play both ways. And it was wild-card substitutions where whole teams had to go in. At any rate, my sophomore year we won the Big Ten thanks to a senior-dominated team. I was the backup quarterback and played some defense. Karl Holzwarth was the place-kicker, and I did some punting. I also played baseball at Wisconsin. The coaches weren't very happy going into the spring practice after my sophomore year, since Hackbart was going to graduate, that I wasn't going out for spring football because I was playing baseball. That didn't sit well with the coaches because I was the one who had the most experience as a returner. I did play baseball my sophomore

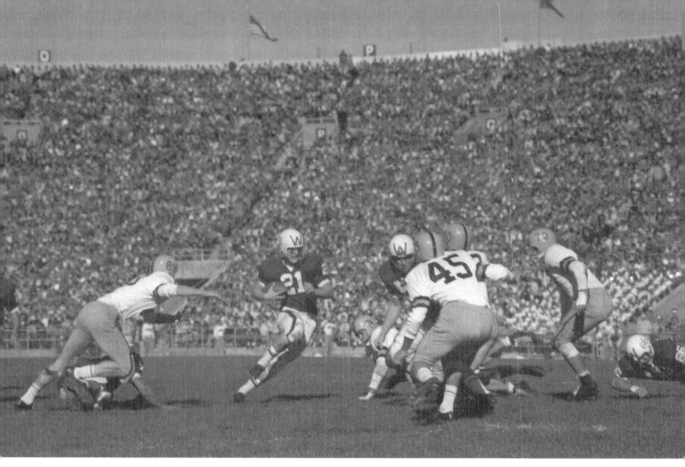

Jim Bakken served as backup quarterback his sophomore year but excelled as a punter/kicker. He twice led the Big Ten in punting average (1960 and 1961).

year and then didn't play baseball the rest of my career at Wisconsin because of spring football and my commitment to the football program. The difference between the systems my sophomore year and the next two years—when Pat Richter came on board and they had some good offensive ends—was that we went to a passing attack. My skills weren't in the passing area, I was more of an option quarterback, so I ended up playing mostly on defense my last couple years and did the place-kicking and the punting.

Milt Bruhn, our coach, had a thing with Ohio State during my senior year. He always felt maybe there was someone spying on our practices the week we played the Buckeyes. So I told our trainer's son that we were going to have some fun with Milt one day. I said to Mo Bakke, the trainer's son, "About halfway through practice, get a hat or a coach and go up on the north edge of the stadium and kind of peer over the top of the stadium and leave the rest to me." And, sure enough, I looked over at the top rim of the stadium as we were practicing in the north end and there was Mo—he'd gotten some field glasses and he had this hat, and he was peering over the edge and looking down at practice. I kind of walked over to Milt and said, "Milt, don't look now, but I think someone's spying on our practice." "Where is this?" Milt asked. "Well, look up there at the north end," I said, and there was Mo Bakke up there looking in. It was all put on. I don't know if he ever knew it was me, but that was a good laugh.

There were a couple of memorable games. Personally, there was a game down at Northwestern, I was the backup quarterback and did the punting and so forth. I had a good game, and a highlight was a 90-yard punt that kind of turned the difference in the game. I also had a 46- or 47-yard field goal and intercepted a pass for a touchdown. Then I threw a pass to Pat Richter, so that was fun. I was named the Midwest Player of the Week, so that was probably my best game. Then the last game of my career was at Minnesota. They scored late, and they were trying to tie the game with a two-point conversion. I was playing defense and was able to get a hand on a pass in the end zone to knock that down and preserve the victory for Wisconsin.

23

It's hard to compare what we did back then to what the players have to go through today—the off-season training. When I played, it was, when the season was over, we'll see you in the spring. There was limited weight-room experience, so it was more of a seasonal thing. I'm just amazed right now at the amount of commitment that players have to make to be as good as they are now. And back then players could play other sports—Pat Richter played three sports and I played baseball one season, but you don't see much of that anymore. In my case, I was able to place-kick and do some punting, and I caught the eye of the Rams. Plus the roster sizes when I played in the pros early on I think it was 37 or 40 players, but the more you could do as a player, in my case punting and place-kicking and play a little defense, that allowed me to get drafted by the Rams.

I guess I took it for granted that I'd play football at Wisconsin because in high school we had a good football team, and why not just move on to, as they say, the next level. And Wisconsin was right there in Madison, so it wasn't a big deal. You just move on to the next level and compete. You'd see new players coming in from Illinois and get acquainted with a player from Ohio or St. Louis, and you say, *Well that's fine, we can compete against these people.* It was something that kind of just happened. And then Richter and Steve Underwood came on from East High School, and there were several players from West, Dan Lanphear and Karl Holzwarth, who had moved on to Wisconsin. So there was an experience of players who were like me, if you will, who moved on to Wisconsin and played Big Ten football, so I never gave it a thought. This is what we do! Play football and move on. Thinking about it today, the players traveling around the country getting recruited by all the big schools—I never took a visit to anywhere else. I remember a couple schools were kind of serious about wanting me to come down and visit, but I was going to play down Monroe Street, right down there at Wisconsin.

I think the pride in playing for Wisconsin has really gone up since I played there. I think when we played, the exposure of Wisconsin nationally, ratings weren't as prolific. You kind of concentrated on the rivalries between Minnesota and Ohio State and Iowa. I guess those were the three—Michigan wasn't that good when I played—so I guess you kind of took all those things for granted. Back when I was playing in St. Louis in the pros with players from Michigan and Ohio State and various places, they'd say, for example, "I'll bet you a hamburger on Ohio State." We had good teams back earlier on, but there was that lull. Then when Barry and Pat took over and did their thing, the pride really started to swell up because you knew you played at the same place, the same stadium, traveled to the same places—Iowa City and East Lansing and Columbus, etc.

The friendship I developed with Pat Richter was a highlight, too. He and I were roommates on the road my senior year, and I obviously followed his career up through the business world and was able to work with him and for him during the 1990s, when Barry and Pat and the rest really turned the program around. That's something that's really satisfying, that Pat had the confidence in me to add me to his staff. I thank him for that every time I can.

Jim Bakken, a native of Madison, Wisconsin, twice led the Big Ten in punting average and served as a Wisconsin team captain in 1961. He was chosen by the Los Angeles Rams in the seventh round of the 1962 NFL Draft and went on to play 17 seasons for the St. Louis Cardinals. Bakken later became an administrator in the UW athletic department under director of athletics and former teammate Pat Richter.

PAT RICHTER
END
1960–1962

IGREW UP ON THE EAST SIDE OF MADISON on a dominant block in the neighborhood. Gary Messner was about five doors down and was an offensive lineman on the '53 and '54 teams. I was eight or nine years old, and he'd bring some players to the house and say, "Hey, so-and-so's coming over"—Paul Shwaiko or Ameche or whoever—and we could come down and get autographs. My father played football at Madison East, and he was a good football player. He was all-city and was going to go to the university, but he lost the sight in his eye and didn't go. But he was a very solid player. I supposed that's how it started. He never pushed, but we had a great neighborhood, a lot of young kids who played football and some older guys who were willing to let us play if we could come close to their abilities. I think that probably is the biggest learning experience if you have the chance at eight or nine years old to play against guys who are four or five years older than you are—faster, stronger, bigger. Unless you got close to what they were doing, they wouldn't let you play. So you had to really force yourself. I played tackle football, no pads, things like that, and everybody had a nickname. It was a lot of fun. That was probably the biggest learning experience. It was nothing organized. We never had any organized football until ninth grade, and that was when we first started with pads and things like that. And, of course, you listen to the Badgers games and Packers games and you'd go out and play on Sunday afternoons. It was just what you were supposed to do that time of the year. As little kids, we kind of focused around the Wisconsin football team. There was just a lot of local involvement with the players, and I think that's what kind of spurred us into sneaking into a game and things like that. It was just part of growing up.

In ninth grade you played against the city teams, West, Central, and Wisconsin High, and I was playing tackle at the time. Between my sophomore and junior year I was moved to end, and that's where I started to catch passes and develop a little interest. So I started receiving a lot of letters. I remember getting a letter from Navy's Steve Belichick, Bill Belichick's father. I never thought much about it because it was basically just letters at that time, or somebody would call. I remember the Air Force Academy was interested. And then basketball, that had generated some more interest and, I think, between junior and senior year I was selected on the *Parade* All-America second team. Bill Raftery—we still laugh about it—we were on that same All-America team. So that began the recruiting process and then, of course, I played baseball in spring, so I didn't really start football at East until I was a junior. I was about 6'3", 210 as a sophomore, then I was about 6'4", 215, then 6'5" 225 as a senior. So you get a lot of interest. At that time it was more or less size and weight that generated interest and letters.

I actually was thinking that I enjoyed baseball. I really thought, as a professional sport, baseball was more well-known. So I really hadn't thought of playing football in college. I was recruited by Kansas—Dick Harp was the basketball coach there and that was one visit I did take. They had Wayne Hightower and Wilt Chamberlain, and I look back on it and think what a crazy time that was. Now, looking at what the recruiting process is, I actually went to Kansas—they never even took me into Allen Fieldhouse, and I still signed a letter of intent to go to Kansas to play basketball. Then I talked to a friend of mine, Gene Calhoun, who told me I'd be better off playing baseball in the Big Ten than the Big Eight. So I changed my mind and decided to come to Wisconsin. At that time you didn't really do a binding type of letter, it's more or less you signed a piece of paper. At that point, we sat down with John Erickson and decided to accept the scholarship to Wisconsin.

I really hadn't intended to play football, but as they got into that time of the year, it was kind of ingrained into you that, now it's time to play football. I had a basketball scholarship and I hadn't talked to anybody about playing football. So I bumped into one of the football coaches somewhere downtown and said I'd like to go out for football but I didn't know if the coach would let me do

Though he led the nation in receiving as a junior, as a player Pat Richter (88) is perhaps best known for his involvement in the Badgers' 1963 Rose Bowl fourth-quarter comeback and almost-victory.

this. So they basically went to Erickson and asked him if he minded, and he agreed as long as I kept up my grades. I went out for football and played end and defensive end. Pat O'Donahue was one of my coaches. I really enjoyed playing defense at that time. So then we went through the normal process of football. I was freshman cocaptain with Dale Matthews, who ironically had left school during our Rose Bowl year and ended up marrying my sister years later. Then in spring I played varsity football because you couldn't play baseball as a freshman. So at that point you just had to go out for spring football.

Looking back, a couple things stand out. My first year, I only played four or five games and three plays and then I broke my collarbone—I caught a pass at that time, tied a record for the number of passes in a season, and broke my collarbone. I didn't play the rest of the season. A fellow I knew, Brad Armstrong from Janesville—we played against each other in high school—was on the freshman team. When we were sophomores, his girlfriend knew this other gal, Renee, and I had wanted to meet her. I asked Brad to tell Renee to meet me at the drugstore. I went to the drugstore, and she came in. I introduced myself to her, and she looked at me like, "Who are you?" Brad hadn't talked to her, so it was kind of a cold call, and I just backtracked a little bit. I think the team was away that next week and the week after. I also bumped into another gal I dated once, and I forgot that I'd given two tickets to both her and Renee, so they were sitting next to each other at the Michigan game. After the fifth play, or whatever it was, I broke my collarbone catching a pass and went to the hospital. Renee had gone to the hospital to see me and found out I was Lutheran. She was, too, and she didn't know too many Lutheran boys, apparently. We had seen each other occasionally before that time, but nothing serious. Then we started dating, hanging around, going to movies, and things like that. It's a true story. But for the fact that I gave them both tickets, it might've turned out differently.

And then the next year as a junior, Ron Miller was a good quarterback who liked to throw the ball, and so he and I kind of hooked up. The highlight of junior year was the last game of the season we played against Minnesota. They were going to the Rose Bowl, and we played up there. On the first play of the game, Minnesota had the ball, Sandy Stephens under center looked out, and Tom Hall was out there waving at him. There was nobody out covering him, so he threw it out to him and went 80 yards for a touchdown. But we ended up beating them. At that point I think it kind of gave us an idea that maybe we had a pretty decent team.

The next year, they tried to get another year for Miller, but it didn't happen, so we really didn't have a quarterback. Hal Brandt was a sophomore, and Ron Vander Kelen came back and he probably would have today been considered a fifth-year redshirt or something. We still didn't know what kind of team we had until we beat New Mexico State 69–13; we scored a lot of points. I can remember as a senior it was fun, we got to be on the same page, and they would actually let us call a formation, and I could call the pass pattern. So it was great. You look out and think you might go for a touchdown or something and it would work! We could call our own plays, and I think a highlight was when we played Northwestern and beat them pretty good. So we started getting recognition, although being ranked No. 1 and No. 2 wasn't a big deal back then. It just was not like it is today. Even when we played in the Rose Bowl against Southern California, no big deal.

Of course the Rose Bowl in '63 was a great experience and, I think, looking back on it years later, the thing I take away from that is invariably people look at it as the epitome of what sport is—people say what a great game it was. They really don't care who won or lost, nobody would say who won or lost, they just say, "What a great game," or, "Remember that?" When we got to the 1994 Rose Bowl, Barry and I met Tommy Lasorda. Barry walked up to Tommy and introduced himself and then mentioned my name. Tommy went on about the 1963 Rose Bowl. It just was one of those things, something people remember.

I think what it means to be a Badger has changed over the years. Initially, with some of the early years around the Badgers and the Rose Bowl, those are the kinds of things people really hang their hats on. But obviously it is a great school, great education. Then there were times when things were pretty tough when, what it means to be a Badger, you try to probably keep quiet. But around here now, it means pride. A graphic example came in '89–'90. A lot of guys weren't wearing their football letter jackets, they were embarrassed, people were making fun of them at the grocery store and things like that. And I think you can appreciate athletics more now and the importance it plays and how people look at the university, even alums. And I think that's why Donna Shalala made the moves she made [with the athletics director position]. It was very strategic. It wasn't just change for change sake. Now you have a chance to hold your head up high and be proud of Wisconsin for all the reasons, not just because it's a great academic institution, but because they have a good, solid program and success that's nationally recognized. I think for participation, the pride is just being in that fraternity of people who represented the university. Now, I think we put more emphasis on the wins, losses, all that kind of stuff. Back then it was a little different, I think, just because of the proliferation of the media, television, much more emphasis on that. We've lost a little of what we had back then—the experience was a little bit more, I don't want to say pure, but it was a little bit more defined and you kept it closer in. Now it's become a little bit more exposed with everybody in terms of what's going on.

When I got to school, I received a letter from Betty Schreiner, Dave Schreiner's sister. I had been selected for a scholarship, a Schreiner scholarship, and it was pretty neat because she said even though she had never met me, her brother would be very proud, and it seemed like I had some similar characteristics to Dave. That was kind of the first time you really started to think about what you've done, what it means to be a Badger, the legacy.

Pat Richter is one of the most decorated athletes in Wisconsin history. A three-sport letter-winner, he led the nation in receiving as a junior. He was a consensus All-America end in 1962 and helped lead the Badgers' legendary comeback in the 1963 Rose Bowl. Richter played eight years in the NFL after being a first-round draft choice of the Washington Redskins. He served as UW's director of athletics from 1989 to 2004, overseeing a revival of the school's athletic program. He lives in Madison, Wisconsin.

RON VANDER KELEN

QUARTERBACK

1962

I GUESS AS ANY YOUNG MAN GROWING UP, you think of football, baseball, basketball, hockey—I tried them all. I just played a little bit with a lot of friends in the neighborhood and, when I got to the high school level, I just decided I'd go out for the team. I never really knew what position I was going to play or what I was going to do. The school I went to, Green Bay Preble, had a really good quarterback who transferred there. So they made me the third-string quarterback because I was a good basketball player and that way I wouldn't get hurt playing football. Well, it turned out I started the first game, and we went undefeated for three years.

Playing in college was always a dream. I always followed on the radio—at that time they didn't have many games broadcast, but I always followed the Wisconsin Badgers on the radio and tried to stay interested. But Wisconsin never called me in for an interview, so I only had a couple options for college. Then all of a sudden I got a call just before I had to make a decision where I was going to go to school, and they asked if I'd come down because they wanted to talk to me about enrolling at Wisconsin. That was always my dream, so I went right ahead and did it and skipped the other schools.

Preble High School was a small school with about a couple hundred kids in it. It had just started up as a brand new school. When I got to Wisconsin and saw how *big* it was in Madison and all the people, I was overwhelmed. I had never been to a Badgers football game and I had never stepped foot on the campus. But I had said that I wanted to go to college and I wanted to learn something. I grew up in a family where nobody had ever gone to college. As a matter of fact, most people didn't even graduate high school from my family. For some reason or other, I just wanted to go and play. I wasn't looking to be the world's greatest star or anything, I just wanted to play and get an education. They offered me a scholarship, and I grabbed it.

My freshman year, we were ineligible to play at that time—no freshmen could play on the varsity team. When I arrived for the first day of practice my freshman year, I think there were, like, 13 quarterbacks on the team. They had posted on the board, and I went down the list and found my name listed as No. 11. So I got into practice, but that was about it. We had scrimmages and all, but I hardly even got in to play. By the end of my freshman year, they took a lot of those quarterbacks and made them receivers or running backs or whatever, or they dropped out. My sophomore year was the year Wisconsin went to the Rose Bowl, it was the '59 season and the '60 Rose Bowl. I ended up being third-string quarterback. Dale Hackbart was No. 1, Jim Bakken was No. 2, and I sat there. I got in one game at the beginning of the season against Marquette as a defensive safety. I played 90 seconds and then, obviously, I was on the team so I got to go to the Rose Bowl in 1960, but we lost pretty big. Then in 1960 I had a really good spring practice, but in the last scrimmage of the season, I blew out my knee. I got tackled as I was running the ball, and the guys hit me from the side and blew out my knee. I had to have knee surgery and so was out for the 1960 season. I still was in school, but I couldn't play and couldn't practice that season. Then in '61 I had a good spring practice. My knee recovered, and I was able to play again, but I had some trouble academically and had to sit out a semester. So I sat out the fall semester of 1961 and then came back to school in January 1962.

If it wasn't for Milt Bruhn and the staff—and in today's world this wouldn't happen—they would've dropped my scholarship. Somehow he must have had something in his mind that I might be a good quarterback. He kept me on scholarship all the way through this time. We started out with about six or seven guys competing for quarterback, but I just had a tremendous fall training camp as a senior in 1962. Milt made me the starting quarterback, and every game we got better and better, and it ended up being a great season, but it still was a heck of a lot of work. At that time, which most people forget, you had to play on both sides of the ball. It was quarterback on offense for me, and I played safety on defense. You were playing not quite

Quarterback Ron Vander Kelen was named Big Ten MVP in 1962, his only year starting at Wisconsin.

60 minutes a game. They could only put in substitutes one or two at a time, and so they kind of picked out different guys they knew were going to do well on defense. In a lot of cases, I played probably 80 or 90 percent of the game on both sides of the ball.

I remember our last game of the regular season. Minnesota had a great team. They had one of the best defenses in the country. We went into the game knowing it was going to be a bitter battle, and it ended up being worse than that; it was just a dogfight. We struggled very much against the Minnesota defense, but in the last couple minutes of the game we were able to put together a drive, scored a touchdown to go ahead, and that eventually won the game. But we still had to kick off to Minnesota, and they drove all the way down the field. Luckily, one of our defensive backs picked off one of the passes and we got the ball down on about our 10- or 15-yard line, and all we had to do was run out the clock. Coach Bruhn just wanted me to run quarterback sneaks so the clock would run. Unfortunately, on my second quarterback sneak, one of the Minnesota guys hit me right in the mouth with his elbow, knocked out all my teeth, broke my nose, shattered my face mask, so I had to leave the game. Somebody else came in and took the snap, but we won the game.

As for the Rose Bowl in '63, for every kid in the upper Midwest—and I think it's still true today—the goal of all football players is to get to the Rose Bowl. That was a dream, and I think we were "wowed" with the surroundings and everything else. That was the first time in the history of college football that the No. 1 and No. 2 teams ever faced each other. So we knew USC was good, they were undefeated. We got on the field, we were very competitive with them, but we made a few mistakes and got down in the game, and then all of a sudden, it looked like USC was going to blow us out of the stadium. I don't know what it was, I don't know how it happened, but when we got into the huddle at the start of the fourth quarter, we were pretty much embarrassed. I know I was. We'd got embarrassed in 1960, I didn't even play, but it was Washington that just kicked our butts all over the place. We just said, "We've got to do something. We're a good team, let's just get this thing going, try anything we can." Nobody gave us a strategy from the sideline, all they did was support us. For some reason, I can't tell you what it was, I just decided passing was the only way. We threw on almost every down in the fourth quarter. Nobody told me to, I didn't come up with this great idea, but it was working! So all of a sudden, we scored one touchdown, and I looked in the eyes of everybody in our huddle, and the intensity they had was the highest level of intensity that I saw in any game we played that fall. As it kept going and we kept scoring, these guys were so excited and the huddle was so focused. Nobody talked, they just listened. And whatever play you called, they executed and did really well on it. It was just amazing to have that feeling and be part of that type of team. And, you know, we lost the darn game, but I think everybody was proud of the effort that we put into it.

Pat Richter was my safety valve. And I think if you asked him, the one thing he'd probably tell you is, every time I was in trouble, I'd yell for him. I'd yell, "Pat!" and he all of a sudden appeared somewhere downfield, and I got the ball to him. Why, I don't know, but he has always told that story. I'd scramble trying to get out of a pass rush and just started yelling, "Pat!" and he'd just show up somewhere. He just knew exactly where to go, catch the ball, and get us out of trouble. He was very reliable. He didn't have great speed, but he was tall and, if you got the ball near him, he was going to catch it and find a way to get open. He was just a lifesaver for me.

I don't get tired of talking about it. How can you get tired when people recognize your name, they recognize the University of Wisconsin where you played, and want to talk about it? How could you ever get tired about talking about a game that was so classic? At that time you never saw comebacks like that. You never saw that amount of passing and scoring. It was something very unusual. You get letters from people all over the country saying, "Thank you, you brought us memories we'll never forget." I still get sometimes two or three letters a week where people want my autograph or comments. I get people who call up wanting to do interviews, radio and TV people and things of that nature. It makes you understand that, whatever it was, that game was a classic in college football because people remember it. Everybody participated in that, so I'm not just talking about myself and Pat. The way we played and what we did got the hearts of a lot of fans out in the United States.

I didn't come from a well-to-do family. I had a dream of being able to do something other than some of the menial work that you're forced into when you don't have an education. I wanted a college education and a chance to play football. That chance was given to me, and I did whatever I could to take advantage of it. It's something I will cherish for the rest of my life. The guys I played with, they were a great group of guys, we all got along very well together. Just the experience, especially with the highs and lows that I had trying to get to my senior year, with being out of school and the knee injury and all the other things, to be able to just hang on that long and still be given that opportunity and just having a fabulous season was something I'll never forget. That was one of the greatest years of my life. What happened was like a miracle, and I don't know why it happened. But being able to play with those guys, to be the quarterback on the University of Wisconsin football team was, at that time, one of the greatest joys of my life. My experience at Wisconsin, both in education and in the athletic world—they both had ups and downs—but I wouldn't change one single thing.

Badgers fans are loyal for life. I've run into them in my business career all over the country. They are so proud to be graduates of the University of Wisconsin, and I fall in that category, too. I'm very proud. That's a tough school—you could still have a lot of fun there, but you just don't get grades—you've got to work hard to get grades and graduate. I was able to make it and am just as proud of Wisconsin and being a graduate of the University of Wisconsin as I think everybody is who went there.

Ron Vander Kelen's one year as the starting quarterback at Wisconsin was a special one. He guided the Badgers to the 1962 Big Ten title and a berth in the now legendary 1963 Rose Bowl game. Vander Kelen was the 1962 Big Ten MVP. He was a 1963 draft choice of the AFL's New York Titans, but ended up playing five seasons with the Minnesota Vikings. His post-football career included work in advertising and marketing, as well as in college admissions. He is retired and living in Edina, Minnesota.

STU VOIGT
TIGHT END
1967–1969

I DIDN'T START PLAYING ORGANIZED FOOTBALL until ninth grade or so. My memories of football were that I was not a big kid very early on. I'd say average, but nothing led me to believe that I was going to be a real big guy, so I was more of a baseball and basketball player in the schoolyards. And we played the old touch football games. I remember getting interested early with the Packers and with the Lombardi teams in the late 1950s and early '60s, and they had some success. I always wondered if I was going to be big enough to play football because I always thought all the really big guys played football, but I didn't really get my growth spurt until after ninth grade. I weighed 140 pounds and then got a spurt and, as a sophomore in high school at Madison West, I was a little over 6′ and probably 208 to 210 pounds, so I was big enough. I literally shot up three or four inches and 40 pounds in a year. Then all of a sudden I was having some success, and football became equal to—but never really surpassed—baseball. Lo and behold, because of my baseball I developed a strong arm and was involved in track and field and won the state title in the discus and shot put. I actually set the national indoor record for the shot put. So I enjoyed football, but it was one of three. As I got more and more involved in football and competition and the physicality of it during high school, that's when I really started to enjoy it.

Some of my fondest memories of Badgers football games were that it was a dollar to get into the games, and you sat in the end zone and watched the likes of Dale Hackbart, Pat Richter, and Ron Vander Kelen. Saturday morning usually there was some high school football and there was what was called Four Lakes football over at Madison West, so I watched that and we got a dollar and went down and watched the Badgers play football. And they were good that year or two, so that inspired me. The crowds were wild, and Badgers fans were rabid, and, as I said, the fun people had at football games and the spirit of the Badgers and all the accolades that go along with winning appealed to me. I just assumed then that, boy, I wanted to be part of that sometime.

I was a halfback in high school and then kind of a linebacker, but I was a running back, punt returner, and kick returner. I was recruited playing running back—of course, freshmen were not eligible in college in those days. I was a running back in my freshman year, and my sophomore, junior, and senior years I switched to kind of a variant of a tight end. Of course, that's what I did with the Vikings. But I was always a guy who was handling the ball, running with it, or catching passes—that's what I did best. I always was known for being pretty well coordinated and could catch the ball, so I did that for the main part of my football career.

When I got to high school, Milt Bruhn was the Badgers' head coach and the guy who recruited me. They were not having success. They weren't poor, but they were just in the middle of the pack after those great Rose Bowl years in '59 and '62. I was heavily recruited not only for football but, having been kind of a big track-and-field guy, I had all kinds of offers. I sort of looked for greener pastures, I thought, and took some trips and had my choice of a lot of different schools. I was reluctant to commit to the Badgers at first, but my dad was at the DNR [Wisconsin Department of Natural Resources] at that time working in a state position, so recruiting was different and the governor actually could come over to your house and sit in your living room and talk. I was a little bit reluctant, but through the different recruiting I realized that it really had been a dream of mine to play at Wisconsin, so I signed a letter of intent.

I do look back, but it's kind of tough. You go in as a freshman. Milt Bruhn was still the coach in 1966, but he got fired after that. I couldn't play freshman year, but we had a somewhat highly touted freshman class, and we had a couple of freshman games—we played Illinois and Michigan and won those games. I just assumed the program would get back into the upper echelon of the Big Ten. I fully intended to play football, baseball, and track, and that was kind of what swayed me to come to Wisconsin, that guarantee. I was on the

As the Big Ten's last three-sport athlete, Stu Voigt earned a total of eight letters in football, baseball, and track.

freshman track team, so I couldn't play baseball, but went to spring practice. Then my sophomore, junior, and senior years were not good, we did not win football games. With that, it wasn't a lot of fun playing football. Some of it I'll blame on the campus uneasiness. It was a changing time with Vietnam and all that, and football was kind of de-emphasized, there was so much happening on the campus. I think it took away from football and, looking back, took away from some of the recruiting. My coach was John Coatta. I guess I was maybe naive, but as a freshman going into my sophomore year, we just assumed we'd be winning games and, maybe not winning the Big Ten and going to the Rose Bowl, but be very competitive. That didn't happen, and it was very disappointing. Finally, my senior year I could see things were getting a little bit better and we were playing better. So I've got to say, even today, that it's very disappointing to play in front of your hometown fans and your family and friends and not be successful, but I think in retrospect it made me better in my pro career because it made me hungry.

My senior year, we were so close, everything that could go wrong did go wrong for a couple years, but you could see that the talent was better. We knew that John Coatta's days might be numbered, but the team was better, so we had a feeling it was going to come. When, you didn't know. We'd been snakebit for a number of years, a number of games we'd find different ways to lose. But when success finally came against Iowa in '69, it wasn't a fluke, it was a game we deserved to win, and the fans reacted. You didn't want to turn it into too much of an out-of-body experience because it was just one win and we didn't have a winning season, but it sure felt good for the fans. Then we had a couple more wins against Indiana and Illinois. That was something of a consolation for a couple hard years.

It's cliché, but you get out of a sport or you get out of football what you put into it. It's a lot of hard work, and some of these things, the harder you work, the better you become. So I'm proud of myself and proud of my teammates because we kept working hard and kept trying to get better every year. I think from sophomore to junior and junior to senior years, the improvement was there. The determination and the discipline, you can only take care of yourself. Your teammates have to do the same thing. And maybe we didn't have enough talent or the coaching wasn't what it should be, but nonetheless, I'm proud of the fact that you realize that there's a work ethic that goes into anyone being successful, and I had that. You could either take it and kind of lie down, or you can take it and say, *I'm going to get better. This isn't going to get me down, I'm going to build from this.* I really found when I got done playing at Wisconsin that I was a better man and certainly a better football player.

I was playing three sports at Wisconsin, and the other two sports went just fine. I was the Big Ten's last three-sport guy. I got eight letters and couldn't play baseball because I was required to play spring football my sophomore year. I always had track, and I did play baseball my junior and senior years. I wanted nine letters to match Pat Richter, but that's the way it went. The Badgers were Big Ten champions in track every year, and I went to the NCAAs [for track] as a sophomore and played baseball and was the leading hitter and all that. That was fine, but obviously football was my main interest. I was a little bit of a "tweener" in that I started as a tailback, then was kind of a fullback, wingback, and then, because a different offense got put in, kind of a tight end. That was totally new, and I was a little bit undersized, even in those days being just a shade under 6'2″ and about 225 or 230 pounds. I was a little small for a tight end, but I thought I'd give it a try. I had confidence. I had gone against and seen first-hand some of the great players in the Oklahomas and the UCLAs, so I felt I could play at that level. If they were going on to the next level, then so was I. When you go to training camp with that kind of confidence and willingness to work hard and do what it takes, well, I was eager to play more football after college, let's put it that way. I wasn't ready to give it up; I started to really love the sport and didn't want to quit after my senior year at Wisconsin.

I've stayed very close to the program. Being from Madison, I think I grew up with it. Not just the football, I watched when the Badgers beat Ohio State way back when Ohio State had that dream team, so I'm a sports fan, something of a historian of Badgers sports. I always see how the Badgers are doing. It was always my dream, and guys from high school are still friends of mine today, and we're Wisconsin graduates, as was my mother and father and sister. So we're Badgers through and through. I made a point to meet all the coaches, broadcast the games for WIBA there for some eight or nine years with Paul Braun, so I've been involved, and that's kind of fun. I'm a Badger through and through even though I live in Minnesota and my wife is a Gopher. I keep track of all the sports and have gotten to know all the coaches and especially treasure some relationships.

I grew up wanting to be a Badger. I went to Badgers practices for football, basketball, and baseball. Going to West High, growing up on the west side of Madison, I was literally a couple miles from Camp Randall, so I remember going to games even before high school, collected programs after the game, then I'd run all the way home thinking about the Hackbarts and the Richters. I think it was always my destiny to be a Badger. I wanted always to be good enough to be a Badger in one of the sports. I kind of went through the process of looking at different schools and I had the choice of different schools, but it was in the back of my mind. When you grow up with it, and it's so ingrained—my parents were season-ticket holders way before I got there and way after I got there. That's just what you wanted to be.

Stu Voigt, a native of Madison, Wisconsin, was the Badgers' team MVP in 1969 after leading the team with 39 catches for 439 yards. He was a 10th-round pick of the Minnesota Vikings in the 1970 NFL Draft. He played in three Super Bowls during an 11-year career with the Vikings. Following his pro football career, Voigt worked in banking and real estate. He is retired and living in Apple Valley, Minnesota, with his wife, Linda. He has a daughter and a granddaughter and serves on the board of directors for some area businesses.

The SEVENTIES

LARRY MIALIK
TIGHT END
1969–1971

I STARTED PLAYING FOOTBALL IN THE 10th GRADE. I was always too big for those little league games, not that I'm that big now, or ever was, but I guess I was a big guy when I was younger. So I really didn't start until I was a sophomore at Clifton High School in Clifton, New Jersey.

Clifton High School was pretty much a powerhouse team back in the day. On the East Coast, particularly in New Jersey, there really wasn't a team that you followed in college. There was, of course, the state team, but it wasn't much of a power at that time, and people were either rooting for Syracuse or Penn State. High school football was played on Saturday mornings. Kickoffs were usually at 11:00 in the morning, as hard as that is to believe. I know *Friday Night Lights* is pretty famous, but high school football was pretty big, and it started probably at 10:00 so people would get home for the college game of the day. There wasn't a freshman team, and my high school was a really large high school—we had around 3,300 kids in the 10th, 11th, and 12th grades—so it was a pretty big deal. And everybody wanted to be a Clifton Mustang.

I was a halfback, a pretty big halfback. We dressed, for the first day of football camp, easily 160 or 170 guys. There were two other guys who contributed as sophomores, and we averaged probably about 190 pounds back then. I remember being in line in the backfield line to go get a rep, it's funny, about 15 deep. I never thought I'd get a turn at it. After a little while, apparently I showed something to the coaches—all three of them, I might add, coaching 150 kids—and I started to get a little playing time.

Neither one of my parents was college-educated; they were both factory workers, and college was not on my radar. I didn't give it a thought. I played in the same conference with Jack Tatum, who later went on to star at Ohio State and in the NFL. In my early childhood, Jack probably lived about two blocks from me. I lived in Passaic, where he went to school. I went to Clifton High School, and he went to Passaic High School, and we played against each other in his senior year. The game decided the state championship in New Jersey, and we won 7–0. I knew he went to Ohio State, but, still, it wasn't on my radar. After the high school season was over my senior year, I started getting letters, and coaches were showing up at the school. It wasn't something I was aware of, and it kind of took me by surprise. And the recruiting process was all a surprise to me! Getting on an airplane, going to visit a college, it was like a fantasy!

I remember my visit to Wisconsin perfectly well. It was January 1968. I had just been down to North Carolina, actually at Wake Forest, the week before and came out to Madison. It gets cold where I grew up, but not Wisconsin cold. I came out to Wisconsin with a raincoat with a lining in it. I got off that plane and it was 10 below zero and there was snow everywhere; I'd never seen anything like it. I remember asking Roger French, who was my primary recruiter, if it was always this cold. And, of course, he said no. I got to Madison late on a Friday night, and it was dark and I didn't know what was going on. So I got to the Edgewater Hotel, and, when I opened up my drapes in the morning, it was blinding white! I was looking at Lake Mendota, but, I remember saying to myself, *What is this field? It's the biggest field I've ever seen!* At breakfast someone told me that it was Lake Mendota, and I started to think maybe it is cold here more than they led me to believe.

45

I can't say that I came to Madison and saw Wisconsin beat Ohio State on a 70-degree fabulous October day, having beaten the No. 1 team in the nation. My decision to attend Wisconsin was probably a combination of things. Quite frankly, I realized back in those days you could sign more than one letter of intent, but only one in a conference. I signed with Wake Forest down in the ACC and I'd signed with Wisconsin and a few other teams in other conferences. I just don't know what it was about Wisconsin. I got recruited pretty hard. Back in those days alumni could make contact, and Alan Ameche called me, and different alumni from the area would call. Of course, Alan Ameche was fresh in my mind, even in '68, because I remembered watching as a little guy the Giants game, the 1958 NFL championship game where he scored that winning touchdown. I'd like to say that it was, "Wow, what a great academic institution, the weather was terrific," you know, but none of the above. I went to the UW Field House, I remember, and watched a basketball game. I thought that was pretty exciting and got a flavor for "On Wisconsin" and "Varsity," and that was pretty impressive and kind of got to me from an emotional standpoint. These people were really into their team. My final decision to come to Madison? It's still a mystery to me to this day.

I remember when I came to Wisconsin, obviously from a media standpoint, it was just a different day and age. I knew "On Wisconsin"—I knew they'd been to Rose Bowls, I knew it was a Big Ten football school. I thought the facility at the time was awesome. And, of course, it was awesome for the time. We didn't really have a weight room or study center or any other terrific center that all athletes get to take advantage of today, but I can remember woefully thinking, *What am I doing here?* Being a blue collar guy from New Jersey with a couple of factory-working parents, I didn't get the whole protest thing, and it was all kind of news to me. I came here and thought, *Am I missing something, or are these people crazy?* Quite frankly, I was starting to feel that a little bit, but I became more comfortable with, *Well, if this is Madison, it's a multifaceted kind of a place. There's a lot of diversity in the way people think.* Once I got over that, it was kind of all engines on go.

We struggled our first years. In 1969, when we broke that long losing streak, it was against Iowa at Camp Randall and, rumor or truth, they say that they drank State Street out of beer! That was a pretty big turning point. Stu Voigt was a senior that year, and I also came here as a fullback and got switched to tight end, which at the time, I really wasn't altogether that happy with. It was such a complete change for me. Well, John Coatta, who I really thought was a terrific guy, got fired. So the coaching staff that brought me in, they were gone.

Coach [John] Jardine came in and, with all due respect to every staff that's ever coached here, put together one of the greatest staffs ever: Paul Roach, who went on to coach in the NFL for years and years; Charlie McBride, who was at Nebraska with Osborne for all those years; and Bob Zeman, who played here, coached with the Raiders and the Broncos, and played in the NFL. There were some really top-flight guys whom John brought in, and I think the light switch went on for me—I remember the first touchdown that I caught was against Texas Christian. It was a 50-yard touchdown, and I thought, *Oh, this tight end position is not so bad.* Then, of course, we went on

Tight end Larry Mialik set a school record for average yards per reception (21.3) in 1970. He went on to play professionally for Atlanta and San Diego.

to beat Penn State. It's been written about many times, and I had a big game where I caught a couple touchdown passes and had more than 140 yards in receiving, and we beat Joe Paterno and, boy, that was a highlight! One thing I kind of take pride in is that team, not just myself. The next year we played against an LSU team that had an All–American named Tommy Casanova, and that was the first time that Camp Randall had ever been sold out since the upper deck had been built. We turned the corner and came to believe we could win again.

I joke that it only took me three terms to graduate from Wisconsin: Nixon, Ford, and Carter. But I did graduate! My older sister wasn't prepared for college, but she ultimately graduated from college. I had an uncle who, after World War II, went to college on the GI Bill, and of all the immediate family, uncles and aunts, he was the only one. So it was a pretty big deal for me, no question about it.

After my pro career was over, I didn't really know what to do or where to go. I remember I told my wife that, for me, the safe harbor is Madison, let's go back to Madison; I don't know what I'm going to do, but let's go there and see what happens. And, of course, I've been in Madison since 1980. I think what I find most interesting, now that I'm starting to get a little long in the tooth, is what great memories fans have. Maybe it's generational. But I've been here for a long time, and it amazes me when someone says they remember me. It's been a welcoming place for me; it's changed a lot in the last 30 years, but it's still kind of the same. The atmosphere of a Camp Randall weekend, going to the Kohl Center, watching the Badgers play hockey or basketball, the Union Terrace. You come to a school like this and, for me, it was hard to leave. I've never not been a part of the University of Wisconsin, at least in my mind. My wife's father played for the 1942 Badgers. Then, of course, I came along. And then my son came to Wisconsin and played football. Once a Badger, always a Badger!

48

Larry Mialik was a first-team All–Big Ten tight end in 1971. He was selected by the Atlanta Falcons in the 1972 NFL Draft and played four seasons with the Falcons and San Diego Chargers. Mialik, whose son, Matt, later played for the Badgers, was also on the crew of *America³* when it captured the 1992 America's Cup.

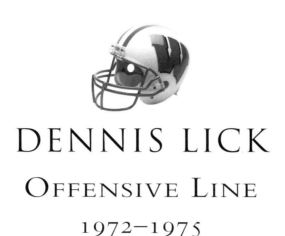

DENNIS LICK
OFFENSIVE LINE
1972–1975

I STARTED PLAYING FOOTBALL BACK IN GRAMMAR SCHOOL and, actually, I'm the head coach there now, where I used to play, at St. Mary Star of the Sea in Chicago. It's on the southwest side by Midway Airport. In fact, I built a house and live right next door to where my mom lives, where I was born, so I'm still in the same neighborhood. I played in seventh and eighth grades, and we weren't very good at the time, but we have Catholic League schools, and it's kind of a feeder program for all the Catholic schools in the area. Back then they could give scholarships to high schools. St. Rita's saw me play and liked me, so they gave me a scholarship, and I went from St. Mary Star of the Sea to St. Rita High School in Chicago.

I was a lineman as a kid. These days, since I've been coaching, we're in a different league, and there's unlimited weight as far as linemen go. When I was there, you had to be 135 to go out to be a back, but in seventh grade I was, like, 170. I figured I weighed 174—if you were over 175 you couldn't play. In eighth grade I went out and played basketball and had to keep my weight down. I got taller and slimmed down, so I was actually 173 in eighth grade. I just made it, but was able to play.

Our freshman team in high school was very good and went undefeated, but the varsity was 0–9. Then a new coach came in, Pat Cronin, who was a legend in Chicago. I started as a sophomore, and I think we were 4–5. Then, by my junior year, most of the guys I played with as freshmen were starting,

49

Offensive lineman Dennis Lick was a first-team All–Big Ten lineman in 1974 and 1975 and was a consensus All-American in 1975.

and we had to win the last game to make the playoffs. We made a run and won our final games to win the Catholic League and play in the Prep Bowl, which in Chicago was the big thing. Back then they only had the three TV stations, but it was on Channel 2 in Chicago, and there were, like, 70,000 people in Soldier Field. Somehow we made a run. We had lost to the team that won it the year before, Loyola, 35–8 about three weeks before. Then we beat them in the Catholic League championship and then played them in the prep bowl, which, again, was the big thing to play in. And we wound up winning that championship. They didn't have a state championship, it was a mythical state championship then; there weren't state playoffs yet. That was The Game—it was Catholic versus public, they'd done it for 50 years. After that we started getting recruited. The rules are a lot different today. When I was playing, you could see the guys as much as you wanted. Actually [Wisconsin assistant] Charlie McBride started recruiting me as a junior. He became good friends with the family and kind of lived at our house. He'd come from a Wisconsin game and got to be good friends with the family and spend the night. So, from my junior year on, they recruited me. Then the following year we were ranked the top team and had everybody coming back. We went undefeated, went to the Prep Bowl, and won the championship again.

I started getting recruited by almost every school in the country. I guess I was the top pick in the state or whatever. I started to look at different schools. I remember Woody Hayes came in, which was unheard of back then—he just stayed in Ohio and Pennsylvania, but he came, and my high school coaches were all excited because he was kind of a hero. So they were all excited, telling me, "Oh, you've got to go to Ohio State!" Back then, you could visit as many schools as you wanted to. I was playing basketball also and on the weekends would go to different schools and take a look. I narrowed it down to Illinois, Colorado, and Wisconsin, finally, at the end. I always wanted to stay in the Big Ten, close to home so my family could see me, so that eliminated Colorado. I remember the one time Bo Schembechler came to see me, and Charlie McBride from Wisconsin was out with my dad the night before and was sleeping in the other bedroom. Charlie walked out and said, "Hey, Bo!" and Bo looked at me and said, "We don't have a chance, do we?" And I said, "No." I kind of always knew. First, it was close to home. Second, the Wisconsin head coach, John Jardine, was from Chicago, Charlie McBride was from Abilene Park, born and raised, so there was a Chicago connection. A lot of the kids there were from Chicago, and it made a lot of sense. It was a tough decision. You've got so many people calling you all the time. I remember talking to Coach Jardine when I was at the Founders' Day here in Chicago, and he told me that, at some point, I'd need to make a decision, and this might be a good time. I walked up there at Founders' Day and committed to him, so everybody was happy in Chicago. That's kind of how I came to Wisconsin.

I came to Wisconsin the first year freshmen were eligible to play, and they really didn't know what to do with kids then. I was the main guy and was a pretty good player, and they moved me up immediately. But they still had a freshman team back then. The next year they just put everybody together and eliminated the freshman team. I was on the varsity immediately, which was kind of a difficult thing because one other guy came up—it was Duane Johnson, I believe—he was up there too, and we were sort of in limbo; we weren't freshmen but we weren't part of the varsity. The freshmen were playing their own games, so it was kind of a difficult situation. And for the four years, the freshmen went through a different thing than I did, so I didn't quite get to know them as well as I would've liked to. But that's why they switched it the next year, and everybody played together the whole time.

My junior year was definitely a high point. Wisconsin is a great place to play. I was there in Madison when just a few years before they didn't win a game. The attendance was way down, and then John Jardine came and kind of brought the fans back. We always had 70-some thousand there, we were always competitive. We lost some tough games, but we got better and, in our junior year, we beat Nebraska, we lost to Michigan by just four points, we were right there. We seemed to turn the corner there. We were 7–4, but there were no bowl games except the Rose Bowl back then for Big Ten teams, so we didn't get to go to a bowl game. We had great expectations for our senior year, but unfortunately we opened up with a Big Ten game, against Michigan. I wish we'd had a chance to play a few games before that. We started out with a senior quarterback who had not played much—Dan Kopina—he didn't lose the game [on his own], but it was a tough game to lose. We were inside the 20 a bunch of times and only scored two field goals. Losing that first one, you're kind of in trouble when you can only go to one bowl game. They made a switch to a freshman quarterback who was more athletic, but he wasn't really ready, and we lost a tough game at Missouri that we could've won. The season kind of went downhill; it was a disappointing year for us. We were 4–6–1. We were expecting big things but, unfortunately, it didn't work out.

It was great to play with guys I grew up with. Terry Stieve was from Chicago, he was in the Catholic League and went to Gordon Tech. Of course Billy Marek and Joe Norwick started and were from St. Rita. And when I was a senior, we had my brother on the team, and Joe Lerro was also from St. Rita. We had a lot of kids from the Catholic schools back then. We still see each other and are still friends today.

Wisconsin is obviously a great school. When I was recruited, Michigan and Ohio State wanted me pretty badly. But John Jardine said he was trying to turn things around at Wisconsin, and I'm disappointed that, unfortunately, we couldn't quite do it. I think maybe we started something there, brought it back a little bit. But I think you could see that if we could start winning, people would get behind it and support it. There are great people in Wisconsin. That's always the No. 1 thing any place you go—it's the people, it's not the buildings or anything. Wisconsin people are great people, the fans, it's just a wonderful atmosphere, and I'm just glad they turned it around completely and are one of the best programs around now. It's kind of hard for me to get back to Madison for games because I coach the grammar school—we usually play Saturdays or Sundays or I've got practice on Saturdays. I haven't been there in about three or four years. But, sometimes if I don't make the playoffs, I'll stop back.

I think the people in Wisconsin are tough, hard-nosed people. I love the way the Badgers play now, and that's how we played. The offense is similar to that, run the ball, throw the ball a little bit. But it all comes back to the people. With St. Rita, I talk to kids and try to get them to look at Wisconsin, look at the people, the alumni, the people who have been a part of it. Things have changed since I was in school there, but they're still great people, very loyal, with Midwestern roots, which I have and which I really enjoy. I've been very fortunate to stay in the area, the Midwest, which I love. I love Wisconsin, I came back to play for the Bears, and everything worked out. I wish we could've done better during my college years, but I think we kind of helped in our little way to bring winning football back to Wisconsin.

53

Dennis Lick was a first-team All–Big Ten lineman in 1974 and 1975 and was a consensus All-American in 1975. He was a first-round selection of the Chicago Bears in the 1976 NFL Draft and played for the Bears from 1976 to 1981. He still lives in Chicago and, in addition to coaching grade school football, works as a freight broker.

BILL MAREK

Running Back

1973–1975

I FEEL THE SAME WAY I ALWAYS HAVE, that Wisconsin football has always been about hard-working, diligent, disciplined people. It's never been high-flying, all about speed, all about deep passing. It's about just a tough work ethic, you just keep coming on every play and you try to execute. You're not fooling anybody. You are who you are, and I just love that style of football. As you go through and look at your life, that's what you'd like to be—hard-working, disciplined, and making sure that you take care of your business every day. It's a pleasure watching it.

Where we lived in Visitation Parish, on the South Side of Chicago, there was a maybe 30-yard-wide boulevard, a big strip of grass, down the middle of 55th Street (also known as Garfield Boulevard). We played football there all the time when we were kids. And then everybody in the neighborhood, of course, did play grammar school football. My brother, Glen, was four years ahead of me, played football in high school, and I kind of followed.

A guy I went to grammar school with and I actually walked on our fresh-man year of high school. At that time, most of the kids were being recruited on scholarship. They really can't give football scholarships anymore, but myself and a friend both walked on—he played quarterback on our fresh-man team, and I played defensive cornerback. I think we were the only two in the starting lineup who walked on, and everybody else was on scholar-ship. At the end of our freshman year, the head coach on the varsity was let go, and the varsity didn't win a game after they let him go. I came in at spring ball and at some point moved to fullback. When we came back in the fall, I was actually the third- or fourth-string fullback on the varsity as a sopho-more and, of course, Dennis [former Wisconsin All-America tackle Dennis Lick] was starting. As that year went on, it was the second or third game, we were getting trounced by Loyola and, at some point in the second half, they stuck me in at fullback, and I had a nice long run for a touchdown. They moved me the next weekend to tailback, and from there it just worked out.

When we were juniors, there were a lot of coaches coming around, espe-cially to see Dennis. And we wound up having a good junior season and win-ning the city championship. More coaches were coming around. Coach McBride from Wisconsin was around a lot. And, of course, going into our senior year, there were a lot of guys on the team who were getting heavily recruited. We had known Coach McBride the year before, and he was just a great guy, just our kind of guy.

Our high school really prepared us. We had a tremendous program. We had winter workouts right through, just basically weight-training workouts, and you went right into running track and spring ball, where we had 30 days of solid practice. When you had a break at all, we wound up having doubles and triples. Junior and senior year, we went away to training camp in the summer for 10 days. One year we were in Holland, Michigan, at a seminary, then the next year we were at St. Joseph's College in Rensselaer, Indiana. We were on one side of the room, the Chicago Bears were on the other. It was really serious football. It was very tough. They worked us hard, so when we got to Wisconsin, we were used to really difficult workouts and a lot of time involved, so I think we were well-prepared.

Rufus Ferguson was a senior at Wisconsin when I was a freshman and, being it was the first year freshmen could play, there really just wasn't a lot of that. That opportunity may or may not have developed, but Rufus was a senior, and he was tremendous. Just getting to know him was fun. There weren't a lot of people behind him. I think the guy behind him hurt his neck, so there was a little bit of a void, and I think there may have been an opportunity—I was on the sophomore team at that time, on the JV squad. At one point I was traveling with the team, but they only put me in for one play, and it's kind of tough to come off the bench on a cold day in the fourth quarter, so that didn't work out. And that was really the only chance I had.

55

Running back Bill Marek's 44 career touchdowns still rank second in Wisconsin's record books.

We had a great group of guys. You look across that list, Terry Steive, Dennis Lick, Mike Webster. When we were sophomores, there were just so many great linemen, John Reimer and, of course, Joe Norwick from high school. You had Jack Novak one year at tight end, the next year you had Ron Egloff and, of course, Larry Canada and Mike Morgan—you can go on and on. We had a lot of great offensive players who went on to play pro football, so we had the really powerful offense. In fact, I think at one point, it just seemed that we had a great opportunity to score in every game. They were all good guys.

You can see it pretty much every year at any level of football, as you go through the year, your timing gets better and better. You look at Wisconsin, even in 2010, running the ball the last few games as opposed to the first few games, you see how all the timing's working, and the backs at that point start to read the blocks a little bit better and have a little more patience. It just comes as the year goes on. And it was pretty much the same when we were in school. Today you have incredible facilities for conditioning, gaining weight, and getting faster and all that. When we played, it wasn't that way. At that time, a 255-pound guy was still a big guy. You get a big guy like that who can run, it's not that much different than today. There are a lot of similarities. Basically we were a little bit lighter, but the movement and everything was pretty much as it should have been for that time. So as the season goes, if you've got talented guys who can run on the line, they can do a lot of things. Our guys were that way, Steve and Dennis and Webster and all those guys, they were very mobile. And you see that today the same way. It's just a matter of, as the year goes, that timing just improves.

57

At the time, or even now, you look at it, and it was just a great opportunity we had to move the ball so well on the ground. We could throw the ball well enough that it would keep the defense backed off. Gregg Bohlig was an accurate passer. We didn't have much of a roll-out game with Gregg, he was more of a drop-back passer, but he was very accurate. We also had good receivers—Artie Sanger and Jeff Mack, we had a bunch of them. So we had enough of a pass threat to keep the DBs back, and with that, as we had a lot of talented linemen, you start rolling along, they get in sync, and good things happen.

I remember being on the bench with a guy when I was a freshman, we were at a road game, and he looked at me and said, "You know, we've never won a road game." I almost fell out of my chair, *Are you kiddin' me?* I had no idea. You come into a program when you had just left a high school that all we did was win, and now your team is down and struggling like that—you just can't let that bring you down. You're there to win ballgames, you're there to get better. If you contribute in any big way, that's a bonus. So I never really considered or thought about that. I just felt like every chance we had to play a game we could win that game. We felt when we finished our junior year that we really had something special going. Our senior year was a disappointment;

we had lost Ellis Rainsberger as the offensive coordinator, we lost Gregg Bohlig, so we were a little disjointed, and I don't think we ever got our legs underneath us our senior year. We expected so much more. I think if Gregg could've come back our senior year, it could've been as good if not better than our junior year. We really felt like we left the program in good shape. Add a couple of key pieces, and we'd have been rolling.

When you're in college, you're kind of in the moment and not thinking about a long-term perspective. When you first get out, for a number of years you're so ingrained with your family and children and your career that you don't think about it. But as we start to get along and kids move on and you have a little more time to enjoy free time, you start reflecting more on all the guys you knew back then, whom you played with. Heritage Hall [inside Camp Randall Stadium] is a wonderful place because it's a nice room where we can all gather and say hello to guys we haven't seen in years and years. I go there every time I go back to a game at Camp Randall now. Every time we go, it seems like there are more guys coming back. I think Barry [Alvarez], Pat Richter, and Coach Bielema are all very much aware of the program's past, reaching out to us and having us get more involved, and it's great. There were many years that went by that we weren't as connected as we are today, and I think it's just wonderful now.

Serving as honorary captain of the team for the Northwestern game in 2010 was fantastic for me, and I don't know that anybody other than myself would realize at this point that I received so many emails from guys whom I played with, whom I hadn't talked to in years and years. So it really keeps that cycle going of bringing back a lot of the guys who have been somewhat disconnected. All of this is fantastic. As you start to age and reflect a little bit because you've got a little more time to do that at home, you're fairly well set in your career. I sat with my wife recently, and we looked at each other and just said, "Wow, this is really incredible. How lucky are we to be involved with such an unbelievable program?"

Bill Marek left Wisconsin as the school's career rushing leader and presently ranks fourth on the list with 3,709 yards. His 44 career touchdown runs still ranks No. 2 at Wisconsin. Marek currently lives in the Old Town neighborhood of Chicago and is president of a sales agency called The Competitive Edge.

DAVE CROSSEN

LINEBACKER

1975–1978

W HEN I STARTED PLAYING FOOTBALL in Rhinelander, Wisconsin, it was never with a leather football, it was always with a rubber football that was half-deflated. I really kind of grew up on a lake, and my mom taught in Rhinelander, just a small community, a family environment. For me, it was the Green Bay Packers and listening to Earl Gillespie and wanting to be a Badger. Football was big up there, with Jim Moore and Brad Jackomino, who also came down to Madison with me and played from Rhinelander. I also really fell in love with basketball and was recruited by John Powless and Dave VanderMeulen when Bo Ryan was down here as sort of a teaching assistant. That's how it all started, but football became really great after meeting the folks at Wisconsin. They brought us in as a package, the three of us, not just one of us.

I think I wanted to go to Wisconsin partly because Mike Webster played there. Our high school didn't have a winning tradition. We kept getting beat by Antigo High School, so we wanted to develop a history, and we beat them for the first time in 13 years, and that's when Jackomino and Moore and myself got named to some all-state teams. That was my senior year. We came through and won the league title. That's also when Mike Fixmer was play-ing. With Mike, we actually had four people from Rhinelander, a little town whose high school program was never very good, eventually starting at the UW, so that was really cool. LaVern Van Dyke actually helped recruit me. He was an older gentleman who was a defensive end coach and just like a father figure. That's what was so cool about the John Jardine era. I had never been to a Badgers football game. I was hunting, fishing, trapping—stuff that northern guys would be doing. Sports weren't my only thing. I never thought I'd be good enough to play at Wisconsin.

When I got to Madison, it was a huge culture shock. It was like when I joined the Atlanta Falcons and Tommy Nobis was introducing himself to me. He came up and grabbed me, his hand wrapped around my hand twice. That was the culture shock in Madison. Coach Jardine already had Dennis Lick, Billy Marek, Terry Stieve, and Ronny Egloff. Those guys went to the pros, to Super Bowls, and were No. 1 draft picks. I thought, *Wow, what am I doing here?* But after getting to know some of the people and really going after it, things just became second nature. It was just lucky that I was around good people.

I remember the Purdue game in 1977. I remember when they gave me the game ball because nobody would look at the stats—that was kind of a running back thing to do. Jardine's thing was, when he came, he wanted to be fast and light, and he picked me, as did Charlie McBride, who went and coached at Nebraska under Tom Osborne. But they had designed a defense that would accommodate me, and they were looking for a person like me or Steve Wagner from Oconomowoc, a driving force on defense, to be quicker and faster. That was kind of their game plan. It wasn't I who really made the 28 tackles, it was in conjunction with the game plan that they were looking for. It was timing.

I'll argue with Coach Jardine's son—and I love his oldest son, Dan. There were things we could have done a lot better as a football program, but, boy, if you needed help—and who doesn't need help being 19, 20, and 21?—that's what John was about. The staff all cared first and we won second, but we had a good showing. We had some good players, and I think they all think that about him. He just treated you real. You'd have a broken hand or be homesick or something—I can't tell stories about other players, but everybody that needed help got help.

I never really got to know Dave McClain very well. I was brought in by a guy I really loved, who was Coach Jardine. I'm not saying I didn't love Dave McClain, it's just that at that young an age, I was really for John Jardine. I was for Coach McClain, too. I guess part of my heart went out, because I saw Coach Jardine booed off the field. But we were dealing with

Linebacker Dave Crossen was the team MVP in 1977 and the 1978 team captain.

a real tumultuous time in Wisconsin history because it was going from a coach who brought the program—with [UW athletic administrators] Elroy Hirsch, Otto Breitenbach, and others—lots of respectability. I certainly loved John Jardine and played for Coach McClain and I'm very proud of it. But I guess my heart was left on the field with Jardine.

I had the opportunity to get elected by my peers to lead our team as a captain when I was a senior, and that was a pretty cool thing. Getting to know those people who elected you, getting to know the coaches, that's special. I think one of the best things in my recollection was Earl Gillespie—the voice of Wisconsin football—what a great guy. He knew history inside and out and he was just…that's part of what made it. You take Elroy Hirsch, Otto Breitenbach, Mike Webster, Earl Gillespie, then we had the Dennis Licks and the Billy Mareks. We have a great history to tell coming from Alan Ameche and so on. Tim Krumrie? Coming out of a small town and making it that big, being that great? We've had a lot of home-grown talent. They always used to say that Woody Hayes owns Ohio, Bo owns Michigan. Well, we got to own some of that. When McClain came there was a little bounce, and when Alvarez came, we kind of came back. It was cool to see little-town guys who were never supposed to make it get a chance and contribute to a little history in Wisconsin.

Look at Mike Webster, look at Jimmy Leonhard, look at Jason Doering. Look at how many people from Rhinelander, Wisconsin, are among your top 100 players! The history is so cool, that's what the Big Ten is all about. I fell in love with it, I got hooked. I would say the integrity and the personality of the state of Wisconsin is meaningful to me. We're farmers, blue-collar workers, we're people who get up at 5:00 in the morning to go to work. And I think that's the integrity. The personality is the ability to really relate to people. And that goes back to Jardine or McBride or some of the great people we've had. They have great integrity. Wisconsin has never been the most talented team on the field, but we showed up every Saturday or Sunday or Friday or whenever we were playing and played the game to the best of our ability and were coached by the best people. That's pretty cool.

Dave Crossen, Wisconsin's team MVP in 1977, set a school record for tackles in a game when he made 28 against Purdue that year. Crossen was a team captain in 1978. He currently lives in Oregon, Wisconsin, and works as a sales manager for Outdoor Products Sales Association representing The North Face.

The
EIGHTIES

DAVID GREENWOOD
DEFENSIVE BACK/PUNTER
1979–1982

I WAS NO. 8 OUT OF 11 GROWING UP, and all my older brothers were athletic, as were my sisters. I started playing football, neighborhood football, because we didn't have any organized football until I was a freshman in high school. We were the River Rats and always competed against the Town Hogs in our little community. We wore towels, or whatever, on our shoulders for shoulder pads or whatever we could put over our heads. I was fortunate enough to have an older sister who had gone to the University of Minnesota, and my first helmet was a Vikings helmet. So I was pretty pumped about that. I think I played one freshman game, then got moved up to JV right away.

I didn't leave the field. I was quarterback until our running back got injured, and then I was a running back. My sophomore year in high school I was a safety. Then my junior and senior year I was the middle linebacker, just went and blew people up. I punted, I kicked off, I received punts, I received kickoffs. I didn't leave the field. We didn't win many games going through my high school career, so respect came through knocking people out. I did make the all-star team my senior year. I played one play at wide receiver, the last play of the game they threw the ball up, and I went up and got it and scored a touchdown. Next thing you know I'm an all-state wide receiver.

I was receiving letters right after my freshman year in high school. Oklahoma, my sophomore year, I was getting letters from them every week because I won the high jump my freshman year and went over 6′6″ that year.

They heard that, hey, there's a guy up there in the north woods who's kind of wild and crazy and a good athlete and you may want to check him out. I really didn't pay too much attention to Wisconsin because they were losing, and I had enough of losing throughout my high school career. I didn't care to play for the Badgers. So I tried to steer away from them and tried to send subtle messages that [I wasn't interested]. I remember that when Dave McClain came in, there was a big change, and Dale Steele, who was a recruiter under McClain, was there every time I turned around. I just remember him breathing on me. I was pretty set going to Minnesota, I'd gone to one of their football camps, and Cal Stoll was still there back in the day. Michigan was also recruiting me, and I kept getting snowed in at airports; I never did get to Michigan, otherwise I probably would have gone there. Bo Schembechler, he was pretty direct, firm and direct with me over the phone, being a young lad. My dad was pretty firm and a disciplinarian, and it seemed like I had two dads. Whenever someone would say, "Hey, Michigan's on the phone," I'd say, "Oh no, here we go." Schembechler would say, "We need to get you up here right away. I know you got snowed in, but we need to get you in here."

Well, toward the end of my recruiting, I was supposed to make trips out to California and Colorado and this and that, and I was getting kind of tired of it toward the end of the year. I had Bart Starr calling me, I had Mike Webster calling me, I had Mike Kalasmiki and other players calling me, saying, "Stay in state, stay in state." Bart Starr, that was pretty inspiring. [Wisconsin] had everyone calling me, so finally I got tired of receiving phone calls and I said, *Okay, yeah, I'll go to Wisconsin.* I did have to take one last call from Bo Schembechler, and he chewed me up and down for about five minutes straight just screaming in my ear. And I just said, "Coach, I'm sorry." I just sat and listened. I was a young lad, I didn't know how to take that. Which made it kind of gratifying after we beat them at home! I did make sure I ran by him and waved at him.

From my freshman year to my senior year, track-wise, I got down to Madison. But I didn't go on campus. In basketball my junior and senior year we went to state, so we did play in the Field House. Of course, in football we didn't do anything. Track and basketball got me into Madison, but until I gave them a verbal, I didn't step foot in Camp Randall Stadium. I didn't care to go to Wisconsin. In my mind, they lost everything, and who wants to be a loser? My goals were to go somewhere we could win.

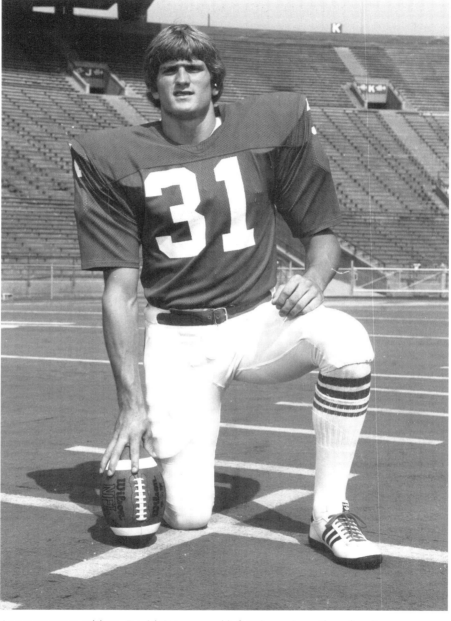

66

As a two-sport athlete, David Greenwood left Wisconsin as the school's career punting yardage leader and won the Big Ten outdoor high-jump title as a junior.

I was brought up to be humble. We walked a bit with a swagger, but then again, I don't know. I may have looked like I was confident and in control, but there was a lot going on inside. I learned how to just forge forward, but we were winning a lot of games and we did have respect of the fans around us and we knew that. We were just on the verge of turning things around and Dave McClain, he did a heck of a job because of what he was faced with. I was an average student. By junior, senior year, I was on the honor roll because I had to get my grade-point up. The study tables after practice—6:30 study table—I didn't have to attend those because my grade-point was up high enough. But half the group was going to study tables at 6:00 AM. Dave McClain gradually got the trust of the academic staff, and things got better as the years went on. Of course, winning changes a lot, too. My senior year was a lot different than my freshman year as far as roaming the campus. You could actually wear your turf shoes, which were pretty comfortable anyway. You could wear them anywhere and you didn't mind being seen as a football player.

67

I was a two-sport athlete, although track was just a hobby. But I won the Big Ten outdoor high-jump title, and that was after spring ball. I was on my way home, and our track coach called and asked me if I wouldn't mind coming to Minneapolis to help them knock off a few points. It was kind of on my way home, so I agreed. That was a crazy weekend because I got with my cousins. It was Friday night, we pulled in, and I stayed with my cousins. I didn't have to jump until Sunday, and the coaches weren't checking rooms like [they do in] football. We enjoyed ourselves for a couple nights and even got shot at Saturday in the park! That's when I turned to my cousin and said, "Look, you gotta take me back. If I get shot, Coach is gonna be mad. He needs me to jump tomorrow." Sunday morning I went out and got into a jump-off. I think we both went 7′2″, and I beat him.

In high jumping, my oldest sister, Bonnie, taught me how to plant my foot when I was in first grade. I was jumping over four feet when I was in first grade. I was in grade school and would go up and watch the high school guys. When they'd get done, I'd tell them to leave it on the highest height, and I'd go jump over it. They were like, "Who's this little punk?" I didn't really have to practice high jump, it just pretty much came naturally.

Ed Nuttycombe and I were pretty much buddies. I was thinking about doing the decathlon and participating in the Olympics, or trying to qualify for the Olympics if I didn't go in the first round in the draft. But since I went in the first round, I decided to go play football.

My football highlights at Wisconsin are all team stuff, like beating Michigan and the gratification of being able to look at Bo Schembechler and waving at him and letting him know that Wisconsin wasn't a bad decision. Anthony Carter was their star wide receiver, and it was always a battle—Greenwood against whoever was the star. I was going to knock their heads off, so they had to look out for me. And I did force Anthony out of a game. I remember him sitting on the sideline, kind of pouting. I played hard and was still trying to knock people out. I think I learned that through my high school career, trying to gain some respect. But that's how I played, I was reckless and didn't hold back. I was a free safety my freshman year. Free safety's a lot easier to play than strong safety. Free safety, you're just flying around, knocking people out. Freeman McNeil was the running back at UCLA and later player for the Jets. I did blow him up on the sideline a few times, and he just looked up and he said, "Man, great hit." As a freshman playing UCLA—those guys were giants! Moments like that were special. But so were the team moments like beating Michigan and Ohio State.

What's it like to be a Badger? It's like they say in *The Wizard of Oz*—there's no place like home. Having Bart Starr calling me telling me to stay home and Mike Webster telling me to stay home, but not really understanding what they were saying until recently. I really appreciate what Barry Alvarez has done, and obviously I'm proud to be a Badger. But being able to go home and have been part of being a Badger, being recognized as a Badger is special. I live in SEC country, in Florida, but I'm all Big Ten. I defend the Big Ten, but the Badgers, it's more personal because I have a hard time watching them. I get nervous watching the Badgers. And I do get nervous watching the other guys, especially if they're playing outside the conference. But being a Badger, we're having success, and that's because of what Barry has done, largely. I see him down here in Florida sometimes and thank him whenever I see him. Everyone's got a place in history, and it takes the whole body to make it go. Barry played a huge part and has done a great job, and I give him props for that. It means a lot to me to be a Badger because I came and I am family. If I would've ended up being a Wolverine, going home wouldn't be as special.

David Greenwood, a native of Park Falls, Wisconsin, intercepted 10 passes and left Wisconsin as the school's career punting yardage leader. He was a two-time first-team All–Big Ten selection. Greenwood played three seasons each in the USFL and the NFL. He lives in Lutz, Florida, where he works for Pryority Food Marketing Inc., Builders Millwork Inc., and is a PGA golf professional.

MATT VandenBOOM

DEFENSIVE BACK

1980–1982

I WAS GROWING UP IN WISCONSIN during the Lombardi reign, so as a six- and seven-year-old I was already a rabid Packers fan, just watching those championships and sort of living and dying with the Packers. That, of course, promoted our neighborhood games over at the park and on the street. We played a lot of football in the neighborhood as kids. That evolved into some parks and rec, playing football as we grew up. I did not play any organized Pop Warner football, things of that nature. My first organized football was my freshman year in high school.

I played at Kimberly (Wisconsin) High School, started as a flanker, wide receiver on offense, was also the place-kicker and punter, but did not play any defense. We sort of platooned back in those days, played one side of the ball. I was one of the sort of go-to guys on offense, built up some stats, was a first-team unanimous all-conference receiver my junior and senior years in high school. And I was a second-team all-state high school receiver. So those accolades led to options with state schools.

I was recruited primarily by state schools. A couple of schools in the Ivy League—Dartmouth and others—showed interest. I had some preliminary contact with Northwestern when Rick Venturi was coaching there. Wisconsin was sort of passive, although they were encouraging me to enroll and walk on. I actually made a couple of trips locally and was very close to signing at UW-LaCrosse with Coach Roger Harring—I was going to play baseball and football and was extremely excited about that opportunity, but still undecided. Then my dad sort of pulled me aside in that process and asked me where I wanted to get my degree from. And it was the most important question that I had been avoiding, getting caught up in the hype of recruiting and so on. I knew when he posed that question almost instantaneously that I wanted to get my degree from Wisconsin.

I had very little recruiting contact with the Badgers. Coach Mario Russo at the time had contacted our high school coach and watched us at the high school Shrine all-star game. There was brief contact, but it was a more passive, we'd-like-you-to-walk-on sort of thing. There was no extreme pressure there. So largely I made my decision to go to Wisconsin to pursue my degree there. I was thinking pre-law at the time. And, of course, I wanted to walk on to see where it would go.

Initially it was very intimidating. I was all of 6′2″, 185 pounds, and they saw me as a scout team tight end. Here I am lining up across from Dave Ahrens, who's an All–Big Ten defensive end. So it was somewhat humbling. But I did note in one of the early practices, I was lined up outside, and they were doing some skeleton pass, and I had a chance to just show what I could do catching the ball, one of my strengths. I was literally catching the ball over our defensive backs a week into practice. I remember saying to myself, *I can do this. I can compete with these guys.* I even got kind of a look from Doug Graber, who was the defensive backs coach at that time. I remember looking him in the eye, and he was like, "What are you doing to my DBs? You're only a walk-on." Later he became my coach as a defensive back, so it was somewhat ironic that it started that way and that I eventually ended up working with him.

71

I earned my scholarship sophomore year. I had a good freshman spring, was voted the offensive most improved player, and things started happening on offense. I went through sophomore year with very little opportunity to play and, very frankly, I went home for the sophomore Christmas break and read in the newspaper that I was being moved to defense. It wasn't a consult. So it created a little bit of a challenge for me. I thought, of course, about quitting many times in those early years, and that gave me cause to think about it again. But I actually showed up at the spring practice as a sophomore, began to learn the defensive side of the ball, and started to become a special teams player. I was literally on all special teams my junior year. My fourth year, senior year, progressed to the point where I got my starting role. And, of course, my first game was the Michigan game in '81, so it was kind of a rude awakening to the role of free safety, but that turned out pretty well. We continued to grow as a team and build a winning program, and that led to some personal accolades, All–Big Ten recognition, and ultimately the All-America honor. I was voted team captain by my teammates, which was maybe the biggest honor I had.

By the time we played top-ranked Michigan to open the 1981 season, I think as a team, we had gotten to a point where we didn't fear anyone anymore. In previous years we had gotten stronger, we played them tougher, we were more physical, we had a group of seniors and a group of players who we were confident could play with Michigan going into that game, and that was maybe the biggest difference between '81 and previous years, where they had beaten us pretty well. As a free safety in my first start, I was obviously an emotional wreck really until the first play. Then we just beat them pretty much in every phase of the game. It's interesting, as I watched the game many years later, I thought defensively we controlled that game. I thought it was really the defense that set the tone for that game. We were so focused on what we were doing. When you came to the sideline, you were on the phone with your coaches talking about the next series. Watching that game many years later, I didn't realize how well our offense played. We just beat them in every phase of the game. It was obviously a great day for Badgers football and a heck of an initiation for me—I had three picks that day—and it really sort of kicked things off for that year and, really, the wins that followed.

Coach McClain brought that winning attitude. He and his coaching staff started from day one, when they arrived the same time I did, with the discussion of a bowl game and how our goals were to get stronger and better. He had a real air for discipline, a real air of respect for the classroom. You couldn't go a week without hearing about getting the work done in the classroom. So I thought he provided the leadership that set the tone for turning that program around, so to speak.

We were at the Independence Bowl in 1982, and there was the banquet the night before. Part of the banquet was sort of a talent show. Kansas State was a little more organized than we were. They had a guy up there on a guitar, he sounded like James Taylor. And they were just rattling off, and they went first, of course. Well, now Dave McClain went up and we were terribly unorganized. And he said something like, "And now, Matt VandenBoom, one of our team captains, is going to come up and sing a song." Out of

Matt VandenBoom was a first-team All-American in 1981 and a first-team All–Big Ten selection in '81 and '82, but he counts being elected as team captain as his biggest honor.

nowhere—I had no inkling that this was going to happen. So I humbly got out of my seat, knees shaking, and walked up to the stage in front of this massive crowd. Something clicked in my brain, and I said, I'm not going to go down alone here. I was going to sing a capella. So I invited my seniors up there, and the rest of the seniors came up. It was the holiday season, and I thought of doing some Christmas carols to get the crowd involved. So we saved the day, we turned it into a kind of fun thing. We were walking off the stage and were high-fiving—we were horrible—but we were together. The crowd was doing stuff with us, it was a good thing. As we were walking off the stage, my roommate, Mark Subach, grabbed the mic and began to do standup! They had to peel him off the mic! They couldn't get him off the stage! It was absolutely hilarious. But Coach McClain—he did it absolutely intentionally—he tended to try to take his kids and put them in situations they could handle, but he would test them. We were at the Japan Bowl and were sitting at the table, and he was coaching us, saying, "Now, Matt VandenBoom is going to lead us in prayer." Well, no prep, he'd just put you on the spot. And, again, I saw it as his way of helping us grow. It was just another way of rounding us out as men.

Clearly, the bowl win over Kansas State in 1982 was a big win for us. It represented us attaining one of our goals that we had begun four or five years earlier. Getting that win was the culmination of a lot of work and the commitment to the program and obviously a celebration. You look back on it now fondly because it was the first in the program's history, and to be a part of that was a special thing.

I was focused on education from the start. As a humble walk-on, you don't know where it's going to lead. So to get a job someday, I was pretty focused. I was fortunate to have been a good student and just really thrived in the environment, enjoyed the academic atmosphere, got lined up with the business school, and thought about going on to law school, but got involved in professional football. As student-athletes, we had a very rigorous agenda, a very rigorous schedule, but one that worked well with me and my personality. It really helped me stay focused in both areas, and I look back on the degree very fondly and appreciatively. It was a heck of a combined education—the academic side and the athletic side. I wouldn't trade it for the world.

Being a walk-on really allowed me—and I think this was actually a benefit—to grow, stay focused on academics right away. The demands on me as a walk-on were not as great, for example, as the highly recruited kids who were freshmen. There was more expected of them, there were more rules to follow, there were more study tables to go to. There were just more demands. I was able to sort of drift in and out to practice, and go back and be a student.

So it allowed me to really focus on my academics early, and yet get bigger, stronger, faster, and really mature in the program without as many demands. Of course, that changed in my sophomore year, but initially that allowed me to get my feet wet and get focused.

My experience at Wisconsin was survival, initially. Then it was really the transition into making contributions. And then it sort of culminated with leadership. And it was that progression and being a part of a program that was turning around, we were beating the Michigans and the Ohio States. There was a sense of pride in being part of that team and accomplishing some of those things with your friends and teammates. Back then it was just a tremendous privilege and honor to be a part of it. And the academic side was there, of course, as well. What it means to me now, it's more reflective of our little piece of history as it relates to the heritage. I'm much more humbled by the overall heritage of being an alumnus of the University of Wisconsin and certainly being an athlete in the athletic department. It's part of a bigger universe, if you will. Just a great appreciation of what that means to young people and the education it provides, the way it prepares them for life beyond. It's a little more thoughtful for me now than it was then, and it sort of honors the bigger picture and what that total education provides a student-athlete.

I look back at the friendships—and they're lifelong friendships—now that I appreciate having been a Badger—the connection with the university, the opportunity to give back as the W Club president, and really just to acknowledge the W Club as the best letter-winner organization in the land. Those are other things that I appreciate now as much.

Matt VandenBoom was a first-team All-American in 1981 and a first-team All–Big Ten selection in 1981 and 1982. He was the Big Ten's coleader with six interceptions in 1981, including three in a win over top-ranked Michigan. A fifth-round selection of the Buffalo Bills in the 1983 NFL Draft, VandenBoom now works as a financial planner and lives in Combined Locks, Wisconsin.

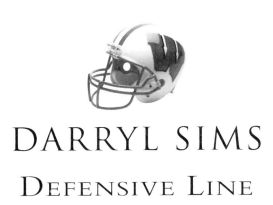

DARRYL SIMS
DEFENSIVE LINE
1980–1982, 1984

My INTRODUCTION TO FOOTBALL actually started out in the backyard with my older brother and my younger brother, and then some neighbors and some other guys in the neighborhood. I guess I couldn't honestly say it was organized, because a lot of the rules never seemed to get applied during the course of our play. But that is certainly where it all stemmed from. We would watch college football on Saturdays and pro football on Sundays, and then we'd go out in the backyard and try to emulate what we just saw. I grew up in Winston-Salem, North Carolina. Wake Forest University was on one side of the town and Winston-Salem State University, a historically black college, was on the other side of town, so there was quite a bit of football to watch, or just athletics, period. Then certainly the University of North Carolina was down the road in Chapel Hill, and they were doing well back in those days. So between those three institutions, there was a lot of football right in the immediate area that we watched.

We played other sports, too. It was big-time basketball country. My younger brother really was the basketball player of the family. He grew really tall and really spent a lot more time working at basketball than I did. I would come in and butcher up people and foul out and would be done for the rest of the game! I had a high of about four points or something, six fouls. It was something that you ended up doing because it was a part of what you did as a family and a neighborhood. If we were going to be playing basketball that day, then everybody played; if it was going to be football, then everybody played; if it was going to be baseball, then everybody played.

I moved to Connecticut to finish up high school. We have family members who lived up there, and a guy who had just been hired at Bassick High was a former NFL player by the name of Frank Brown. Frank had played for the New York Jets. So my uncle would call and speak to my mom every Sunday—this was a family tradition. They'd talk on Sunday just to check in and see how everybody was doing and all that good stuff. One Sunday he had shared with my mother that this Coach Brown had gotten the job as the new head football coach and would love to talk to me to see if I would be interested in transferring.

I spent two years in Bridgeport, Connecticut, playing for Bassick High School, which was not a perennial powerhouse by any stretch of the imagination. When I got there, I don't think they'd won any games in a number of years. So they were really looking forward to Coach Brown coming in and doing well. I recall quite vividly we won, like, two or three games one of the two years we were there and we got the key to the city! It was pretty interesting. During the recruiting process, I remember Coach [Arnold] Jeter coming and talking and having discussions with my family, and subsequent visits from him and then head football coach Dave McClain about the positives of Madison and what have you, and they convinced me to take a trip. At that time in my life, I had never been to Wisconsin. I jokingly say to people, it's one of those states as a young kid, when you have to do the map and fill out each state, I'd always kind of miss that one because I could never remember where it was! I was really intrigued about going, and it sounded really great, and we spent a lot of time reading up on the school and its history. They certainly had struggled over the years with the Ohio States and the Michigans of the world. But it sounded like Coach McClain was really headed in a different direction and had some great ideas about how the new teams were going to be under his tutelage.

So I remember like it was yesterday, landing in Madison by way of Chicago. Back then, there were no ramps that would come out to the plane and you could get off right to the terminal. You had to get out of the plane and walk across the tarmac and into the building—and this was in late December and January. I didn't even get out of the terminal before I was saying, "You know, I'm not quite sure this is going to work." But we ended up getting to campus and had a great recruiting trip. A lot of the guys who were

Along with teammates Al Toon and Richard Johnson, defensive lineman Darryl Sims was a first-round draft pick in 1985.

on that recruiting trip are friends of mine still. A lot of the coaches I ended up working with during the time I was in Madison are still friends of mine to this day. When it came right down to it, we were looking at Miami (Florida); Michigan, because we had family members in Detroit and they could kind of keep an eye on me; and then Madison. The thing that really sold it for us was Dave McClain and the staff; they were very professional. They were very fair and honest, and the things that they suggested were going to take place, actually, we felt were very realistic, and so we as a family decided to enroll at the University of Wisconsin in Madison in 1980.

What really jumps out to me when I talk about Madison, Wisconsin, or the state of Wisconsin, are the people. You're talking about a guy from North Carolina by way of Bridgeport, Connecticut, who came to Madison, Wisconsin, and really didn't have a whole lot of ideas about what was going to be taking place. I didn't have a really firm grasp on living in that part of the country and experiencing that kind of culture and doing all the things you need to do to fit in and make it all work. But the folks of Madison, and the people of the state of Wisconsin, I know they embraced me, I know they embraced a lot of my teammates, treated us like family members from day one—and still do to this day—and I will never, ever forget that. And having lived in the state now for a number of years and calling it home, I try to emulate those things that were shared with and done for me and how folks helped me along the way. I was just so moved and so touched—and my family felt the same way—that there are just unbelievably nice people on the planet, and a great deal of them live in the state of Wisconsin.

Individually, certainly there were times when things went really well. My junior year was really my breakout football year, and I look back on that with fond memories. I remember being in the race for the conference sack title with a guy from Ohio State, another defensive lineman, and he and I were going back and forth to see who was going to have the most sacks of that particular year. But like everything else in life, you don't get an opportunity to have that kind of success or to be able to do those kinds of things if you don't have good people around you helping you out. My teammates my junior year were obviously equally good and in some cases even better, so that there wasn't a lot of attention put on me, and that allowed me to be in one-on-one situations so that I could have that kind of success. I'll never say that the success I got or gained as a Wisconsin Badger was something I did all by myself; that certainly was a result of my teammates, it was a result of the coaches coming up with schemes that put people in specific situations, then you really just have to go out there and get it done.

Coming to Madison, especially on the recruiting trip, I remember hearing a lot from nonbelievers. You're introduced to the people in town, and they talk about the real challenges that the football program had to endure over the year with the Michigans and the Ohio States and how it's just going to be an uphill challenge for us to be able to overcome all that. The thing that Dave McClain did for me, personally, was, we never really talked a whole lot about that. It was really simple and straightforward. This is who we've got this week, this is how we match up against those guys and, if we execute and if we do the things we need to do, we'll be successful. And everybody believed that; everybody bought into that. I don't recall there being any hesitation. We just reveled at the idea that we would get an opportunity to play those guys because we knew that they weren't going to take us very seriously, and that was a mistake that a lot of people made from 1980 to 1984. When we started to win—and one year we beat Michigan, Ohio State, and Purdue—we put ourselves in a very advantageous position. I think then folks really started to believe that Coach McClain was recruiting quality people and had a plan that was obviously working. All we needed to do was support him and be able to buy into his plan and his direction and we would be okay.

I tell people all the time that there is no question that Barry Alvarez and his staff over the years have come in and done an unbelievable job. We're all the better having had him on the staff as a head football coach and even more so now as an athletics director. But prior to Barry's arrival, Dave McClain, in my humble opinion, was the guy who really brought back and put Madison on the map. It was the bowl game in East Rutherford, New Jersey, something that we hadn't been to in many years. Unfortunately, we lost to Tennessee. A year later, we were in the Hall of Fame Bowl down in Birmingham, Alabama, and then two years after that, we were at the bowl game in Shreveport, Louisiana. Were they BCS bowls? Absolutely not. But they were bowls nonetheless, and the program had certainly come out of obscurity and was where folks really had to take us a lot more seriously than they had in the past. We were building. Recruits were coming in, and we were talking to them about the way it used to be, the way it was right then, and the way it was going to be in the future as long as Coach is here and everybody buys in to what he's doing.

I have a tremendous amount of satisfaction for really not so much the success that I had individually but what we had collectively. When you finally leave intercollegiate athletics or college and get out into the real world, a lot of the tools, a lot of the skills, a lot of the attributes that you learned as a student-athlete—working with the team and doing things for the betterment of the team—I use in my job now every day. So there's an enormous amount of learning that takes place, life learning skills that take place that I've been able to bring with me and have been able to utilize in every aspect of my life as a husband, as a football coach, and now as an athletics administrator or athletics director. Being a Wisconsin Badger is something that will be with me for the rest of my life. It was the start, really, of my adult life. It was the first time I was away from home and on my own, interacting with guys from different parts of the country, building relationships, establishing friendships, and working with folks at the university.

Al Toon and Richard Johnson and myself were all first-round draft picks in 1985, and there's a lot of projection, there's a lot of speculation. A lot of the experts will tell you where they think guys are going to go and all that kind of stuff, but you really never know, obviously, until you get the phone call and you accept the position or you accept that they're going to draft you. Then you're all good to go. The day of the draft I got a call from the Chicago Bears, who told me they were going to take me if I was going to be there. But the Steelers picked before the Bears, and the Steelers were on the clock. I got the call from Tony Dungy, the defensive coordinator at that time. Tony said they'd like to draft me at this position, that I'd play end for them, and he asked me how I'd feel about that. I said, "Coach, I'd love to be a Steeler!" At the end of the day, I learned that Richard had gone and that Al had gone—actually Al had gone earlier than I went. It really didn't hit me until later that evening that we had made history for the Badgers. So, I guess it really goes back to Dave McClain and his staff. Somebody had to recognize the talent Richard Johnson, Al Toon, and Darryl Sims possessed, and they had to bring us in and put us in situations where we could be successful.

81

Darryl Sims was a three-time All–Big Ten selection at Wisconsin. He was chosen in the first round of the 1985 NFL Draft (one of three Badgers selected in the first round that year) and went on to play four seasons in the NFL with the Steelers and Browns. He is currently the athletics director at the University of Wisconsin–Oshkosh.

AL TOON

WIDE RECEIVER

1982–1984

M Y BEGINNING IN FOOTBALL BEGAN just playing sandlot football down the street. I typically ended up being the quarterback. I did that for a while and then I got away from playing football. It wasn't a priority; it was just a game at the time. It's not that I had a huge passion for football; it was just something to do because everyone else was doing it. But, later on, I did go out for the Pop Warner league for basically one day, and they wanted to make me a lineman. I wasn't having that, so that ended—I was probably about 10 at the time. That's when I began playing a little bit on the street, sandlot style, and then, after that passed, I started running track my sophomore year in high school. Prior to running track, I went out for JV football and ended up getting cut. This was my first time doing organized athletics, and so I got cut from the JV football team and tried track and ended up becoming an All-American, actually, as a track athlete. That's really where organized athletics started for me. I decided I was going to try football again as a junior. I wanted to prove to myself that I could do it.

My junior year I started playing and actually made the team. I started out as a defensive end and was second-team tight end, but I don't think I ever played a down at tight end. Art Price, who would also be a Badgers football player, was a senior at the time and was a starting tight end, and he played some defense, too. He was recruited by Wisconsin, and apparently they saw me on film, and the connection with football was there. The other connection was that my head football coach was also the father of one of the assistant track coaches at Wisconsin, so I was recruited as a track athlete, too. As a senior, after having such success the year before, I started getting recruited. But my focus was primarily on track, and I wasn't sure if I was going to play football my senior year. Finally I was convinced to play, ultimately by my girlfriend in high school, believe it or not, and went out for football my senior year. The coach gave me the option to play pretty much any position I wanted, so I ended up playing free safety. I started at free safety and tight end, and the letters continued to pour in, or increase, at that point. I was third in the nation in the triple jump. I was a pretty good hurdler and jumper all around, and then I did pretty well as a football player, so I started getting recruiting letters as a football player. My parents weren't able to afford to send me to college, so I was going to go into the Air Force. I was in ROTC my sophomore and junior years in high school until I realized I was going to go to college and get a scholarship, so I shifted my focus a little more intently on athletics. I had a pretty good season both on the football field and on the track as a senior, and I ended up going to Wisconsin for my first visit. I really liked it and went to one more visit [at Kansas]. I had planned to go to Hawaii, UCLA, and California, as well, but I decided that I really liked Wisconsin. So I didn't even finish the rest of trips and chose Wisconsin.

Dave McClain put together a very good recruiting staff, so we had some pretty darn good recruiting classes. I think the class prior to mine was a very good class and there were several others, including mine. So the players were there. In later years I realized that we were loaded with talent, and I look back and wonder why we didn't have more success as a team. However, we went to the school's first bowl game in decades my sophomore year, so there was significant progress made as a program. We ended up going to three bowl games in my four years, so I feel like it was very successful at the time. As far as Coach McClain goes, he was obviously smart enough and a good enough coach to get us back on the map, bring in some quality players, and help push Wisconsin football forward.

Balancing track and football was not very difficult for me. Obviously, they are in opposite seasons, so that was helpful. But Wisconsin was one of the schools that were okay with me participating in track, exclusively, during the spring. Once the football season was over, I spent all my time on the track and never actually went up to the football offices during track season. It was just like how during football season I never went to the track offices, so it worked very well for me, and there were no real conflicts or issues. It was just perfect.

I thought Dave McClain was a good guy. His untimely death was a big hit to the program; I think it took the program a few years to transition back into its winning ways again. So that was difficult, but, personally, I guess the person who stands out the most was my receivers coach, Fred Jackson, who ultimately ended up being the best man at my wedding. He was probably the most influential in transitioning me from being more of a track person to being able to deal with the rigors of football. The sports are obviously totally different, and he was a tremendous friend.

I would say most of the people who walk up to me who were at our 1982 game against Illinois ask me about the infamous bounce pass. It was a play that we practiced during the week for a few weeks prior to actually executing in the game. Apparently there were a few high schools that had successfully completed the play, and some of our coaches had seen it, so we thought it might be a good play to have in the arsenal. I remember right before the play was called, we had to inform the officials of what was going to happen because we didn't want them to blow the whistle prematurely. The coaches called the refs to the sideline and talked to them about the play, what was going to happen. The play was called, and I was hoping it worked because it wouldn't look good if it didn't work. So our quarterback, Randy Wright, called the play, and the ball was snapped. I stepped back, caught the ball, and pretended like it was a dead pass. Then I looked into the line of scrimmage, and we thought a few linemen were coming at me, they figured it out. Finally I had to look for my target, who was Jeff Nault, sprinting across the field, and just as I released the ball, I got pummeled. I was thinking, *Boy, I'm glad I'm not a quarterback!* I didn't actually see Jeff catch the ball, but I did hear the crowd, so that was an indication that it was successful.

The week prior to our 1983 game at Purdue, I wasn't even sure I was going to play. I had a knee issue I was dealing with and didn't practice all week, so it was a game-time decision. Coach Jackson, who was the receivers coach at the time, did a lot of work, was exercising his best sports psychology techniques possible in trying to get me to not focus so much on my injury and just focus on the possibility of being able to play and not worry about it so much. As a track athlete, you always felt like you had to be 100 percent healthy to be productive, and I was still kind of developing that mentality. So game time, I was warming up, felt pretty good, it was a great day, and I loved

Al Toon starred in both track and football, leaving Wisconsin as the school record-holder for career receptions, touchdown receptions, and receiving yards.

playing on grass. So all the stars lined up, and from the first couple plays of the game I just felt great and caught, I think, a long ball for my first catch, and it just kept going from there. I was just kind of "in the zone," as they say, and I just stuck my hands up and the ball was there. It doesn't happen like that all the time. [Toon set the then–school record for receiving yards in a game with 252.]

It was a blessing to have an opportunity to go to college. It was something that wasn't in the cards for me early on, and I was blessed with enough talent where a school felt like I could contribute. That was No. 1. No. 2 was the educational opportunity the university offered was outstanding. It gave me a chance to leave the confines of Newport News, Virginia, and experience life outside the East Coast. So that was spectacular. I was allowed to participate in two sports, one that I really loved coming in, as a freshman, which was track, and one that I grew to love, football. I was just kind of blessed with the ability to play, and I kind of grew to love it. The other thing college at Wisconsin allowed me to do was meet my wife. I met her my freshman year, and we've been happily married for almost a quarter century now, so that's been good. Moving into the next generation, obviously I have a couple of kids, Kirby and Nick, who are student-athletes at Wisconsin, so it's been tremendously rewarding and tremendously exciting for my family and me.

Elroy Hirsch was around at the time I attended Wisconsin and was part of helping create this. He was a very special person. I really liked him, he was very personable. He made me feel like I was special, and he did that with everyone. I'm sure that was an important part for a lot of players who came here to the university and had the opportunity of meeting him. Dave McClain is obviously no longer around, but his wife, Judy, has followed up and been a great friend. Coach Jackson was a great man and a great coach and helped make me who I ended up being as a football player, but more importantly, as a person.

As for us having three first-round draft choices in 1985, I was fully aware of how difficult it was to, first of all, get drafted, and then to have three from the same school get drafted in the first round. We were followed by some other high-round draft choices on the same team—it's just amazing. As you mature, as you get older, you get a better sense of things with time. Maturity brings more clarity to history.

Being a Badger embodies the spirit of the college experience. I think I know that Wisconsin does that as well as any university or college or post-secondary school in the nation. The alumni's passion, the alumni's contributions, the current players, and the players who aspire to be Badgers all have this drive or this passion to be a part of something and continue the legacy of Badgers athletics. It's just a great experience.

Al Toon left Wisconsin after the 1984 season as the school record-holder for career receptions, touchdown receptions, and receiving yards. He was the 10th player chosen—by the New York Jets—in the first round of the 1985 NFL Draft and caught 517 passes for 6,605 yards and 31 touchdowns during his eight-year career with the Jets. Al's son, Nick, is a wide receiver for the Badgers, and his daughters, Kirby (Wisconsin) and Molly (Michigan), play collegiate volleyball.

JOE ARMENTROUT
Running Back
1983–1986

My first experience with football wasn't organized. My brother was a year older than me, so I'd always tag along with him wherever he went. We grew up in Elgin, Illinois, a couple hours south of Madison, and their Pee Wee program was incredibly competitive. All the stuff you don't wish for your kids: parents with the cowbells, you beat this team and we'll offer you a bike—some pretty random stuff. But I basically just followed along with my brother and got started when I was eight. We were on the Redskins and, when we joined the team, they hadn't lost a game in three years. There was a lightweight and a heavyweight. The eight- and nine-year-olds played light, 10 to 12 you played heavy. My five years at least, we went undefeated, as well. We were a west-side team, and the Packers, of all things, were an east-side team, and we made it to the championship. I'll never forget when I was 12, literally, they had banners, they were offering bikes, they were offering boom boxes, they were offering whatever you can offer. So it was pretty competitive. Again, probably not what you would hope for nowadays, looking back at it. But I was just kind of tagging along, following my brother, looking up to him, wanting to do what he did.

They started me at offensive guard and middle linebacker when I was eight, and I hated it because my brother was a running back and a linebacker, so I thought I should be that. And when they gave me No. 65, I hated it. When I was nine years old, they put me in an all-star game [because the coaches] thought I was my brother. I got three touchdowns, so they left me at running back from there on in.

Our high school was a pretty good-sized school. We were a 6A team in Illinois, which was the division with the largest populated schools. The varsity coach was the athletics director, as well, and had been there 35 years and didn't want to bring anybody up. So as a sophomore I got called up for the state playoffs, and we made it all the way to the semis against East St. Louis–Lincoln, which was just a fantastic team, very athletic. We ended up losing by a touchdown to them. I got a little experience as a sophomore, getting to run down on kickoffs, nothing too big. Seldom did any junior start, but I got to start as a junior. My brother was a senior then and was our quarterback, and I was a running back. We ran the wishbone and had some success. Then, prior to my senior year, our school district had a teachers' strike. School wasn't in for literally three weeks, which meant we forfeited those games. One of them was a conference game, and we couldn't catch that team that was ahead of us, so we didn't get to go to the playoffs; we had three losses right out of the bat. In addition to that, a lot of the schools that were recruiting the Chicago area kind of ducked out on me. I would have told you after my junior year, Iowa, Stanford, and UCLA were probably the three that were hot and heavy on me, and they'd go watch other guys and kind of prioritize those guys and rank them. So that was bad, because I thought I was losing such an opportunity with different schools, but it turned into a blessing to be able to come to Wisconsin. It really did. It limited my choices as far as recruiting trips. I went on six, like most guys back then, and to me it was really a clear-cut decision to come to UW.

89

My mom raised us with not a lot of money, so literally whatever school would ask me to come visit, my mom would drive me to O'Hare, give me my bag, I'd get on a plane, I'd fly, they'd dump me off. I was a bit of a late-bloomer, personally, because of the teachers' strike. So I took my six trips in a month. I missed a number of days of school. For instance, when I went to Wisconsin, I flew back into O'Hare, my mom gave me a new bag, and I flew to Purdue.

But I had a great time visiting Wisconsin. There's one story I always remember about Coach McClain. Bill Dudley was our old coordinator, so he recruited me in the Chicago area. After you were done with the recruiting trip, there was a 10-minute session with the head coach. I was the second or third of about 15 guys. We sat in there for 45 minutes, which screwed up the

Running back Joe Armentrout was selected as the Badgers' offensive team MVP as a junior and senior. He also was the 1986 team captain.

entire day's schedule for him and all the other coaches and players. He didn't ask me one question about football. It absolutely amazed me that he asked me about my family, my brother—who ended up at Southwest Missouri State and who'd been recruited lightly in the Big Ten—my sister, my likes, my dislikes, what I was looking for in a school. Everywhere else you went, it was just "let's talk about football" and nothing else. And I found it really unique. When I got to O'Hare Airport and my mom asked how it went, I said, "I think this is the right school." She asked why, and I said because the coach didn't care if I played football. That was my perspective. We just enjoyed talking, and he never brought up once, "We think you're a running back, we think you're a D-back," any of that. It was a great time. When I got on the campus, it kind of overwhelmed me with not only the size, but the lakes and things you're just not really used to.

My redshirt freshman year I was running with the third team because one of our fullbacks got hurt. I didn't know how hard to go against these guys. I had read up on all of them—guys like Darryl Sims and Tim Krumrie, Matt VandenBoom and David Greenwood, and just a bunch of monster—All-America type players, all future NFL guys. We were running just a simple toss to the right and were just in shoulder pads and helmets, so I was even more confused how hard I was supposed to go. And Greenwood came through and hit me as hard as I've ever been hit, right through my hips, just knifed me. He picked me up and said, "You might want to get it together and go a little harder, or you're not going to be around very long." This was the third day wearing pads, and I was thinking, *Okay, I guess that was an easy lesson if my body's still in one piece.* He and I have become very good friends, and I appreciate everything he's done.

By far my greatest day at Wisconsin was the Hall of Fame Bowl on December 29, 1984. Our son was born that day. My wife went into labor at 3:00 AM and had the baby, Zachary, about 3:00 PM. We were having our team meal, getting ready to go to the field to play Kentucky. We lost the game, which stunk, but by far that was certainly the highlight of mine. That whole week just flew by, and it was draining and difficult. To have all that happen and then get to play. I had met my wife at the Lakeshore dorms. She's from Greendale, left the dorms after the second year, we got married and had Zachary. His middle name was almost "Fame"—I'm not kidding, it was going to be Zachary Fame—then we thought we just couldn't do it to him. So my mom and my mother-in-law were in Wisconsin at the hospital, and I got a call at about 2:30 or 3:00 that afternoon, an hour before we were going to the stadium for the Hall of Fame Bowl. That was absolutely the highlight.

Certainly the most difficult part of my time at Wisconsin was Coach McClain passing. My family and he and [McClain's wife] Judy had gotten pretty close. There were three married guys on the team, but I was the only one with a child. So Judy would always be looking out for us, and Coach McClain would as well, to make sure we were okay. Then the following year, we had our second son, and he didn't think it was so funny anymore. He told me to knock it off! But his death was really hard because Craig Raddatz and I were the captains going into that year, which would have been our fifth year as redshirts, our senior year. And we were all quite close to him. I vividly remember being at my apartment in Madison, and Pam was in class, and I was just with the boys and saw it scrolling across the bottom of the TV that he had had a heart attack. And Craig was one of the people who walked in, literally right after it happened. It was really difficult. I think they handled it as well as they could. But I don't think you can understand the magnitude of it at that age. I think the assistant coaches played a very substantial role. Father Mike Burke played a huge role in trying to comfort everybody. But we took a pretty good team coming in as seniors, eight guys drafted and a couple free agents, and Paul Gruber and Glenn Derby and a couple guys behind us who had a nice role in the NFL, and we just laid an egg. You had anything from 17- to 22-year-olds who were kind of bumping around, not knowing how to react. So that was certainly the most difficult thing we had to go through.

The staff just broke apart. Coach [Jim] Hilles really didn't have a fair shake at it. He was plugging holes to try to help people whom he cared for, kids he recruited. Dave [Coach McClain] was a wonderful man. He cared more about you growing up and doing the right thing than winning games. I'd be really curious to see how he would do today in kind of a cut-throat industry now. But he truly cared more about you growing up as a young man and turning into a man. He was fabulous that way. And dearly missed. He truly believed it didn't have to be the best guy, it just had to be the right guy. I think there's a lot to be said for that, being able to pick those guys out. He had an awful lot of success. He was a fantastic guy, and it was meaningful to have the Coach of the Year award in the Big Ten named for him.

The thing about being in the Big Ten and competing, it's always a highlight when one week you're playing Pepper Johnson, the next week you draw Carl Banks, and then you get Rod Woodson at Purdue. It's just off-the-charts good. You can see they're going to be really good professionals, they just look so much better on film than anybody else, so it was always fun comparing and competing against those guys.

I get goose bumps thinking about my time as a Badger. Young people, when they're in the process of getting recruited, whether they're 16, 17, or 18, don't understand the magnitude of that decision. Then you get here and are going through the process—you feel the tradition to a point, but you're really just trying to work through practice and the weight room and get along with the upperclassmen, adjust to school, help win some games, and actually get on the field. As you get further removed from it, you see kind of the legacy and the tradition of what it means to be involved in Wisconsin football and be around the fans. I not only appreciate the team effort, but also the camaraderie among the administrators, coaching staff, and former players. I'm incredibly proud of being associated with the program, being allowed to come to Wisconsin and play. I think you find that a little bit more here, you're a little more humble that you're allowed to get that scholarship, or even preferred walk-on and get to play and participate and do the best you can do, and kind of leave it at that. Just be judged off that. We had a lot of ups and downs for a lot of reasons, but as I get older, I appreciate the integrity of the program and how they treated me, how Coach McClain wanted me to be a good person as much as a good player. I'm just really proud to be involved in it.

Joe Armentrout, a team captain in 1986, was selected as the Badgers' offensive team MVP as a junior and senior. He was a ninth-round draft choice of the Tampa Bay Buccaneers in 1987. Armentrout lives in Madison and is broker/owner of Pinnacle Real Estate Group LLC.

PAUL GRUBER

OFFENSIVE LINE

1985–1987

I LIVED IN THE COUNTRY OUTSIDE OF PRAIRIE DU SAC, Wisconsin. Most of the time, at least while I was in grade school, things were pretty active. We lived on Lake Wisconsin, so we water skied, played basketball in the driveway with my neighbor, and just played backyard football type of stuff. I didn't really start playing organized football until I got into middle school, which is when it started for us. Through middle school and high school, I always played tight end as my primary position, and I played defensive end, as well. It was a middle school program, and we played other teams that were in the Badger Conference, if I remember correctly. As far as organized sports go, prior to that in elementary school, I played a lot of basketball—played in a league. I went to camps for basketball, but not so much for football.

Maybe two or three times a season my dad would get tickets from someone he did business with, so we'd go to a few Wisconsin games a year. I can remember Rufus Ferguson and Billy Marek and, even when I was in high school, David Greenwood. It was fun following those guys.

It was a little different back then. I participated in track, as well, quarter mile, shot, discus—actually went to the state tournament in all three of those events. Then I went to basketball camps and stuff, played in leagues during the summers. But I didn't really get recruited for basketball; I got mostly Division II offers. When I was a junior in high school, the senior class ahead of me had some pretty good athletes, and we went to state playoffs that year, which was the first time in quite a while for our high school. Then those guys who were the year ahead of me were getting recruited, mostly for Division II schools. By having success as a junior, and having some of the upperclassmen on the team scouted, it helped me get scouted. I was a tight end in high school, so that was what I was being recruited as. I wasn't really heavily recruited. I was recruited by Wisconsin, obviously, and then because they were recruiting me, Minnesota and Michigan State recruited me, as well. I think I wanted to play tight end and, growing up in that area, at that time I think Jeff Nault was a tight end at Wisconsin—he was a U.P. guy, I think. My dad died while I was being recruited as a senior in the fall, and at that point Dave McClain was the head coach. He took kind of a personal interest in me. It wasn't much of a choice at that point where I would go, just because of the relationship I had with him. I didn't really look at the other schools.

By the time freshman camp was over, I was no longer a tight end, I think I moved to defensive line. My first year I was redshirted, so I was there for five seasons. I started my first year playing defensive line and at some point during that season switched over to offensive line, primarily because I really liked the offensive line coach, Ron McBride, and I wanted to stay there. They wanted me to go back to defensive line, but Coach McBride was a great guy and a really good coach, so that's really when I started to enjoy playing offensive line.

As far as highlights at Wisconsin, my first couple years the program was doing well, we went to a couple smaller bowl games. But at that time Wisconsin wasn't where they are now, where they go to a bowl game every year. I remember while I was still in high school they went to a bowl game for the first time in quite a while. So that was good the first couple years. Then I guess it would've been after my third season, and really the first season I was a starter, when Coach McClain had a heart attack. I can't remember what our record was at that point. Then Jim Hilles took over on an interim basis for a few years, then Don Morton, and my last couple years weren't quite as successful. I guess they weren't successful at all. I would say the highlight would be from my third year, my first year as a starter, when we went down to Ohio State. They had a really good team that year with Pepper Johnson, Keith Byars, Chris Spielman. We ended up beating them down there in a pretty low-scoring game, but that was definitely a highlight.

Coach McClain's death was a really tough experience. Just the whole thing, it's not something you expect. It was definitely a tough situation. He

Offensive lineman Paul Gruber was a first-round selection of Tampa Bay in the 1988 NFL Draft. He played 12 seasons with the Buccaneers.

had done a good job of building the program and recruiting. Maybe my second year there, we had quite a few No. 1 draft picks. He had gotten some talent as far as recruiting was concerned. I was a senior in high school when Wisconsin had beaten Michigan for the first time in a long time. I think when I was at Wisconsin we beat Ohio State three years. So he started that tradition, and his death was a big hit to the program. It's hard to recruit if there's not stability at the head coaching position. In some ways I think it was almost unfair to have Jim Hilles in an interim position—it just didn't work. I think it would've been interesting to see what would've happened if Coach McClain hadn't passed away because the program really was in good shape from year to year.

I appreciate my years at Wisconsin probably more now than I did at the time. I don't know if it was just kind of the proximity of growing up close to Madison. You definitely appreciate the fact that you got to go play in your own backyard, in front of your friends and family. And I also just appreciate the opportunity to go to such a great educational institution at the same time. I think going out and seeing other places and being around guys from other schools, you realize what a special place Madison is—the fans and I would also say just the academic tradition. It's definitely just a great college environment.

Anytime your alma mater is doing well, and especially as an athlete, especially when you're playing professional football and you are around guys who are all football players, there's a lot of pride that goes into that. I guess post-graduation I kind of reaped the benefits of Wisconsin's presence. When I was playing professionally in Florida, it seemed like we played with a lot of guys from Florida State and Florida, SEC and ACC, so they all have the programs that have a winning tradition and have been successful. There's definitely an element of pride in those programs. I think that definitely has happened at Wisconsin, and I think it started during the McClain era.

Paul Gruber was a first-team All-America offensive lineman in 1987. He was a first-round selection (fourth overall) of the Tampa Bay Buccaneers in the 1988 NFL Draft. Gruber played 12 seasons in Tampa Bay. He currently lives in Edwards, Colorado, and works in the real estate business.

DON DAVEY

DEFENSIVE LINE

1987–1990

I'M THE FOURTH OF FIVE CHILDREN IN MY FAMILY. My three other brothers all played football, so I kind of grew up with it around the house. I grew up in upstate New York, and we had a Vince Lombardi league—kids played tackle football at the age of five, in kindergarten. As soon as they let me, I put on a helmet and joined the team, and I've been playing football ever since. The hardest hits I ever took were in the backyard when my brothers would beat me up! When I look back on it, I played football from the time I was five until age 31. Much of my life has revolved around the football season.

All the time growing up I was either the quarterback on offense or a nose guard on defense—a pretty odd combination. I loved playing on defense, and I loved playing on the defensive line. I loved playing in the middle because I could always run from side to side and, no matter where they ran the ball, I had a chance to make the tackle. As I started growing in junior high and then into high school, it became obvious that quarterback wasn't going to be the position for me. I moved to the offensive line and played center in high school at Manitowoc High. We had a fabulous high school program. Ron Rubick, who passed away just a few years ago, was the coach, and the program won 48 games in a row. We had the longest winning streak in the nation. It was a terrific kind of three-yards-and-a-cloud-of-dust type of offense and tough, hard-nosed defense, and that was the personality of our coach. We had a bunch of really good athletes who came through over the course of two or three years, and we loved to play together and, by the time we got to high school, we had some pretty solid teams.

My junior year, I was the only junior starter on a predominantly senior team. We won the state championship that year, so going into my senior year I was getting a lot of notoriety for having won a state championship. It was shortly after that season, when we won the state championship again, that there were coaches from Northwestern, Michigan State, and the Badgers showing up in my basketball practices. And pretty soon all the Big Ten schools started showing up. I really didn't know what to make of it, quite honestly. I was kind of a bruiser in basketball. I could have played Division II, probably, or maybe some state schools; I do remember being recruited for basketball by some state schools. Football was always my passion. I always say football, basketball, swimming—I love all sports and I played whatever I could, but football was always my sport.

I was a straight 4.0 student since grade school and I was valedictorian my senior year. Recruiters loved me because, of course, all the programs were trying to build their programs around great football players who were good students, too. So I think that enhanced me as a recruit and maybe was as much of a reason why I was recruited so heavily. Two of the guys who were instrumental in me going to Wisconsin were Jerry Fishbain and Mario Russo of Coach McClain's staff. I remember coming down for the spring game in April and watching them play, and it was that weekend when Dave passed away and Jim Hilles took over. So by the time I reported my freshman year, Jim Hilles, the defensive coordinator, was the head coach. He only lasted one year, and then Don Morton came in for three years and was fired, and my senior year Barry [Alvarez] came in for a season. So, in five years, I guess I went through four coaches.

I chose Wisconsin for a number of reasons, but first and foremost to me was that they had a phenomenal engineering program. As passionate as I was about football, I was also equally passionate about math and science. I knew early on that engineering would be a good fit for me and, as much as football, I chose Wisconsin because of the engineering program. I showed up in the fall on campus and redshirted that year. Most freshmen who walk onto campus are pretty wide-eyed and don't know what college they're going to go in, never mind what major. When I came in, I'd done all the research and knew I wanted to get into engineering and graduate in four years. Engineering was 135 or 140 credits—you have to take a demanding schedule every

Defensive lineman Don Davey chose Wisconsin for its excellence in athletics and academics. He is the NCAA's only four-time Academic All-America selection.

semester if you're going to do it in four years. I came in my freshman year and sat down with my advisor and told him I was going to take physics, chemistry, calculus, and a foreign language—it was, like, 18 or 19 credits. And they said, "Hold on, we get all kinds of kids come through here who think they're smart as a whip and then get into the university setting, and it's a whole different ballgame down here." I went back to my position coach, Dave Anderson, recruiting coordinator Jerry Fishbain, my head coach, Jim Hilles, and all of them were trying to talk me out of that schedule. So I told Coach Hilles I would back off to 14 or 15 credits, but they had to promise to leave me alone if I showed I could handle it. I got a 4.0 that first semester, and I remember coming back after winter break, and the coaches and academic advisors sitting me down and saying, "All right, you're on your own, Davey, you can schedule whatever you want." I was taking 15, 16, 17, 18, or sometimes 20 or 22 credits with a lab—and the 7:00 AM labs were on the other side of campus. I was always a full-time student first and then I'd squeeze in the football around that.

I started playing my second year. I had a pretty good training camp. It was a young team that wasn't all that good, and I was a redshirt freshman who ended up starting. I'll never forget when I played at Michigan. We went to Michigan, it's the Big House and it's 105,000 people or whatever it is, and I was a redshirt freshman. That was a real eye-opening experience. I went out and did the best I could. I was a pretty good player, but I probably wasn't a Big Ten–caliber defensive lineman just yet and I played my butt off and hustled like I always did. We lost that game 49–0 in my first start. So we came back and watched the films. Coach Morton came up in Sunday film session and announced that I was the defensive player of the game. So the newspapers back in my hometown read: "Don Davey was the defensive player of the game in Badgers 49–0 defeat." It was kind of a dubious honor—I don't know how well I could've played if we lost 49–0. No matter how good you are, like when you jump to the pros, you never quite know how you're going to stack up at the next level. But freshman year I got defensive player of the game maybe five or six times out of the 10 or 12 games I played. It just kind of gave me that confidence that, *You know what, maybe I'm not quite big enough to play yet, but I have some ability here and I think I'm going to succeed in this place.* In my four years I played as a starter, we won seven games. Our best year we were 3–8. I have had people tell me I could have gone to Notre Dame or USC and played for national championships and gone to bowl games every year, but I wouldn't change it for anything. We didn't have a lot of success on the field, but the friendships I made, the education I got, the fun I had, it's just a special place. I wouldn't change one minute of my college career even if I could go back. My college roommates to this day are my closest friends. Those experiences, even the bad experiences of losing—I really feel like it builds character, it builds discipline, all those things that helped me be successful later on in life.

Don Morton was fired after the season after my junior year, so heading into my senior year they announced over Christmas that they had hired Barry

Alvarez as the new head coach. Our very first meeting in January, when we came back, we were all in the meeting room when he walked in. He just has such a presence about him. He looked us all straight in the eye and said, "Take off your hat, if you've got an earring in take it out, sit up straight in your chairs. Eyes up on me, I'm Barry Alvarez, I'm your new football coach, and we're going to win in this program." In one sentence, he completely turned things around. The attitude, the culture, the feeling sorry for ourselves a little bit. We'd been struggling the last three seasons. He came in with instant credibility, he'd just been fighting for national championships at Notre Dame and was quite honest. He said, "You're going to work harder than you've ever worked, but that's what it takes to win." We probably had 15 guys quit the team that first off-season because he worked us so hard—5:00 AM every day, all winter long, doing every kind of drill that we could imagine. He wanted to weed out the guys who weren't committed to this thing. And he told us, "You guys that are committed to this thing, and that are going to stick it out, we're going to win championships here. I guarantee you that." And my senior year we didn't have a lot of success, we only won one game, but we knew when we left, my class of seniors, that it wouldn't be long at all before this would be one helluva place to play football. He did exactly what he promised.

I rave about the Badgers, and I rave about how much fun my five years in college were, how well they prepared me for the rest of my life. I really can't pinpoint one thing. It's the whole experience. The campus is just beautiful. The football program now is one of the best in the country. Academics are as challenging as any university in the world, no matter what your discipline is. It is just a fun place to go to school. I had more fun than anybody on campus, and I finished with a 3.5 in chemical engineering and a master's degree, and I was an All-American football player, and I managed to get drafted. My wife and I fell in love during those years. My best friends to this day are guys I shared a locker room with during those years. I just look back on those years with such fond memories and wouldn't change any of it. The funny part is, having played in the NFL for eight years, I played with guys from every school in the country, and so many of those guys who played at Notre Dame, played at USC, played at Cal, they hadn't been back to campus in 10 years or 15 years. I get back to campus every chance I get. My wife and I go back up there, we take our kids up there, we spend weekends up there and try to get back there as often as we can because we had just such a phenomenal experience there.

Don Davey, a first-team All–Big Ten defensive tackle in 1990, is the NCAA's only four-time Academic All-America selection. Davey was chosen by Green Bay in the third round of the 1991 NFL Draft and went on to play for eight seasons with the Packers and Jacksonville Jaguars. Davey lives near Jacksonville in Atlantic Beach, Florida, and manages his three companies: Disciplined Equity Management, an institutional money management firm that caters to high net-worth individuals; DKSS Subs, a holding company for several Firehouse Subs franchises in Central Florida; and Parrothead Properties, a real estate investment company with residential and commercial properties in Florida and Wisconsin.

The
NINETIES

TROY VINCENT

DEFENSIVE BACK

1988–1991

IPLAYED PLAYGROUND FOOTBALL FOR THE MOST PART—nothing real organized. One year in the fifth or sixth grade I played organized football for the local Pop Warner league, but my whole time growing up, I really thought I was going to be a basketball player. I went on and played one year of high school football, went out my senior year. I couldn't play my junior year because I had moved from one state to another, and the rules wouldn't allow me to play. A gym teacher came to me during the summer prior to my senior year and spoke to me about coming out for his football team. I think he probably saw me in gym class, moving around. In most cases, generally, basketball players are pretty good athletes. And he probably just saw my movement and at that particular time, in a public high school, you want as many people out for your football team as you can. You want the best athletes. He told me to come out, and I just took a shot.

I came out, played well, the team had some success, and I had some success. Then I started to be recruited. I had basically committed to Syracuse. That was my first visit—Coach [Dick] MacPherson was the coach—and at that time I canceled all my other visits that I had set up. When my high school coach found out, he said, "Hey, you can't do that. You get five official visits. Let's just take one visit in each conference so at least you can see what else is out there." I had totally turned off the faucet. *Okay, let's try Wisconsin in the Big Ten*. There were some other Big Ten schools that were recruiting me. *Okay, I know I'm not going to go here, let's take a visit here.* And that's kind of how I got on campus. The only visit my mother took with me was to Wisconsin. A week before signing day, we were sitting down, and she said, "Where did you decide to go?" And I said, "Well, I'm going to go to Syracuse." And she looked at me and said, "No, you're not." And I was like, "Why did you ask me?" She said, "You're going to Wisconsin." The rest is history.

I ended up signing with Wisconsin under Coach Morton. I came in, and they asked me what position I wanted to play. I had the least amount of experience as a corner, so I was trying to sneak through the system at that time. I ended up playing corner. The first two years were good. I was an instant starter. I played well on Saturdays. Then Coach Alvarez came in my sophomore year and just kind of rejuvenated my enthusiasm about football, about who I was as a person. When you lose, you kind of lose confidence in yourself, or you second-guess your purpose. He just rejuvenated that inner spirit that drove us. He told me I had a chance to play on Sunday.

I've never asked my mother what attracted her to Wisconsin. Probably it was just me getting away—she just felt like I needed to be removed from where I was. And I didn't need to be in a place where people could just casually come visit me. So that's why it was no to Penn State, which was three hours away. No to Pitt, which was three and a half, four hours away. No to Temple, no to all the local schools. Syracuse was even four hours. No. When she dropped me off, it was very cold. There was no crying and "we're going to miss you." It was like, "Don't do this, don't do that, and don't do this." And last thing, "Don't be calling home talking about how you're homesick." Boom, door shuts.

When you're playing, you always think that you have a chance—even though you know you don't have a chance—but in your mind, you're fixing to say, *Yeah, we do have a chance.* Outside of Northwestern and Minnesota and Iowa because it was such a rivalry, you're not going to beat Michigan, you're not beating Ohio State. But you're playing. *Hey, I'm on scholarship, I'm not going to complain. I'm getting my education. Line up and play.* And that was kind of the attitude. I didn't complain about it, we just weren't good.

When Coach Alvarez came, it's not that we were loose, we weren't. We're Wisconsin, I mean, we were losing, so we weren't like we were just a bunch of wild wolves. We weren't that way. Coach Alvarez brought what I would consider today when you look at Nebraska, you look at Notre Dame, and

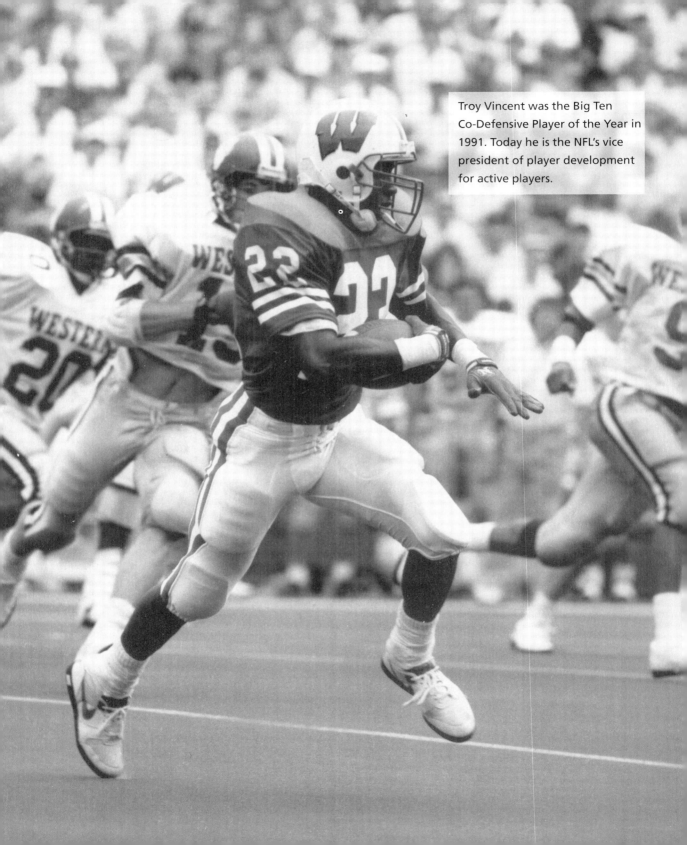

Troy Vincent was the Big Ten Co-Defensive Player of the Year in 1991. Today he is the NFL's vice president of player development for active players.

what those programs were built on—discipline, high character, detail. Sure, we were going to get a sprinkle of good athletes, but for the most part, we were going to build from within. We were going to build from our core market and then get a sprinkle. And we were going to do it this way: no names on the back of your shirt 'til you earn that. I'll never forget. If you want to put names on the back of your shirt, you're going to earn that, you're going to win some football games to get that. And it was just that, obviously, he reviewed tape and when he came to me, again, he didn't have to worry about me leaving school, even though I might've been what they saw as the athlete or the player on the team. I was generating all the offense on the defense, but I wasn't going anywhere. He gave me hope again. He said, "Hey, I've been coaching this guy, I think you're better. I know you're better. I've just watched some tape on you. I know you're better. Just kind of believe in my system, just stick with me." He said it very nicely: "If you stick with me, son, I think you're going to play on Sunday."

You couldn't second-guess Coach Alvarez because he just beat the No. 1 team in the country in the Orange Bowl two weeks ago. He won a national championship at Notre Dame, who's going to question the credibility? And it wasn't like it was just a one-year wonder. Notre Dame was at the top at that time, they were the cream of the crop. And so you don't question it. It was the first time I'd ever been part of a firing. That happened at the high school level and you hear about it in the streets. So it's, *Okay, new guy in town, he's won a national championship*—and you just say, *We don't have anything to lose. Let's go.*

One play in my career strikes me more than any. I'll never forget I had a 68- or a 71-yard punt return down at Ohio State. We were underdogs. It was one of the first times we wore the white-on-white jerseys—white jerseys, white pants. I'll never forget going up that sideline, making a couple people miss. I'll never forget Paul Jette coming to me saying, "Guess what, we got a Heisman candidate over on the other side of the field, Desmond Howard, and you're going to shut him out today." Those kinds of moments, taking on a guy of Desmond Howard's caliber at that particular time. Moments like going down to Illinois and, potentially, this guy—Jeff George—was going to be the No. 1 pick, and it was going to be a chance to show my stuff. I'll never forget punt returns versus Iowa and Western Illinois. But that Ohio State game because it was at the Horseshoe, I'll just never forget going up that sideline.

The one thing that sticks out about my experience at Wisconsin is, when I came in, there was a mentorship program they offered to scholarship athletes. I was appointed to both Jane and Irv Piliavin, who were professors at UW. They were my surrogate parents. When I could not go home, they allowed me to come by for two or three hours and just get me out to eat a real fresh egg or toast. It was that support that allowed me to see people and families that I wasn't accustomed to seeing in a different manner. They didn't know me from a can of paint. I just happened to be a student-athlete at the University of Wisconsin. Everyone was taking turns sharing information, I became part of the family. And it taught me core values. So, throughout my time, there were different people who touched my life and gave me hope that inspired me, and I continued to do better.

Then I left. I came to Madison and had a great experience. I had a unique opportunity, unlike others, to be drafted within the first 15 minutes of when the draft starts and to play a long time. I was able to do something, and this doesn't always happen. I look at the things I do today, the way I process things, the way I treat people, and it's because of the relationships that I had at Wisconsin, the respect. I didn't run around, and they weren't always getting me out of trouble. I respected them: "Ma'am, yes, ma'am," "No, sir." They remember you, and you're always embraced. And that's important to me. At the end of the day, it's all about relationships. I wouldn't be welcomed back to the university if I was a knucklehead. Whether it was the collegiate level or the pro level, Wisconsin fans are still watching me. Wisconsin allowed me to think about life differently. It allowed me to be free. It allowed me to respect and honor tradition. I was drinking from a well that I did not dig. All of us are. There have been a lot of people who have come through the UW—engineers, teachers, scientists, you name it—and we're all drinking from a well we did not dig.

We talk a lot about tradition. At the end of the day, the Brent Mosses, the Terrell Fletchers, the Lee DeRamuses—they built this house. Ron Dayne and Lee Evans, you were great. Thank you, Al Toon, Troy Vincent, thank you Nate Odomes. Hey, Joe Thomas, thank you Paul Gruber. That's the history. I go back to Joe Rudolph, Cory Raymer, Joe Panos, they paved the way. Someone asked me what drives me every day? It's because I'm accountable. I'm responsible for what I say and what I do. I'm responsible for that "W," because, God bless him, Irv Piliavin, if he didn't touch my life the way he touched my life, I don't know if I'm here today. If I didn't get that support from that family and Russ Middleton when he was a professor, I can't tell you that I'm here today. It wasn't the athletics that kept me at Wisconsin or kept me inspired, it was these people who were placed around me on campus.

Troy Vincent was a first-team All-American and Big Ten Co–Defensive Player of the Year, as well as being a semifinalist for the Jim Thorpe Award, in 1991. He was the No. 7 overall pick (to Miami) in the 1992 NFL Draft. Vincent, a cornerback, played in five Pro Bowls during his 15-year career and was named the Walter Payton NFL Man of the Year in 2002. He served four years as president of the NFL Players Association and is currently the NFL's vice president of player development for active players.

JOE PANOS

OFFENSIVE LINE

1990–1993

I STARTED FOOTBALL AS A KID, just playing in the street with my brothers. I played one year in eighth grade. That's the first time I played organized football. I was always on the bigger end, somewhat tall, but I was never a big thick kid until I started hitting the weights, and that wasn't until high school. I started seeing I was tall, with big hands, big feet, then I started to fill in, so we started to hit the weights later in high school, early in college. Nowadays the kids are way more advanced.

It's kind of funny, you ask a kid when he's younger, "What do you want to be when you grow up?" they'll say football player or basketball player. Eventually you get older, and it changes to engineer or whatever, realizing that football or basketball or baseball is not an option. For me, it was always football. Even at the time I thought I wasn't going to be a football player, I still said football because that's what I wanted to be, and I was pretty determined to become a football player. I was okay in football in high school. There were a lot better guys. My freshman, sophomore, junior years I was on varsity and I started. I wasn't anything special, but I was pretty good. I was big, I had a nose for the ball on defense, and I could block pretty hard and play on offense, but I was nothing special. My senior year I had a pretty good year on a somewhat bad team, but didn't make all-conference. I remember when I made honorable mention, I was heartbroken. But I wasn't ready to give up my dream of playing football. I didn't get any offers, obviously. A friend of mine called the coach at UW-Whitewater and said, "I've got a kid who wants to play, he's a pretty big kid, and he's a good kid, and he'll work hard for you." I hit the weights pretty hard, worked on my training, and was a defensive lineman at the time. I got pretty good and got to play my freshman year at Whitewater, got to start at the end. I left high school at 225 pounds. When I was at Whitewater, I was 250-something. And then in January 1990, Coach Alvarez had a press conference saying that he was the new coach at Wisconsin and all spots were open. I wanted to give it a go and decided to transfer to Wisconsin. So I wrote a couple letters, said I wanted to transfer to Wisconsin, wanted to walk on, and he let me.

My father taught me what a hard day's work is. He taught me a ton about responsibility. My father owned his own restaurant; he owned a couple restaurants back in the day. When I was a little kid, when everyone else was playing on the weekends, my brother and I were at the restaurant bussing tables, peeling potatoes, washing dishes. The only way we knew how to do it was to work hard. So we never backed away from work. When I heard Coach Alvarez at his press conference, I said, *I'm going to give this a shot. I'll work as hard as anyone else on that field, if not harder, and eventually I'll find out if I can or cannot. I was a good student and my dream was to play football.* I always tell my kids not to say, "I should've or I wish I could've, I wish I tried." At the end of the day, if I tried and I didn't make it, so what? At least I gave it my all. I hate the guys who are sitting at the bar or sitting in the stands at a high school game and say, "I could've done this, but my coach didn't like me," or, "I could've done that." I would never do that, and I don't want my kids to do that.

I wasn't with the old regime at Wisconsin, I was with Barry's team. The first training camp, the only thing I know is Barry was trying to weed out the guys who weren't going to buy in. He didn't have to run them off; they'd quit on their own. If you made it through his couple of training camps, tell you what, you worked pretty damn hard. You're going to survive and if you survive, you're going make it on this team. If you made it through his training camp, the first couple training camps, the first couple winter conditionings, you're going to be alive. As time went on, the more we realized, No. 1, he knew what he was doing. And No. 2, if you noticed, the first couple years playing, Coach had a lot of his guys on the field. I'm talking about a lot of true freshmen, true sophomores playing. So he knew which guys were going to end up making it, and he knew that the guys who started that early would end up being three- and four-year starters.

We had a pretty good team in 1992, but we just didn't know how to win games. We were close to winning a lot of games. We lost five games by a total of 11 points, and some of those we had leads in the game, some of those we couldn't finish. A blocked field goal at Iowa, last-second touchdown against Indiana—I remember this stuff. We just didn't know how to finish. We were one play away from going to a bowl game in '92. So we knew we were close, and after that Northwestern game we lost at the last second, I said to myself, looking on paper who was coming back, looking at the depth chart, I said, *You know what? We're going to have a good football team next year.*

I was extremely confident about our football team, and I believed in our guys, and that comes from Coach Alvarez. We all believed in him because he made us believe in ourselves. The senior group in 1993, the guys on the field, those were his guys, those were guys who bought into his program and believed exactly what he was telling us. So we knew people were talking about who was the Big Ten leader, and I said, "Why not Wisconsin? Give me one good reason why not us. We have four out of five returning offensive linemen coming back, we've got a quarterback coming back, we've got two of the best linebackers in the Big Ten, if you ask me, coming back, a great defense, the best coach. Why not Wisconsin?" I truly meant it.

Coach told me to just lead the way I knew how. I learned from him that it's better to be respected than it is to be liked. There are guys on a lot of teams I played for that I didn't like very much, but I respect the hell out of them. And there are guys I liked a lot—great guys, a lot of fun—but I didn't have any respect for them because they just didn't take their trade as seriously as they should have. I want to be the guy who everyone respects. Being liked is not my goal, it's not a popularity contest. I want the respect of my teammates. And the only way to do that is to set an example. I was a senior, a captain, and I had my place there, I had the run of the team. But if they see the captain running out there doing the extra stuff, working harder than anyone else, people will listen. I didn't think I was better than anybody. I associated with everyone on that team, and I think the guys appreciated that. As far as being a leader and captain, my job, if you ask me, was to have Coach not have to worry about the little stuff; I'll take care of the little stuff. He wanted me to feel the pulse of the team. He'd ask me how we were doing. I would meet with Coach every week, and he'd ask, "What's going on?" and we'd go from there. If I could handle a situation, I did. If I couldn't, I'd bring it to Coach's attention.

Offensive lineman Joe Panos was a team captain his senior year—the season the Badgers won the 1993 Big Ten title and the 1994 Rose Bowl.

Coach Alvarez just instilled confidence in us. He didn't use smoke and mirrors, it wasn't fake confidence. He knew that if he coached us the way he coached us and prepared us the way he prepared us, all we'd have to do is go out there and do what he taught us, that we'd have a chance to win. Confidence and toughness—I hate bringing this up because people think I'm being egotistical, but we were a tough, tough group of kids. We worked pretty hard, all of us, and we were a mean group and, boy, we stuck together. Really, really stuck together. It was as close a group as you can get. We went out together, we worked together, we played together, you name it. We did everything together. It was a bond like no bond I've ever seen before or since. It was a special group, a really special group. And it was because of the time we put in. We were 1–10 the first year. We had some lean years. We dug out of a big hole, and that meant a lot to us. I always said I never was a confident person. I never feared anyone when we played, but I played in fear every game. I feared letting down my teammates. When you've got that kind of pride and that kind of love for one another on the football field, I use the expression, you're going to be a tough out.

What happened in the student section at the Michigan game in 1993 was tough. [A number of fans from the student section were injured at the end of the game when the they tried to come down onto the field to celebrate. Panos and others helped to save some of the injured.] But we went to the hospital and, once we found out they were okay, it was business as usual. We were a very focused group. Those first couple days were tough. We knew what was on the line and did not need any distractions. Everyone was okay. It was a near-tragedy, but everyone survived, and it was back to work. Work kept us focused.

Clinching the Big Ten title in Japan [against Michigan State in the Coca-Cola Bowl, a regular season game] was unbelievable. We knew the week before, on the bus headed to the game at Illinois, right before we got to the stadium, Coach Alvarez said that Michigan just beat Ohio State, which meant if we won, that we would control our destiny. The second they told us that, it was a rout. We knew it was done. That was it. We needed a little break, we got our break, and they could've called both those games right then and there. Illinois didn't have a chance. Not a prayer. We went to Japan and were all business again. We had a lot of fun afterward, but it was a business trip, big time. We knew what was at stake. Talk about distractions, we were flying across the planet to play the game that was going to determine whether we're going to go to the Rose Bowl or not. But it was a tough group, a well-disciplined group, everyone was focused to do what needed to be done to get us to the Rose Bowl.

The Rose Bowl was weird, surreal. For whatever reason, that game was really choppy to me. I haven't seen that game in probably 10 years, and I'll forget stuff that happened in that game, but I haven't forgotten the overall experience. The thing is, I forgot about it the week after it happened. Everything was happening so fast, it was such a big game, and it was so exciting. It was over before I knew it; I didn't even remember the score until years later. [Wisconsin beat UCLA 21–16.] I think it's because there was so much going on and so much going through my head. It was just one play at a time. When that play was over, I moved on with the next one. I just remember what happened afterward. I remember the feeling I had afterward. I remember going out there before the game, but I don't remember many of the plays. I remember yelling at the referee at the coin flip, because he called us Washington for whatever reason. Everything else is a giant blur.

I take great pride in the time I was at Wisconsin. Coach, I remember, nonstop, he'd say, "Leave your legacy. How do you want to be remembered?" We wanted to be remembered as the first Rose Bowl–winning team ever at Wisconsin. That was really big for us. We all wanted to do that, to leave a legacy, and we did. We had a lot of pride in the fact that we were one of the best teams ever to walk out of Camp Randall. There have been some really good teams that have walked out of there. We kind of paved the path for other Rose Bowl teams, and the fact that we were one of the first, and I was a captain, I take great pride. Coach taught us a lot. I learned more in my four years at Wisconsin than I could ever learn the rest of my life.

Coach Alvarez put a stamp on this team, a stamp on this university, and a stamp on this football program. I think it starts and stops with him, and he passed it on to Bret [Bielema], and he took off running. Bret is a great coach and a great man, and I'm proud as hell of the job he's done, as well. He's carried it on.

Joe Panos was a second-team All-American, first-team All–Big Ten choice and team captain as he led the Badgers to the 1993 Big Ten title and 1994 Rose Bowl victory. He was selected in the third round of the 1994 NFL Draft by Philadelphia and played seven seasons with the Eagles and Buffalo Bills. He lives in Hartland, Wisconsin, and works as a certified sports agent.

LAMARK SHACKERFORD
DEFENSIVE LINE
1990–1993

I PUT IN PROBABLY ABOUT FOUR YEARS OF PLAYING Pop Warner ball. And then I didn't play football again until my freshman year in high school. I played a lot of offensive and defensive line. Sometimes I had to move up a weight class because I was heavier for my age group. At that time, it was just fun. That's what a lot of my friends did. It was just an activity at first, and I just developed a love for the game at that age. I enjoyed going out and playing. That set it up because I always liked football, even when I wasn't playing, I would watch it until my freshman year in high school.

At the time my football coach didn't really start freshmen on varsity, so we had a freshman team and we were good, we were undefeated. We had a small schedule, we played nine games and went 9–0, and then my next year I moved up to varsity. I didn't play any junior varsity games because I was start-ing on the offensive line my sophomore year in high school. So I played a lit-tle defense, but I cracked the starting lineup on offense.

The guys I played with as a freshman were still together by senior year, and we moved all the way up to second ranking in the state in our class. We only had about 30 people on the team, being an inner-city school, but we were ranked second in the state. We had the No. 1 offense, and that right there started to solidify things. We were good, and I started seeing some talent in myself, and before I knew it, I started getting inquiries from colleges. I played both defense and offensive line.

[UW assistant coach] Kevin Cosgrove recruited me. The background is that Coach Cosgrove was first at Colorado State, that's where he started recruiting me. So I was getting ready, and he came back and said he was at Wisconsin now. I liked Cos, so I checked out Wisconsin. I had just seen the Colorado–Notre Dame game when Barry [Alvarez] took the job at Wisconsin, the interview after the game when they were in the locker room—I remember that. So I took the visit at Wisconsin there because Cos wanted me to. He didn't have to talk me into it because I was ready to go to Colorado State. So I just said, *Okay I'll take a visit to Wisconsin.* I liked all the coaches, and they seemed like they were eager to go in the right direction.

I felt that I could come and contribute, but I didn't realize I was going to be starting my freshman year. I just wanted to come in and contribute my part and show that I could play on that level. I was one of the last scholarship players taken in Barry's first class. I felt I had a lot to prove. I think that's what every person who comes in to play college football feels—they want to prove something and show how good they can be. It's up to the player. We started recruiting the kind of player who wanted to show—not just talk it, but walk it. So that's how we started gelling like that. We were so close as a team, we wanted to prove to everybody else that we belonged on this stage and we could play with anybody. So that's what drove us. Not as individuals, we wanted to prove as a team—everybody. Nobody else outside of the team, nobody believed that we could do what we did in 1993, but we knew.

You point to that Ohio State game in 1992—when you beat a team of that caliber you say, *Okay, we can play with these teams. We are as good as people who are the top teams in the conference.* It still was a work in progress because we still didn't have that winning season yet. That Rose Bowl season, I would say the game against Michigan really made a statement, because I felt we had been pretty good, and we just dominated this team. That was the confidence booster right there. I think that really made us believe we could play and beat anybody. I remember the fans being into the game and just felt the energy—it was just electric. At that time, we were riding on a good season already, so them coming to town was just big—it was a huge game for everybody. I remember the electricity of it. Everybody offensively just rose to the occasion. We didn't come out in awe of them at all. We stepped on the field knowing we could beat this team.

I was elected captain in 1993 by my teammates. They felt that I came to play every day and I put my heart into the defense on this team. And I was a good

Defensive lineman Larmark Shackerford was a team captain in 1993 and helped the Badgers capture the Big Ten title in Tokyo, Japan.

leader. I kept the calm of everything on the field, when we were in the huddle and everything was getting kind of crazy. I was a senior and stepped up and solidified that defense, so I think a lot of the cats followed my lead. We gave each other the confidence we needed to play the defense we played and to play at the level we played. But to be elected team captain by your peers, that just shows that they have respect for you, and you just have to give it back to them by never taking plays off, always showing up, always helping the young guys. Everything you would feel like a captain is supposed to do for you.

Joe Panos was the other captain. He was the backbone to why Wisconsin has these great lines they have now. He was one of the founding players, that powerhouse factor they have now. He was a walk-on, he was trying out on defense at first, but I guess he just wasn't a defensive lineman and he went over to the offensive side of the ball and just thrived there. He just showed he'd work hard, and that's what everybody respected about him. He earned his position.

Winning the Big Ten championship in Tokyo was special. Just the chance to go to another country, see another culture at that age of our lives. That was fun—it was like a bowl game within a season. The fans over there were just amazed by American football and really into it at the game. But even with the implications of the game, we were actually relaxed. By that time, before the term you hear all the time about the team having swagger, we had a quiet confidence in ourselves. That's how we were. It was just like another game, but it was in another country, so we got to have some fun at the same time. We stepped on the field, we handled our business with them.

I talked to a couple guys who played the year after I was done, and they got to go to another bowl game. Of course, we went to only one—the Rose Bowl—and to win, you couldn't ask for anything much more than that. A huge prestigious bowl, just the atmosphere of it, the fans, it was like a home game for us, we had so many fans. Even though UCLA played there all the time, we felt comfortable in their stadium. We weren't in awe of the situation, we just rose up to the situation. That's the type of team we were, because of our leadership—me, Panos, Brent Moss, [Darrell] Bevell—even the young guys we had at the time. Those special situations didn't put us in awe, we just always went out to do what we had to do no matter whom we lined up against.

From the start, when I got to Wisconsin, we went 1–10, so I knew at that time there was nothing else we could do but get better. And that meant working hard, working, working, working. I appreciate the fact that I got to play college football on that stage, but at the same time I know we helped build the success that this program is experiencing right now. We helped build that, and it makes me proud that we started it. I hope that our blueprint is used—just work hard and never get intimidated and never take it for granted. I know this is a different era now with the kids and the way they play and the way they're recruited, there's a lot of other things going on in their heads nowadays. The thing I appreciate is that I had a chance to play in the era where it was just really about playing football and working hard. We saw the fruits of our labor, and now you see what's going on with the program, nationally ranked every year, success. We helped build that. It's amazing really.

There are so many team accomplishments: Ron Dayne's great career, having a Heisman Trophy winner in the program, playing in multiple bowl games, going to the Rose Bowl four times, basically dominating the conference for a good run. To be a part of a well-respected program that is always at the top of the conference and to be able to say, *Yeah, I played there,* is special. You'd always be proud to say you played college football, but you could wear that even higher when your program was successful.

I think Barry is a great organizer, and I think he put a good staff in place. He started going after the players he knew would help turn the corner. Barry just makes you want to be part of it, and that transferred into why he has success being an athletics director. He just has that personality and knows how to get things done. He taught us patience. He was always letting us know he had faith in us and the way the program was built. Those were some of the qualities that Barry had. Plus he's a great guy and a great coach to play for. Barry's first Rose Bowl win was special for a lot of reasons. A lot of what's going on now, it helped a lot of people. I'd just like for that to be acknowledged because that was just a special time.

Lamark Shackerford was a captain, along with Joe Panos, for the Badgers' 1993 Big Ten championship team that also won the 1994 Rose Bowl. He was a first-team All–Big Ten nose guard in 1993 and a member of Barry Alvarez's first recruiting class.

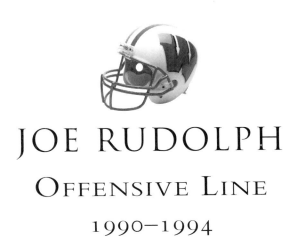

JOE RUDOLPH

OFFENSIVE LINE

1990–1994

FOOTBALL IS VERY IMPORTANT TO THE PEOPLE of western Pennsylvania, and it was important in our family. My dad played in high school and college, so it started pretty early for me. Probably my first memories were watching the Steelers, guys like Jack Lambert, Lynn Swann, just loving that growing up. I was always a guard and linebacker. You don't see that combination as much anymore. When you're out there recruiting, you're not looking for your guard/linebacker combo!

Playing in high school, I was pretty lucky because I had a brother who played, and I had a chance to watch him progress and see his work ethic. I think that was very valuable. It really helped me along in the process. I remember my sophomore year, during camp, we did a drill for linemen, and it was like a one-on-one, rite of passage, manhood type of drill. The guys who win those drills are usually the better players, and I was going against a junior or a senior who was starting. I won the drill pretty convincingly and heard the reactions, and I started from that point on in camp. I started that sophomore year and played tackle, and the next year I played linebacker and offensive guard. I did that again my senior year. I was really just focused on being a good high school player. It wasn't until I was going into my senior year when I started to hear a little bit about recruitment and teams coming out to visit the school and see me. That was obviously fun, neat for our program.

Obviously, the pool of people who recruit you is big at the beginning, and then those people tend to disappear. I actually went to the spring game at Notre Dame going into my senior year. I met Coach Alvarez, got a picture with him shaking hands with my dad. Then, when the offers started to come out, the pool got pretty small as the recruiting process went along. I played my whole senior season, took some senior visits afterward, and went to games at Pitt and West Virginia and kind of all over. Penn State dropped out earlier—that's most likely where I would have gone. I thought I'd go to Pitt, but Pitt went through a coaching change that year, and the recruiting didn't pick up as much after the change. So I'd taken a visit to Miami of Ohio—it's kind of funny because on my visit there, another recruit who was there with me was Mel Tucker, and it turned out we were both visiting Wisconsin the next weekend. So we were on the same trip into Madison, which was pretty neat. But it really kind of took to life because my dad worked at U.S. Steel, and the guys in the mill knew Coach Alvarez, knew the family, a lot of people from the area. I think they referenced his father and said, "Alvarez's boy's up at Wisconsin, you've got to go up and take a trip." We took a trip up and ended up really loving it. I committed a little bit after that.

Coming in, the one thing that really stuck with me from the standpoint of recruiting was that Coach Alvarez said, "You come here, you're going to have a chance to be part of a Rose Bowl championship," and that's a strong statement. There's someone there who's been part of championship teams. It made you excited about the idea of building something. Coming in it was pretty challenging. That first year we were 1–10, there weren't a lot of fans in the stands and it was a different environment after that. What you knew you were getting from Coach Alvarez and that coaching staff that year was consistency. They were demanding a certain level of work, of attention to detail, of execution, and of effort, and those things were instilled in that first year. They were the foundation for what you build on. I think the result in '93 was just seeing that come to life, putting those three years of work in to get to that point. But it was fun. I came in as a linebacker who wasn't very fast, but fashioned myself as being tough and hard-nosed and working hard and really just kind of wrapped myself around the weight room and got as strong as I could. I really made myself into the best I could be athletically. I ended up moving positions the second year, doing scout team work at tight end and defensive tackle. I was all over the place, wherever they needed someone. Then that third year I moved to offensive line and went through camp at offensive line and ended up winning the job in the spring. It was pretty classic to that group—you had a few guys who were different athletically. Guys like Troy Vincent and Don Davey, but there weren't a lot. The first time Coach Alvarez talked to us, he talked about a hard hat and a lunch pail, and I'd seen my dad do that for a long time. So it was pretty easy to understand and grab onto.

The game that sticks out for me in '93 that kind of turned it—because to that point we still hadn't been to a bowl game, still hadn't finished with a winning record—was that game at SMU when we went down there and found a way to win. You know it wasn't perfect, it was ugly, but you found a way to win, but sometimes those are the best teams. You can't always play perfect, but can you win when you don't play perfect. You're not getting all the breaks and the ball isn't bouncing your way, but you find a way to pull it out and win. I think that group gained a lot of confidence on the road winning that one in that environment.

Late in 1993 was a wild period of time. You finish the game at Illinois and you win, you find out that Ohio State loses, and you put yourself in a tie for the conference championship, knowing that if you win your next game, you go to the Rose Bowl. Meanwhile everyone else is done, so you've got one game to play and it's in Japan against Michigan State. It was definitely different. There were a lot of things we did leading up to it—we had a class on Japanese culture that everyone was taking, so everyone knew that game was coming, the trip was coming. It was something that was on our mind from the beginning but no one had any idea of the repercussions that would come from that game. We kind of set the tone for the Rose Bowl. But from our preparation to our trip out, Coach Alvarez, probably the thing you loved about him more than anything was he always wrote the story for you. He did an unbelievable job of just kind of putting words to the setting you were in, giving you that vision of what you needed to do that week in prep. Giving you the vision of what they were doing, what *their* mind-set was. Then laying out the plan for what we needed to do to win. And that's what he did from day one, from prep to practice in Madison at midnight and wearing sunglasses during the day, you had a mind-set that you were doing things smarter and you were working harder, and so that was all pretty neat.

Coach tells the story: we were up and staying awake on the flight to Japan. Our guys went downstairs and saw the Michigan State players sleeping, and he said we won the game right there, mind-set wise. And to a certain degree,

you felt like you had an edge. The thing I remember there is my feet hanging over the bed in the hotel in Japan. Instead of hash browns and sausage,
you had hot dogs and French fries in the morning. I remember the offensive
line guys would walk down the street, and [pedestrians] thought they were
sumo wrestlers, some that were bigger than others. It was fun, but I'd say the
group was very focused. You knew what you had to accomplish. The game
itself was a little bit surreal. The fans didn't really 100 percent understand it.
We'd score a long touchdown run, and you'd hear nothing. You'd kick the
extra point, and the fans would go nuts. The biggest thing was we had a blast.
When you work your tail off and you can have fun doing it with a group,
that leads to success, and that's definitely what I remember most about it.

When I think about the 1994 Rose Bowl, we didn't have a lot of reference
points; we'd never been to a bowl. From the Rose Bowl standpoint, I think
you gain a much better appreciation for just what that game means to so
many people. Now I have a better appreciation for that than I did back then.
What I did know is it was unbelievable. Everything about it was first class—
the way you were treated, how things were handled to going to the field and
seeing how well that was set up. Our reference points were small, but the
experience was more than I could've imagined.

I remember going in, and I think we all knew that Wisconsin had never
won a bowl game. And the Big Ten, around that period of time, had not had
a ton of success in the Rose Bowl. Those two things kind of stuck out. There
was a point in that season where now you have a chance to have a year that
is special, and I think we kind of all took that on. And the thing we probably did best was have a sense of urgency that was with us through Tokyo and
took us deep into December. We maintained that in Pasadena. And it wasn't
all perfect—and guys made some plays, and obviously UCLA made plays in
that game, and you end up just making one more than them—but the sense
of urgency the group had in their preparation was special. The defense on
the field at the end had to get the stop to win it, and I don't think there was
a player there who didn't feel like his heart was on the line or wouldn't die to
be out there to help in that situation. So I think the group really knew how
much it meant to finish it and to win that game. It was very rewarding to do
that, and it kind of solidified the season for me.

Looking back, football-wise, I have great pride in maintaining the program and growing and keeping things moving forward. Probably the thing I
take the most pride in is the consistency of the program. You don't have years

Offensive lineman Joe Rudolph's hard work in the weight room paid off as he was twice named first-team All–Big Ten.

that you don't perform and you don't fall off. The program was built on work ethic and consistency, and that rings true through what the program has accomplished. From the school standpoint, it's kind of funny, you graduate from Wisconsin, you're going to school, and it's a big part of what you do, but football is a big part of what you do. I didn't really have the appreciation I do now for how good an education I received and how well respected the university is. You know that it's respected in the state, but when you talk about it across the country and across the world, it's pretty neat. I probably didn't gain that perspective until I went back to get my master's degree and I saw how well-received the University of Wisconsin was on applications and interviews.

What comes to mind for me when I think about being a Badger is the success of the common man. It's the work ethic, the drive, the fight to finish, the smart play, the dependability, the whole being greater than the sum of its parts. All the things that go into that, that go into team, those are the things that, to me, are what it means to be a Badger. It's not flashy. It could be at times, but it's not intended to be. It's really all about unselfishness and doing things together to accomplish your goal and that toughness. A lot of times I talk to my players about toughness and how that's misconstrued. It's not getting mad and punching a door and breaking it. Toughness is doing that thing that you might not want to do but because you know it's right, and do it as if it's your most favorite thing in the world to do. To me, that's toughness, and that's what speaks to this program over that period of time. I think it's what you see in the success of our players on the field, but then also as they continue to grow in their lives, that they carry that with them, and you can see the appreciation they have for the guys playing.

We're a pretty far-reaching football program when you talk about recruiting and where people are coming from and who makes up the team. The thing that it does for families is it really brings them in, they enjoy every second of it. I think about my family and me being a part of this, and how much they enjoyed every moment of it. And my roommates, I could see how much their families enjoyed it. I don't know if there's anything more important than the coaches who work with our players and their families because their backgrounds are solid, and I think that's an attraction for the kids who come here. They appreciate what it means to be a Badger because it probably relates closely to what it means to be part of their families, and that was something I loved. I loved having my family be such a part of it. Seeing the families now come and see their kids afterward and getting together and sharing, it's pretty neat. So you talk about the whole group, those tentacles reach pretty far from that team and really pull a lot of people in—I enjoyed that part of it.

Joe Rudolph, a member of Barry Alvarez's first recruiting class at Wisconsin, was a two-time first-team All–Big Ten guard for the Badgers. He went on to play two seasons in the NFL before moving on to coaching positions at Ohio State and Nebraska. Rudolph returned to Wisconsin in 2008 and currently serves as the program's tight ends coach and recruiting coordinator.

TAREK SALEH
DEFENSIVE LINE
1993–1996

I REMEMBER WANTING TO PLAY ORGANIZED FOOTBALL and my parents saying I was too young. We used to get together with the other kids in the neighborhood and actually buy pads and helmets to have an unorganized, informal game. I remember the NFL strike season in '82. There was no football on Sundays, so we would get together and play against each other, tackle each other. We obviously didn't know what we were doing, but I really enjoyed it. I remember watching football. My father actually emigrated to the United States in the late '60s, and I was born in '74. We kind of learned the game together. He just became a great fan of the game, so it was really cool watching it with him.

Growing up, I was begging to play, and, when I was about nine years old, he agreed to let me play Pop Warner. I was in a smaller town, so I had to go to the next town over, Seymour, Connecticut, so I could play. Seymour was a blue-collar town, a tremendous town with a bunch of people who really took a lot of pride in how they went about their business, not only at work, but football is also really important to them. And I got an opportunity to play with a great group of kids. It was a peewee league, and we won the state championship and later earned the right to go to Alabama to play a team from Atlanta for the national championship. They took into consideration your record and your grade-point average. So that was really special. We lost the game; that was the only game we lost all year, but what a great experience it was traveling as a team and getting to play. It was one of the most exciting times in my life. It was, for me at the time, even on par with going to the Rose Bowl later, because for a 10-year-old to get to play and go somewhere with your team was truly something special. So it really was a great start for me with organized football, and I'll always remember those times back in Connecticut.

I played Pop Warner football in one town and lived in another town, which was Woodbridge, and it had a public school called Amity High School. When I went into eighth grade, I played eighth grade football, but then they moved me up and I played freshman football as an eighth grader. We had a lot of success there, and there was a little excitement that I could play a little football and could help at Amity. But my grades weren't where we wanted them to be, so I was sent to a Catholic school called Notre Dame High School in West Haven. It's the same high school that [2010 UW All-American] John Moffitt played for. I went kicking and screaming, but they basically told me to go for one year, see how I'd do, and we'd go from there. I went there, my grades started going up, I got my focus, and I paid attention to everything and improved both on and off the field and in the classroom, and made some great friends. The coach, Tom Marcucci, who is still there today, had a tremendous influence on me as a student and as a football player; he made me a lot better. In that one year I was getting Bs, and I actually played freshman, JV, and varsity. Just to dress for the varsity was really neat, and I got a couple snaps. From sophomore to senior year, I started pretty much both ways. It was a great experience, we went to state championship and lost our senior year at state championships. But we had great teams, great people, I got a great education, and it really prepared me for college, not only from a football standpoint but also academically.

I guess the recruiting process started my freshman or sophomore year. Freshman year I got the form letters, and sophomore year I started getting more specific letters. My junior year I was offered by Penn State, and growing up in Connecticut, that's the Holy Grail. I watched the '86 national championship when they beat Miami, watched every play, every ounce of it, and I was dead set if Penn State ever offered me in my entire life I would go there hands down. I really liked Joe Paterno's mystique and the whole deal. Some others were in the mix, too, like Syracuse and Boston College, Vanderbilt, Rutgers, and a bunch of other schools. I was more focused on Penn State.

132

Tarek Saleh set Wisconsin career records with 58 tackles for loss and 33 quarterback sacks. He was first-team All-America in 1996.

Then right in the middle of my junior year, Wisconsin coach Rob Ianello started calling; Rob was a tremendous recruiter, he did a great job and really intrigued me. That year, my junior year, Pete Diatelevi, who's a good friend of mine to this day [we graduated together], turned down Boston College for Wisconsin. I didn't know why he would do that at the time, but I later found out why. Then John Palermo came into the picture and took over the recruiting for Rob, and I really developed a great relationship with him. I got to know Coach Alvarez, and I liked them both. I took my official visit to Penn State and felt I more than likely was going to come to Penn State. Just for my own peace of mind, though, I planned to take a few more visits. The first one was Syracuse and then Wisconsin. Syracuse was fun, but I didn't think it was for me, so Penn State was still top of my list. Then I went to Wisconsin and really enjoyed it. You saw the energy of the staff; you saw it in Coach Alvarez and Coach Palermo and then you have Brad Childress, Jim Hueber, Bill Callahan, Dan McCarney, Jay Norvell, the late Coach [Tom] McMahon. They had that something special, a passion for the game. Then you got to meet the team, and they had a little something more to them. I think you had people from all different walks of life, interests. There was one common interest and it was football; they loved football. It wasn't just a program, you had a lot of guys who were students and football players. I thought there was something special at Wisconsin.

The pressure was coming on to make a decision, and I wanted to take two more visits because it was fun and, as a kid, you want to see all there is in the world. But the pressure was too high, and everyone wanted to know what I was going to do. The night that I made the decision, I was with my high school coach. There was a coach from Penn State outside at my mailbox—he was sitting outside. He came there and sat outside my house, waiting for me to make a decision. So he was sitting outside, my father and I were putting everything down on paper, all the key points that were important for making a decision for a college, or at least what we thought were important. We kept going down the list, and Wisconsin kept winning out. My mom was pacing because she really wanted me to go to Penn State, thinking it was a safer choice. Wisconsin was a great school, but we didn't know the program and how they work with student-athletes—it turned out to be the best thing in the world, but not knowing that, my mom was a little nervous. She was pacing, and the guy from Penn State was outside, but my coach and my dad were really tremendous in helping me evaluate the situation. I told them I had to go to Wisconsin, and we all agreed, and my mom gave me a hug and was happy with the decision, but it was just emotional. So the guy from Penn State came in and told me I had to call Coach Paterno and let him know about my decision. That was probably one of the tougher calls I ever had to

133

make. I was happy to go to Wisconsin, but to call a legend like Joe Paterno and say what I had to say was emotional, and I was shedding some tears and so forth. But the next call I made was to Coach Alvarez and Coach Palermo. I called Coach Palermo first and said, "Hey, I'm going to be a Badger"—that was really exciting. It was a great feeling to know that I believed in something and I was taking a path less traveled.

Well, the lessons learned in my freshman year at Wisconsin were lessons I still carry with me. They came from Coach Palermo kind of breaking me down and building me back up, teaching me how to play the game of football the proper way. I think I had a good work ethic from high school. I think that, in terms of sportsmanship and toughness and how to compete and those sorts of things, Coach Marcucci prepared me very well. But to really play at a high level and to play with good technique and fundamentals, to play smart and within the system, Coach Palermo got me ready for that. It's a big change freshman year, you've lost your friends, your girlfriend. I got my butt beat for the whole year, even though I played. Part of my memory is going to Japan and playing for the Big Ten championship and getting to the Rose Bowl for the first time in 30 years. Those experiences were surreal. All along the way it was really rough on me from the standpoint of being away from home, being undersized, just because I'm a freshman, not knowing the plays. But we went to Tokyo and won the game. Having observed all this as a freshman stayed with me, and you see how to compete. I don't think there's a team that ever competed as hard as that '93 team. That was a reflection of the head coach, Coach Alvarez. He always prepared us the right way and, as a freshman, to take all that in, it really was important and it really helped me as I went along in my career, not only in college but in the NFL. So I'm grateful for that experience. The Rose Bowl was crazy, a tremendous experience. The preparation and the intensity of the whole group was awesome. After practice was over, everybody was friends, but on the field we competed and we fought and scratched for everything, so that made us a tremendous team, and it helped me personally.

One of the things I tell kids is don't confuse effort with results. I needed to be taught that it's not always enough just to give a great effort. That came from John Palermo. One day at practice I remember a fullback running at me, and I stalemated him, hit him as hard as I could. I thought I did the job, but I didn't cover my hole, and the running back ran right by me. And there I was thinking I did a great job. I gave great effort, but the result wasn't what it needed to be. That stuck with me for my entire life. That whole first year was a great learning experience.

My sophomore year I really felt like I got an understanding of the defense and I started all the games and had some success. We beat Michigan at Michigan, a tremendous game, at a place where you're told you can never win. We had some tough games that year, but we persevered and ended up going to the Hall of Fame Bowl in Tampa. Going to Florida for a bowl game, being able to play with Terrell Fletcher and guys like Joe Rudolph, was an honor and a privilege. The next year we didn't go to a bowl game, but one of the most memorable games of my entire life was going to Penn State, where I was recruited, and beating them there the season after they won the national championship. My family was up there visiting, and just to go in to Happy Valley with a group of great guys from the University of Wisconsin, that was one of the most memorable experiences of my life. I'll always cherish that game. We had some good ones that year and we had some tough losses. The next year, Ron Dayne came aboard, and in the fourth game he broke out and played great, broke Herschel Walker's record that year. We fought our way into the Copper Bowl and beat Utah. They were a very good Utah team, and it was a great experience.

I had a lot of great experiences throughout my career, a lot of success. A big part of it was the guys we had, the coaching staff, some great teammates, and being able to go to a great institution like the University of Wisconsin. You know you're going to get a great education, but to be able to get that plus play great football in front of great fans and make some friendships for life, it was just unbelievable. To this day, I live here in Wisconsin. I came back here after playing pro football. It's a great place, great platform to do business and continue those relationships that were formed years ago.

What it means to be a Badger is having the passion and conviction to go out and compete against all odds. You may not be the most talented team, you're not the prettiest team, but you will be the most physical team, and no one will outwork you, no one will outsmart you. You play smart, sound, fundamental football, you love the game of football, you had a lot of pride in your school, pride in your team, you bring your hard hat and your lunch pail every day to work, and you go about your business. You don't worry about the other team, you worry about what you do, and you go out and have a lot of fun, you work hard and you play hard. That's the bottom line, that's a reflection of Coach Alvarez and what he preached. He'd say it's one heartbeat—everybody playing together and a sense of pride and community that is very passionate about football, very passionate about their school, about academics and about getting after it and working hard and having some fun.

Tarek Saleh set Wisconsin career records with 58 tackles for loss and 33 quarterback sacks. He was first-team All-America in 1996. Saleh was a fourth-round selection of the Carolina Panthers in the 1997 NFL Draft. He played five seasons in the NFL with Carolina and Cleveland. Saleh lives in the Madison area and works as director of business development for LIDS Sports Group.

CECIL MARTIN

FULLBACK

1995–1998

MY INTRODUCTION TO FOOTBALL was a flag football league for fourth and fifth graders. Then I did one year of tackle football in sixth grade. It was a weight-restricted league, and I worked really hard to try to make weight. It's interesting to think about a sixth grader actually putting on a gar- bage bag and running hills and trying not to eat too much and almost going through a whole wrestler's dynamic in order to make weight to play football every week. So I did that one year of tackle and I didn't want to go through that anymore, so I didn't play tackle football again until high school.

I got to Emerson Township High School and jumped right into football. Everyone did get a chance to make the team, but there was an A team and a B team, so I remember the anxiety of whether I was going to make the B team, whether I was good enough to make the A team. After going through about a week of practice, they split the teams up—one group was the A team the other group was the B team—and I was an instant starter playing both ways. I was punting and doing kickoffs, as well. It was a really great experi- ence. We lost one game our freshman year to a crosstown rival.

Not having played much tackle football, I was definitely behind on some basic fundamentals, but I think that I was a good enough athlete—I had always played sports—that my athleticism allowed me to close the gap between that notion of being behind in comparison to those who had gone to Catholic school or gone to schools where they had played before.

I moved up to varsity as a sophomore to play linebacker and I just did okay. They pulled me back to the sophomore team. I played both ways, I kicked, I punted, I had a ball just playing football. Then I went back up to varsity for the last three games of the season and was a completely different player. Just getting out there and playing the game over that period of four or five games on the sophomore team helped me to get better, and it helped me to show that I could compete with older kids, that I could compete at a higher level. So that moved me into some exposure-driven opportunities where colleges were getting a chance to hear about my potential. I played my junior year as a starter both ways and had a really good year—not a great year, but a really good year. I ended up going to camp at Illinois and Northwestern. I did really well at both of those camps, which increased my opportunity at potentially getting offered a scholarship to go to those schools. I was generating a lot of interest, but no offers.

It really all came down to how I did my senior year. I had a really good senior year but, when I walked off the football field for the last time, I had no scholarship offers. The two schools I felt most interested in and were in my home state—Northwestern and Illinois—had kind of backed out on me in their own way toward the latter two weeks of my season. So I walked off the field with no scholarship offers. I really had no idea where the recruiting process was going to go from there. I went to West Virginia and had a good visit, and on the way to West Virginia is when Wisconsin set me up for a visit somewhere around the last visit of the recruiting process, that last week of January, which meant that they weren't as interested in me as maybe some kids they were bringing in the first group of the recruiting process. I also visited Iowa and UCLA. Before I went to UCLA, Wisconsin asked me to come earlier, right after my UCLA visit. That was 1993, the year that Wisconsin was getting ready to play UCLA in the Rose Bowl. So I went on my visit to UCLA in the third week, my third recruiting visit, and then I came to Wisconsin during the week, not even the next weekend, but during the week, like Wednesday or Thursday, and there were only three people there, two of which were me and [future Badgers quarterback] Mike Samuel. It was at that moment that I felt as though Wisconsin was potentially the place for me. But I also felt like Iowa was potentially the place for me. I boiled it down to Wisconsin and Iowa and told both Hayden Fry and Barry Alvarez that I was going to make my decision on, if I'm not mistaken, Christmas Eve. And that's what I did. I wrote things and I talked to people, and the reasons I

Cecil Martin was a fullback and captain for the Badgers' 1998 Big Ten championship team that went on to win the 1999 Rose Bowl.

chose Wisconsin were things like the coaches were honest. Azree Commander was my host, and he was a Chicago area guy from Lane Tech. I had played against him in high school, so I always looked up to Azree. I also got to spend some time with another Chicago guy, Tony Simmons. They told me what they thought was the good of University of Wisconsin—the great part of the University of Wisconsin and football program, and some of the challenges that they felt were there. And the honesty, from the coaches' standpoint, I always remember what Barry Alvarez said to me: "I'm not going to tell you you're going to come here and be a star. I'm not going to tell you you're going to come here and be a starter. I'm going to tell you I'm going to let you compete. I'm going to get you a legitimate chance to compete, and if you're ready to compete, if you want a place where you can compete, then this is the place for you." A lot of other people tried to fill you with a lot of banter about "you're going to be a star, you're going to be a starter, you can play wherever you want to." So those are things that are important to me. Aside from that, I wanted to be a teacher. And Wisconsin had the No. 1–ranked School of Education in the country. I did my research on Madison and the university, and Madison was ranked the No. 1 place to live in the country that year. I came to the Ohio State–Wisconsin game during my senior year, and I knew that was the place I would want to be even if I wasn't playing football. So during that period of time when I was evaluating between Wisconsin and Iowa, things like that were the reasons why I chose Wisconsin. For me, once I made my decision, it was all about the opportunity to become a part of something special and leave a legacy with everyone else that I was coming in with that we could be proud of.

I have a number of great memories. My first start was as a redshirt freshman against Colorado at night on national TV in 1995. I was going against this big, wide All-America linebacker, and I can just remember jogging out there on that field. We went out for pregame in one set of uniforms, and then we came running out in a completely different set of jerseys. The electricity of that day was just unbelievable.

Then I think about when we broke Joe Paterno and Penn State's streak in that night game down there in Happy Valley. We were underdogs in that game, but went in there and came out with a victory; that was exciting. I was a starter for that.

I think that when I earned a spot on the American Football Coaches Association's Good Works Team a couple of times, I really felt good about that, being recognized for something other than what I was doing on the football field and what I was doing in school. I took a lot of pride in that. I think of Ron Dayne, when he came in against Penn State as a freshman in 1996. I have a lot of Ron Dayne memories. And, I guess, the 1999 Rose Bowl is a favorite memory. Walking out for the coin toss as a captain with Bobby Adamov and Donnel Thompson and Chris McIntosh was special. I also talk about this a lot, but walking across that stage as college graduate, as a University of Wisconsin alum, something that could never be taken away from you—an education. The experience that I had as a student-athlete kind of brings it all together.

One thing I can really appreciate is that the university has something called the Wisconsin Idea. I've gotten a chance to really engage the notion of the Wisconsin Idea. Each person who's come through the university as a student or a student-athlete has their own experience, but then all of us have almost kind of a collective experience and memories because of the space in which we all spent time. For me, having been gone from the university and obviously having been back, all the places that I've gone, the love that is expressed for the University of Wisconsin by so many people—to be able to share that, verbally, no matter if you've known them for a long time or you just met them, is significant. That connection brings you together in a special way that I think culturally isn't always there for a lot of other universities. I think there's something special about the University of Wisconsin, and to have the experience of what a student has and represent that W in a special way, that's it. There's so much we don't even realize about the university until later on—things like, and this is a fact, that Wisconsin has produced more volunteers for the Peace Corps than any other university in the country. Then you take the other side of that, that the University of Wisconsin has produced more CEOs of Fortune 500 companies than any other school in the country except for Harvard. The more you learn, if you engage in the university, if you try to reconnect and you try to be a part of it in your own way wherever you are, you find out things like that. You just get consumed with so much pride.

What does it mean to be a Badger? I think it's to represent a state of good people, a great university, a great contribution. And to represent a legacy of student-athletes who have come through the university to be the best that they can be. To pass that on to their families, their communities, and leave a legacy on the university and on the athletics department in their own way.

141

Badgers don't mean football. Badgers fall under anyone who's involved with Badgers athletics, and represents the athletics department and Badgers athletics. I think what it means to be a Badger is a culmination of all of those things because you can't internalize what it means to be a Badger without internalizing the impact and the representation you have for so many who have come through the university and so many in the state who are in some way directly or indirectly connected to the university in the state. What it means to be a Badger is to represent that with heart and with strength, with toughness and with leadership, with teamwork and with pride.

Cecil Martin was named to the American Football Coaches Association Good Works Team in college and became a sixth-round draft choice of the Philadelphia Eagles in 1999. He played five seasons in the NFL. Martin works as an educational and motivational speaker.

MIKE SAMUEL

QUARTERBACK

1995–1998

I HAVE THREE OLDER BROTHERS, so football was always part of our lives. I've been playing football since I was five years old. In the street, going outside, in the backyard, tossing a football around, sports were always just the first and foremost thing that I was introduced to, and it came naturally to play football, basketball, baseball—they were the three major sports. My father was a football player in college. It was just part of who we were.

There was an organization called the Frankford Boys Club, and they just kind of donated their time, wanted to be involved with kids. They taught great fundamentals and were dedicated to getting kids to learn team football and all sports, really. I played basketball, football, and baseball with them. I was fortunate to be involved with a great group of guys.

I was lucky I played for an all-star youth organization called the Little Quakers that was started by a guy named Bob Levy. They just wanted to get inner-city kids, kids from around the Philadelphia area, a chance to experience something different. So they would fly us around, going to Hawaii, going to New Orleans, going to Florida, and we'd go on one trip a year. So I played for them and actually got a scholarship to Penn Charter, which was a private school in Philadelphia. Otherwise I would have gone to the local public high school, which wouldn't have been the best situation academically or athletically.

Quarterback Mike Samuel proved himself in a 1997 game against Boise State, and he started every game thereafter.

144

I had some great coaching at the high school level. I was fortunate to have great quarterback coaching, and during my junior year the scholarship offers started to funnel in. [Wisconsin assistant coach] Jim Hueber, who was actually from Philadelphia, came and recruited me in Philadelphia, he knew the area, was a great guy, and we made a connection there. I had visited Boston College and few of the other schools in the area. I visited Wisconsin and just kind of fell in love with the place. I can remember flying out to Wisconsin, and it was cold and they were practicing for the 1994 Rose Bowl, which was extremely exciting. And I just kind of loved the place. I remember when I went in there it was kind of a ghost town because there were exams and everyone had left campus, but Wisconsin was still practicing for the Rose Bowl.

Once I got to Wisconsin in 1995, it was a major adjustment. Just being in the game, that's the biggest thing because everything happens faster, and the level of commitment that it takes to play at the University of Wisconsin is more intense. It's an adjustment, moving halfway across the country, being away from my family. But it's what I wanted, so I was very happy with the way the situation was working out, and it gave me time out to soak things in my freshman year. Traveling with the team is an important thing, as well—because I went on all the road games, I was accustomed to what it was all about.

I started the '96 season, we opened up against Eastern Michigan, went 3–0, and then we hit a rough patch there in the beginning of my first year starting. We lost a heartbreaker to Penn State. We went on the road, I remember, against Ohio State, which was No. 1 in the country, I believe. And we played them tough to the end, and ended up losing that. The most crushing loss that I've ever experienced as a football player was against Northwestern at home that year, and we had the game sealed. I remember there was a handoff between Ron Dayne and myself, and for whatever reason it just didn't happen. We wound up losing that game. What was ironic about that was, the next year, one of the greatest wins we had involved a similar situation against Northwestern in '97, where they had sealed the game up, they were going for a score, we got a fumble late, and Matt Davenport wound up kicking a last-second field goal to win the game. The '96 and '97 seasons were 8–5 seasons. Another pivotal game was Boise State in 1997. I got pulled from the game early because I just wasn't playing well, I had a couple picks. They put Scott Kavanagh in the game, and I just knew it was a turning point. For whatever reason Coach put me back in the game, and we wound up winning late. So I thought that was an important game in terms of what I was going to do at the University of Wisconsin. I wound up starting from then on out. And then we had a couple good wins there, late field goals against Indiana and Northwestern. We wound up 8–5 and went into the off-season really geared up for the '98 season. The 1998 Penn State game definitely stands out to me. We beat them at Camp Randall 24–3 and clinched a berth in the Rose Bowl.

The Rose Bowl was magical. It was surreal being out there, just enjoying and reflecting on it. You just relish the moment, knowing that opportunities like this don't come around every day. So you want to make the most of it, and that's what we did as a team. We had unbelievable leadership in Coach Alvarez and the other coaches, and I was just very fortunate. It was an amazing time, something I'll never ever forget. The week leading up to it was great. They explained everything perfectly, and as I think back on it, the way things shook out was that UCLA had lost earlier in the season, so they were kind of disappointed to be in that game, and they had lost to Miami in a rain-shortened hurricane game. They had to replay Miami and lost to them, so they were disappointed to be in the Rose Bowl. We were big underdogs, and they were playing in their own stadium, they were used to it. To us, it was the event of a lifetime, and we seized the opportunity. They had a dynamic offense, but I knew that we had an advantage running the ball, obviously, from the very first handoff.

The thing that sticks out most for me from my years at Wisconsin is the people. The friendships, the relationships that you make, but people in the Midwest, and specifically Wisconsin, are just amazing. My teammates are what I miss most when I think back on playing, the camaraderie through the struggle, the off-season workouts, the games, the sitting down in the locker room looking at each other and saying, win or lose, we gave our best. It's something not everybody gets to go through in a lifetime at that level. That's what I miss most is the relationships and the teammates, the camaraderie, the coaches, and just being involved with the whole program.

Coach Alvarez was an unbelievable leader. He was a guy you would do anything for, you'd run through a wall for. I can't say enough about Coach Alvarez. He gave me the opportunity to start and grow as a quarterback. I had my bad moments, and Coach Alvarez was always there to inspire confidence. He was a tremendous leader. You can't say enough about him, he was just unbelievable.

As for Ron Dayne, once he got on the field and started to run and you'd see him plow through the line, I think that's when we got a sense of how good he could be. Once he got rolling, yeah, he was something special. When he was first recruited, no, he was just another name, but once he got on the field, he was Ron Dayne, and you could see he had something special.

What it means to be a Badger, to me, is extreme pride. I'm proud when I wear my Wisconsin shirt in Philadelphia and go to football games out there. I think that's all due to Coach Alvarez. Not that Wisconsin didn't exist before Barry Alvarez was there, but he put it back on the map. He is Wisconsin, and

I was proud to be a part of it. It's a great institution, a tremendous learning experience with diverse people and an outstanding faculty and administration. I think the greatest thing I could say about a place is that I would send my children there in a heartbeat. Wisconsin is a great place to live, a great place to go to school, and obviously a great place to play football. Coach Bielema is doing a tremendous job, as well. I really can't say enough about it.

Mike Samuel was a three-year starter at quarterback for the Badgers and helped lead Wisconsin to the 1998 Big Ten title and victory in the 1999 Rose Bowl. He left UW with the second-most passing yards in school history. Samuel is currently a coach and teacher in his native Philadelphia.

RON DAYNE
RUNNING BACK
1996–1999

I STARTED PLAYING FOOTBALL WHEN I WAS ABOUT THREE years old. We had some kind of league, it was like a Pop Warner league, but I couldn't play because I wasn't old enough; you couldn't start playing until you were five or six. My mom knew the coach, and I was as big as the five- and six-year-old guys, so they would let me play. At first, my playing was just talking to the other team because I knew them. I'd be talking and wouldn't be trying to tackle anybody and stuff like that. Finally, we had a game, I think our championship game. I was three or four and got to run the ball. Ever since then, I always wanted to run the ball. One of the things I liked about playing was I could do stuff to people that I couldn't do normally: tackle 'em, lay on 'em, jump on 'em, just different things like that.

When I was eight, I moved to New Jersey and didn't get to play until I was 14 or 15, going into my freshman year, so I was just ready to play. My freshman year in high school, I came in and had just moved in with my Uncle Rob. My cousin Rob was the big-time running back for the varsity. But as a freshman, I couldn't play varsity, so I was just doing good with the freshman team. My freshman year, I had about 29 or 30 touchdowns. That was the first time I got to play since I moved from Virginia. For four or five years, I couldn't play ball. Everybody just kept talking about me. So I was playing, and they wanted me to play varsity, but we couldn't do it. Finally, sophomore year I got to play. My cousin Rob and I were on the team—we were both running backs. When he was getting recruited, I was a sophomore, and they were coming to watch me. I was on most of his highlight films. The coaches were coming to see him but were asking about me. Finally, he went to Tennessee–Chattanooga, where Terrell Owens went. I kind of sat back and waited. He came home and had had a bad experience in college, so in my junior and senior years, I was thinking college was the worst because I saw my cousin come home. But I went on some visits, and my first one was with Wisconsin, and I committed when I first got there. The only other reason I visited other schools is my Uncle Rob wanted me to compare Big Ten teams, so I went to Ohio State. And Ohio State, when I was on their recruiting trip, six running backs committed, so I didn't even go meet the coach. My recruiting days were pretty easy. I committed to Wisconsin, went to Ohio State, and I took a trip to Tennessee to see my cousin, just to see how he was doing, and that was pretty cool. I had a good time.

[Wisconsin assistant] coach Bernie Wyatt was always around, and I got to see him. I don't even think Coach Wyatt came to any of my football games; he came to my track meets. I wasn't being recruited for track, but I had all these different schools at my track meets, and Coach Wyatt would come watch practice. I was kind of shocked that they wanted me to come out to Wisconsin and be a running back. I remember Coach Wyatt said, "I'll have Barry Alvarez, our head coach, tell you that, too." And that's how he and Coach told me, and I was thinking, *I have a chance to be a running back?* I was an All-America fullback coming out of high school and didn't even play fullback. I didn't play fullback since I was a freshman in high school. I guess I was just too big. Coach Alvarez, I just talked to him once, and I guess Coach Wyatt was trying to prove a point: "I told you, you could be a running back." Coach Wyatt was the one who was always around and stayed on me. When I went out to Wisconsin, Coach Wyatt would always come check on me and make sure I was straight. "You need to talk to somebody? You doing good in school? What's going on?" After a while I was just kind of dodging Coach, but it was cool that he stayed on me like a parent. Coach Alvarez was there always. Anytime I needed something, I could go talk to Coach, tell Coach what's going on with me. When my girl, Alia, became pregnant with my daughter, Coach was probably the first person who knew. Coach stuck with me and gave me great advice and helped me handle my situations, especially with practice, and I had to do study table and come home and see my daughter, spend some time with her. Coach would do little things to give me opportunities to go spend some time with my daughter, still get my work done, and still be at practice. That's why I love Coach to death.

My adjustment to Wisconsin was easy because I got to come early. I left the day after we graduated high school and went out to Madison. Coach already had a great program going. He had guys like Carl McCullough to help me out, Brandon Williams, guys I used to hang with when I first got here, and those guys took me under their wings. It just made it a lot easier for me, they helped me with so much, it was just like normal. It didn't even feel like an adjustment. Carl and I still talk all the time, text each other, crazy stuff and things like that. So Coach had great guys around, and that's what made it a lot easier.

Probably the top moment I had at Wisconsin was after the 1999 Iowa game getting to see Coach, how happy he was, how happy I was. Once I broke the [all-time NCAA career rushing] record [at that Iowa game] was probably the biggest moment for me. I'd have to say my best game was probably against Hawaii. We were down there for a week and were practicing, and we were having bad practices and things like that. We were tired, but we ended up playing a great game. And I played really well, even though I didn't even expect it. We were looking at how big those guys were, the quarterback was big, the running backs were big, they were all Hawaiian guys. We were thinking this was going to really be tough. You could just kind of see it— the locker room was kind of down. Then once the game started, it was like we just turned the switch on and, oh man, we couldn't be stopped. Give me the ball, Coach, give me the ball! That was probably my best game, but my most memorable moment was seeing Coach after breaking the record in '99. The atmosphere in the stadium that day against Iowa was just electric, it was amazing. It just seemed like something big was going to happen.

I think we just had so many different leaders and great guys, and Coach just put us together during my years at Wisconsin. We stuck together, we even hung out together. There'd be linemen and we'd be hanging out with the same guys, we were all at the same parties. It was just a team thing. Coach put us together, starting from fall camp at the seminary. Once you started going to seminary, it was just like, *They're going through the same thing I'm going through,* barely walking up the steps, crawling up, taking turns helping each other up the steps. We were feeling each other's pain. The leadership on the team was just crazy because we had so many different guys who were great leaders and would talk, and it might be a down day for one of our leaders, like Cecil might

Ron Dayne set the NCAA Division I career rushing record in 1999. His career total of 6,397 rushing yards has yet to be broken.

have a down day. So we'd have Mike Samuel step up and talk and get us practicing together. We had Big Mac [Chris McIntosh], we had Tom Burke, guys like that on the defense. If the defense was playing bad, Tom Burke would go off and talk. Sometimes Coach might make us start over practice, and guys would call it up as a group, and it wouldn't even have to be Coach. His big thing was recruiting great guys and leaders.

The whole awards circuit in 1999 was kind of tough, but it was good getting to meet all those different guys, the great athletes from other teams, like Drew Brees. I got to visit with a couple guys like Ricky Williams, Kevin Faulk, Randy Moss, Peyton Manning. It was just great to be able to go and do those things. But the biggest one was probably the Heisman. Everybody kind of thought that I was going to win it, but I didn't know until about 20 or 30 seconds before the event, when they came and powdered my face up even though I wasn't even sweating or anything. Chad Pennington was sitting next to me and kind of bumped me, and I just kind of moved over because my legs were shaking. When they called my name, I didn't know what to do. I wanted to shake everybody's hand. I was kind of going through my thing, I want to shake everybody's hand, then come talk to Coach, then go up on stage. But soon as they called my name, I shook Chad's hand and hugged Coach. Coach was talking to me and said, "Ronny, take three deep breaths and you're going to be all right." So I got up on stage, and my eyes started watering, and I was like, *Oh man, I can't cry, because the boys at home, my linemen were like, "You can't be crying on TV, don't be crying, man we're gonna be watching!"* So as soon as I felt the tears in my eyes, I didn't know what to do. I didn't even have a handkerchief or anything to wipe my face, so I took my three deep breaths, and they worked. I kind of looked at Coach, and he gave me the nod, and I went on with my speech. That whole week was great.

The program at Wisconsin, it's just a great program. We've got great people around. I'm getting ready to go back to school, and seeing some of my old tutors and things like that, they're still around and they still show you support. All the guys are great, the fans are definitely great. We've got great coaches, a great staff in all the sports, and they're great people to be around. That's what I think Wisconsin is—just good people. It's great to go out and meet the people, especially those who have never met me. My kids are loving it in Wisconsin. It's just a great place to be.

If it wasn't for being a Badger, I don't think I'd be where I am today. Being around great guys, having great mentors, Coach and all the coaches, and just being here. If it wasn't for them and the things they did for me and the way they showed me what's right and what's wrong—I knew a lot of that stuff—but just hearing it from them made a difference. Being a Badger means everything to me.

Ron Dayne was a consensus All-American and became Wisconsin's second Heisman Trophy winner after setting the NCAA Division I career rushing record in 1999. Dayne led the Badgers to back-to-back Big Ten and Rose Bowl titles. He was a first-round selection (11th overall) of the New York Giants in the 2000 NFL Draft. Dayne played eight seasons in the NFL for New York, Denver, and Houston. He currently lives in Madison.

CHRIS McINTOSH
OFFENSIVE LINE
1996–1999

I GUESS YOU COULD SAY I GOT STARTED playing football because I was the biggest kid ever to come through our school and I was, more or less, expected to play. I didn't start playing until I was a freshman in high school. In all honesty, I literally didn't know the difference between a lineman and a linebacker. Before my freshman year, I went to a football camp and ended up playing linebacker there, thinking it was a newly invented position. I knew nothing about football whatsoever. I never put pads on or a helmet until my freshman year in high school. I feel like I didn't really learn how to play—I was an average high school football player, but somebody saw I had some potential.

I played a bunch of sports as a young kid. Soccer, baseball, but I really wasn't a good athlete. I wrestled in middle school. I was always taller than everybody else but was kind of a chunky kid—I weighed too much for my height. Then, between sixth and seventh grade, I grew six inches in a year and wound up being 6′6″ in seventh grade and only 160 pounds. I was so uncoordinated I couldn't even put one foot in front of the other. And I've only grown an inch since then. So I started to fill in and come into my own and try to figure out how I was supposed to walk around. That was kind of a blessing, a double-edged sword in that I couldn't chew gum and walk down the hallway in seventh grade, but I got my growth spurt out of the way early and it was enough of a growth spurt that I could really come into my own down the road.

Entering my freshman year in high school, I thought I'd be good at football because I was big, tall, strong but I didn't know anything about it; I just figured that was enough to be a good player. In hindsight I look back and I'd say I played way too high, my pad level was way too high. But I was so much stronger than the kids I was going against that I could just compensate for it with strength. I never did play varsity my freshman year because I wasn't any good. The next three years I started on the varsity.

I think my sophomore year was the first time I was invited to come up to Madison for a game. It wasn't until my freshman year in high school that I actually went to a game at Camp Randall. My sophomore year I went to a game, and I remember we were late coming down to the field during pregame and the tunnel was filled with the UW band. This would have been in 1990–1991, prior to that run in 1993, and the band literally wouldn't clear the way in the tunnel for the recruits to come down onto the field. So we were standing up there, and Rob Ianello, the assistant coach, was throwing a fit because it was his job to get us down on the field and give us that experience. We ended up missing the majority of the pregame because they wouldn't let us through. Rob told those band guys, "You know, at one point the fans came here to listen to the band, and what you guys don't realize is that they're going to come here to watch football games." It just stuck with me. It was prophetic in hindsight.

155

After my junior year in high school, I went up to camp in Madison, and when I walked in, the first person I saw was Mike Rosenthal. He was about 320 pounds and would later go to play for Notre Dame and in the NFL. He was literally the first person I saw at camp, and I thought he was a college athlete—he had the college or the pro build. I thought, *Holy cow, I'm out of my league now.* I don't know if it was a three- or four-day camp, but in those days I became twice the football player that I'd ever been. On the last day of camp, I remember Coach Alvarez called Mike and me over and offered us scholarships. I was shocked, absolutely shocked. This would have been the summer of '94, right after the Rose Bowl. He didn't want us to give him an answer; he wanted us to go home and talk to our families about it. So he came down sometime in July, and we talked about it, and I asked him what would happen if I got hurt. I was trying to figure out why should a player, at that stage of the game, verbally commit—what's the upside to doing so? Coach told me if I were to get injured my senior year that they would honor the scholarship. And he shook my hand, and I remember plain as day where I was standing in the foyer of my house. I said, "Okay, that sounds like a deal. I'd love to come play for you, Coach." And he left, and, as I recall, I believe it was the third game of my senior year I tore my ACL and MCL. It was a Friday night game, and I knew I hurt my knee. Coincidentally, I was coming up to the Badgers game Saturday morning, and you can imagine the look on the coaches' faces when I came in.

It was just crushing at the time. So I went up to the UW Hospital, did the reconstruction and I ended up getting a staph infection in my bone, in my femur, and it required three additional surgeries to clear up. I think I spent 21 days at the hospital and lost 40 pounds. I had to administer IV antibiotics to myself for the next 12 weeks or something like that. They took out the screws that were holding the graph together in my knee. It was a really tough time. I was worried about playing football. I remember Dr. Graf looked at me, and I kind of asked a stupid question like when would I be ready for camp, or something like that. And he said he was more worried about saving my leg than getting me ready for camp. That put things in perspective. I'm sure the coaches didn't want to make good on that promise because it probably wasn't looking too good—it wasn't looking like it was going to work out too good at the time, but thankfully it did.

I came to Madison the next year and had put a lot of weight back on. In that time, Coach [Bill] Callahan had left to go to Philadelphia, and Coach Hueber was named the offensive line coach. I'll never forget when I got that call. Coach Hueber called me himself and said Coach Callahan was gone to Philadelphia and that he would be my new O-line coach. He said he only knew how to coach offensive linemen one way and that was to treat them like dirt. Prior to that, I was getting the recruiting talk from Coach Callahan, so it was kind of a stark contrast. I remember sitting on the edge of my bed and putting my head in my hands, wondering how this turn of events came about. But I thoroughly enjoyed my time with Coach Hueber, and he's a good friend to this day. He is responsible for all the success I had. In hindsight, it all worked out.

The first year I started was in 1996 with all the seniors. I was the new kid on the block, and Coach Hueber just rode me hard. His style was to break you down and then build you up. And he broke me down hard. Midway through the season, I began talking to a sports psychologist twice a week. At the time, it was humbling. I didn't want to do it because you believe you're strong and you don't believe in the mental aspects of the whole thing.

Offensive lineman Chris McIntosh fought back from a high school injury to become a 1999 consensus All-American as a senior. His talents contributed to the Badgers' consecutive Rose Bowl victories in 1999 and 2000.

In hindsight, it was probably a blessing in disguise because it really helped me focus on the mental aspects of the game. But that was really my low point. I remember I wrote a note home from fall camp that year and just doubting that I could pull it off.

But there were some great moments, particularly the last two years. There's the one speech I made prior to the 1998 season when we came back from the Outback Bowl. A lot was made out of the line: "I didn't come here to play in the Outback Bowl, I came here to play in the Rose Bowl." But that was kind of the defining moment for me because I wasn't really a captain when I said that. It's just that there was a room with a ton of talent sitting there, and a real leader hadn't emerged, and it just took one little spark, one comment like that. We had some really strong leaders come out of that group and out of that team—Bobby Adamov, Donnel Thompson, Cecil Martin. That team had a really good chemistry about it.

The No. 1 moment for me was when they made a mistake and called the captains out early for the 1999 Rose Bowl. We stood in the tunnel in the corner of one of the end zones so all you could see was one side of the stadium, and it happened to be the cardinal and white side. That was the only national anthem I ever witnessed in college. And then the flyover as probably the last line of the national anthem came over—I had tears running down my face. It was just one of those moments when you realize all the hard work had paid off and it put things in perspective, where you'd come from and where you'd gotten. That game was made just so much more special by the fact that we were such an underdog and we played a great team. They had some unbelievable players, and to come out of there with a win was by far the most cherished moment athletically that I had at Wisconsin. The following season was a lot of fun—it was the most fun I had as a player, actually playing the game, just because I was really confident and it allowed me to enjoy the game more. But the season as a whole wasn't as enjoyable because we weren't the underdog anymore. A lot of pressure was on us to perform, and, obviously, Ron Dayne's rushing record was extra weight on us. We wanted to repeat and go to the Rose Bowl and be the first team to do that. [Wisconsin won the 2000 Rose Bowl over Stanford 17–9.] With the rushing record came the Heisman talk, not to mention the fact that I was trying to put together a solid season because I had aspirations of being drafted. So there was a lot of pressure, but it was probably the most fun I had playing on the field.

What it means to be a Badger, I guess, is defined by the Coach Alvarez experience just because that's the time frame I was there. But what it means to be a Badger is to overachieve, to work hard, to be tough. Coach always talked about the blue-collar mind-set, in the face of critics and people who don't believe, to prove them wrong. You just focus on what you can control and don't listen to the outside influences because they don't know what they're talking about. If we believe and we put in the work, then we can get it done. We had "believe" painted on the walls, so we got 100 players to believe they were the best when, frankly, we probably weren't the best, most gifted athletes. We didn't have the most talent, but he got us to buy in and believe.

Those are little life lessons that carry on with me. What I just described is what I subscribe to at work in my professional life. It's the kind of values I want to instill in my children, so they're good life lessons. I still live in Wisconsin and am a Badgers fan, obviously, and I live among a lot of Badgers fans. You talk to people who just recall that period of time in the mid-to-late 1990s. They kind of lump together '94 through 2000, that seven-year period, and it's amazing how people have some vivid memories of that period of time. I didn't really appreciate it at the time because that's all I knew, but winning back-to-back Rose Bowls hadn't been done prior and hasn't been done since then. So I guess it was a pretty special thing we accomplished and, maybe to Coach Alvarez's credit, it's amazing that we didn't realize at the time just how special it was.

Chris McIntosh was a 1999 consensus All-America left tackle and key component on the offensive line that paved the way for Ron Dayne's NCAA rushing record. McIntosh, who started 50 consecutive games for the Badgers, was a first-round draft choice of the Seattle Seahawks in 2000. An injury forced his retirement from football in 2002. He is the owner/operator of The McIntosh Team (residential real estate); be fitness and wellness center in Delafield, Wisconsin; Body Basix Nutrition; and Dirty Girl Adventure Mud Run. He lives in Hartford, Wisconsin.

KEVIN STEMKE

PUNTER

1997–2000

I GREW UP AS A SOCCER PLAYER. My dad was in the Olympics for the U.S. soccer team in Munich and was with the national team for quite a number of years. I grew up wanting to be a soccer player. I was going to follow in his footsteps. So, actually, just before we were about to report to high school, I was gung ho to be a soccer player, and he actually sat me down one night and asked me if I had ever considered trying football. And I said, "No, I'm a soccer player." He suggested I give it a try. I was interested in all sports growing up, but the only thing I did competitively was soccer. I ended up saying I'd give it a try. So I went out for the football team. I'd thrown the football around some, so it wasn't like I was totally foreign to the game. But growing up in Green Bay and being a Packers fan, you pretended you were Don Majkowski or Brett Favre. You don't picture yourself being Don Bracken. So it wasn't like I grew up thinking I really wanted to be a punter. You want to throw the winning touchdown pass, you don't think about fourth and long and it's two minutes left in the fourth quarter. But as it happened, after the first day of football my freshman year, our coach at the end of practice said, "Okay, show of hands, who's played soccer before?" There were probably four or five of us who raised our hands and had played a lot of soccer, and so he said, "All right, kicker tryouts." It was between us five, and I won the job, and they moved me right up to varsity to kicking field goals as a freshman.

I'm built as a punter. I was a small freshman, so they didn't want me punting or even kicking off because there might be the off chance that someone might come and try to take me out or hit me, and my body would snap in half. So all I did was kick field goals for two years. And then, my junior year, I punted, kicked off, and kicked field goals. Then I went to a camp after my junior year, a kicking camp for all different aspects of special teams. So one of the coaches said, "Kickers over there, punters over there," and I'm kind of sitting in the middle thinking that I do both and wondering what I should do. One of the coaches told me kickers were a dime a dozen, but if you can punt well, you'll have a better opportunity of using this to move forward. So that's when I really started trying to learn how to punt and really tried to focus on that. My senior year I had a pretty decent year punting, so that's how I got started in it.

I had a number of colleges contact me, certainly by virtue of just being in the state and having some success—all of the schools in Wisconsin, from Whitewater to Stevens Point to University of Wisconsin. The first letter I ever got was actually from the University of Nebraska. I remember at the time looking at the letter, thinking, *I'm being recruited as a punter and kicker by a school where it might be the windiest place in the country?* So that was the last time I opened a letter from Nebraska. It wasn't like I had every school in the country beating my door down, but there were a number of places. When Wisconsin showed interest and when they offered the scholarship, it was a pretty easy decision for me. There were other schools that were near the area where my family certainly could have come and watched me play, so it wasn't necessarily being in close proximity to my family, although that was an attractive thing. But when you're a Wisconsin kid, you go to Wisconsin, that's what you do. If Wisconsin was going to offer me, that's where I was going to go.

It's tough to look back. How do you summarize the best years of your life? I met my wife at Wisconsin. I met all my best friends at Wisconsin. My family got to watch me go to two Rose Bowls. The basketball team went to the Final Four, the volleyball team went to the national championship, the hockey team was ranked No. 1. It was this unbelievable time to be at Wisconsin. The highlights, it's kind of easy to pick out the Rose Bowls as the highlights, but the opportunity that we had as student-athletes at that time were great. Obviously, the opportunity to be in the Rose Bowl was unbelievable, but I'll never forget when the basketball team went to the Final

Four—it was nuts! That was crazy! That doesn't happen! So it was really exciting. A lot of who I am, a lot of what I know, a lot of what I believe in, is because of what happened at Wisconsin and the people I was lucky enough to be around when I was there.

When we played at that time, we didn't have a coach who necessarily coached us on the fundamentals and the techniques of kicking and punting. We had a special teams coach, so we would do our special teams period, which was a fraction of a total practice. We were by ourselves a lot of the time. To be able to every day have the self-motivation and the discipline to know that you're going off by yourself and, for example, figure out the best way to pooch punt, to get the ball to sit down, or to bounce left or right out of bounds. We kind of figured that stuff out on our own. The challenges associated with that are anywhere from just the sheer trying to figure it out on your own and being on that island, but at the same time you've got a lot of people counting on you. You've got a whole team of people who count on you to do your job well. But they don't understand and they don't know what we do. To them, we could've been in the locker room sitting on the couch watching TV the entire practice. That's part of the stigma of this position. I always felt it as a pressure to prove myself to my team that my position is important, I work hard, I'm just as important as any other—it was a challenge at times.

I knew who Ray Guy was. I don't know if I really had a full appreciation of who he was as an athlete, not just as a punter. He played safety and quarterback…in the NFL. He was a tremendous athlete. So to win that award was really gratifying and really significant. To be really honest, I look back at my winning that award, and it's crucial that we had the cover team that we had—we broke the Big Ten record for net punting average. And that's not because of me—that's because we had Donte King and Joey Boese running down the sideline. We had Mike Schneck and Mike Solwold snapping perfect balls to me. You've got the guys blocking out in front of me—that, to me, was what was so gratifying. I would never brag about winning the Ray Guy Award because of what I did. It was a culmination of so many things coming together at a time that was really a special thing. So I'm fortunate to be a part of it, I'm fortunate to call myself a Ray Guy Award winner, but the trophy itself, I think it's in a trunk packed up sitting in my basement. It's not something I have out for people to see. I'm extremely proud of it. If someone asks, I'll talk about it. But I think more about the punt team that we had during

Kevin Stemke received the inaugural Ray Guy Award, given to the nation's top punter, in 2000. His 43.5 yard career punting average holds the Wisconsin record.

not just my senior year, but all four years, and I feel very fortunate to be part of it.

I don't think anyone can fully appreciate, fully realize how truly special it is to be part of the Wisconsin program. I don't know that as an 18-year-old immature kid you really grasp how special the opportunity is to run out of that tunnel, to put on the jersey, to wear the gear to class, to have an opportunity to even go to class at Wisconsin. I don't know that you get it. You're in sort of your own little world, in that you go from class to practice. Practice to meetings. Meetings home to study. You wake up, you go to class, you go to practice, you lift, then game day. Then you go to class, you go to practice. It flies by and it's gone. You're sort of in this little world, and, at least for myself, what I failed to realize at the time was truly the enormity of the situation. I can sit back now and see it from an outsider's perspective that there are kids all over the state, all over the country, who would die for the chance to play one play in Camp Randall Stadium. And we got an opportunity to do that for four years and two Rose Bowls and be coached by one of the greatest college football coaches ever, to go to a great school like Wisconsin, to be proud of that degree that hangs in my office. I didn't really get it until I stepped back and had the opportunity to play in the NFL for about five minutes and you run across people from other schools. And now in the working world, you run across people who maybe weren't athletes, they were just students. And you talk to them about their time wherever they were. I remember a lot of conversations where guys talk about, "I had this many interceptions or this many touchdown passes, or my punting average was this or my kicking percentage was that." I look back and think about the team. I know at the time how hard we worked. But it's not until you back off and you talk to some other people that you realize we flat out worked harder than other teams. You care whether you win or lose. You live or die based on how you win or lose. If we lost, we didn't go out, we sat at home and sulked about losing. And we cared, but to step back to see and realize how much more we truly cared than everybody else. That's what I realize now, looking back at how special that time was, is the pride we had in our team.

When I talk to people about Wisconsin and they ask me about my time there, I don't talk about the Ray Guy Award, I brag about Mike Samuel running down the sideline and not pitching the ball to Ron Dayne and running head on into Penn State's LaVar Arrington. They both went flying, and Mike Samuel got up and went back to the huddle before Arrington did. That's the kind of stuff that I brag about because that's Wisconsin. That's a hardworking, working-man's man just going and making a great play. We were special in that way in the fact that we were all just working hard for each other. That's when I look back and realize how special it was, and you can't replicate that. You can't replicate it after college, you can't replicate it before. It's a very unique four-year period. There's nothing like it.

Kevin Stemke was a first-team All-American and inaugural winner of the Ray Guy Award as the nation's top punter in 2000. He set the UW record for career punting with a 43.5-yard average. Stemke played two seasons in the NFL for Oakland and St. Louis. He lives in Athens, Georgia, as a vice president for Replay Photos.

JAMAR FLETCHER
DEFENSIVE BACK
1998–2000

I HAVE AN OLDER BROTHER who's four years ahead of me. Little league starts when you're about seven or eight years old, so I got introduced fairly early, if you will, seeing him play. He was playing little league football. I was always a big football fan, and I loved the '85 Bears, my favorite team of all time. I love the game of football. It was just one of those things. I couldn't wait for football season to come around. I played all sports. I played everything—basketball, baseball, soccer—but there was nothing like football. It just felt right. I started playing little league football from about the age of seven to 12, and then on from there. I was a running back. It's funny how it works, even thinking how they did it. They put you through a little test, they'd have speed tests for us. As a kid I wasn't really thinking, I was just out there having fun. But they put us through these little tests, and before you know it, they told me I was the team's running back. That's predominantly what I played throughout little league, and I was an outside linebacker on defense, things of that nature. So that's where it started.

I wasn't really allowed to focus just on football. Even going through when I was in my younger days playing little league sports, I got called to play on AAU basketball teams, AAU baseball teams, and if you know anything about AAU, sometimes they take you and they want to extend their season. But my father wouldn't let me do that. He told me I was going to play the sport that was in season. I loved baseball; I personally think baseball is my best sport, skill-wise, but football is the one that's most dear to my heart. But once I got to high school, I definitely was geared and ready to go because I went to a high school that has traditionally been a powerhouse, so to say; we are a football school, if you want to put it like that. But I did run track, play basketball, and other sports, but when it came to football, that's where it was at for me, and it kind of grew each year. It just got better and was a beautiful thing.

We were a nationally ranked high school, won the state championship—Hazelwood East High School, St. Louis, Missouri. Junior year we won state and had a lot of Division I players on that team; I wasn't really the team star my junior year. I was a nice addition, if you will, but late in my junior year, I saw a few schools sending letters and things of that nature, but nothing really heavy. It was still mostly not even a lot of Division I schools. But senior year, I took over the reins as quarterback and I still played running back, kicker, punt returner, defensive back, and, as the process went on, schools would start coming in and they'd say, "This guy can play." They came in and toward the end of that year started offering scholarships, inviting me on visits, things of that nature. So I figured this is something I could probably do—go to the next level and play, and it worked out pretty good.

167

Wisconsin, well, it just clicked. I always wanted to play in the Big Ten. I'm a Midwest guy. Growing up, all I ever saw were Michigan games and those states and everything. When the process came and it was time for me to go visiting schools, as other guys have said, it just felt right and it just clicked. And a lot of things played a major factor. The guys who were in front of me—Jason Suttle, Soup Campbell—were pretty much getting ready to leave and there weren't a lot of younger guys. So I saw that I had a lot of opportunity. It was Division I, it was an up-and-coming program. I think they had just won the Copper Bowl the year before I came, so I saw that. I figured I'd come in and play fairly early. I got to Madison, and the campus was beautiful. It just felt like home from the coaches to meeting teachers, professors, other players, it just felt right. It made all the sense in the world to me, so that's why I ended up coming.

I have great memories, both on and off the field. Off the field, the guys I came in with were great. You never forget the guys. You remember back to the time staying in the dorms and having a ton of fun and growing up and being young men and growing together, just building relationships. So, off the field, that was something that I remember and that I will always remember. It's very special to me. Obviously, on the field, going to the multiple Rose

Bowls and winning a lot of games and being recognized across the country as a major program is important. That was very special to me.

I do remember our night game against Drew Brees and Purdue in 1998. I feel I was blessed with some God-given abilities, if you will. I think instincts are big for me; I'm not the biggest guy, not the fastest, but I have knowledge of the game. I think instincts helped me tremendously to have great anticipation. To take you back to that night game we played Purdue, I think that really put me on the map. It was really big for us, it was a big game, it was a tough game, back and forth, and I was able to make a play. And on from there, it piled and piled up as far as making plays. That's definitely a very memorable moment.

The day Ron Dayne set the rushing record against Iowa? We won, it sent us to the Rose Bowl again. We were like, *Man, we're going back to California, back to the Rose Bowl.* And Ron, coming on and breaking the record—that time in particular, coming from winning the first Rose Bowl, playing the '99 season, getting up to that point, and then having the opportunity to go again, we were feeling on top of the world. Everybody was elated. It was, not only for me but for others, one of the best times in our lives. It was one of those days, it was cool, more toward the evening, a later game, we just had the time of our lives. Ron broke the record, we just knew he was going to win the Heisman, and we knew we were going to the Rose Bowl.

Playing in the Rose Bowl is like a dream. You know what the Rose Bowl's about. For me growing up, knowing that the Big Ten winners usually play in the Rose Bowl against the Pac-10 team. I was watching football when I was five or six years old, college and pro, but I was more of a college football fan than anything. To get to play in a game of that stature, the Grandaddy of Them All, you can't beat that. I used to wish I could've played in the Sugar Bowl or the Orange Bowl, but now I think back, the Rose Bowl is the one. And to get to play in that two times? Can't beat it.

When I think about what Coach Alvarez brought to the table, I can't think it would be anything other than love. To get the opportunity when a lot of schools didn't think that I would be able to play Division I football—that alone, just having a belief in me, a young kid out of St. Louis, not highly recruited, and giving me that opportunity and that chance, I will forever be grateful. And Coach Alvarez is just a cool cat, you know, he loves the game, and everything about how he goes about his business, how he teaches us, it makes sense. Everybody doesn't click with a team like he does. So to have

Defensive back Jamar Fletcher holds the Wisconsin record for career interceptions, with 21, set in just three seasons.

that kind of camaraderie, you want to play for a guy like that. His whole aura, it took me in and made me feel comfortable.

Being a Badger, even from the perception of others, is what I give off. Just being an upstanding individual, a winner. A lot of positives, man. Coming from this school, this program, helped me become the young man that I am today. It helped me in so many ways. Sports, that's a bonus, I always say. Life is the most important thing and how you are perceived in life, that's most important. To be a person who now gives that respect, but a person who gets respect. To me, just being a Badger is a beautiful thing, it's a blessing. It's something that I wouldn't trade for the world.

I definitely appreciated my experience at Wisconsin at the time, but I appreciate it even more, down the line, now that I've left and am away from the program, away from the campus and things of this nature. I definitely do appreciate it that much more because this was the best time of my life—the people I met, the guys I played with, we still all hang out and built strong relationships. You look back, you fast forward 10 years, and, man, it's a wonderful feeling. I wouldn't trade it for anything. I loved those times, and I loved everything about Madison, Wisconsin.

I think Madison is one of the best-kept secrets. People just don't realize how great it is. To be able to come from a place like St. Louis, Missouri, it's different, obviously, from Madison. And other young adults come from cities and states around the country, but then you come here. Everybody has a perception. I was made fun of when I said I was going to go to the University of Wisconsin—people said "Wisconsin?" But they just don't know how beautiful this place is and how beautiful the people are. You don't have to love it; I'll love it for you! Madison is one of the most beautiful places in the world, and I'm very grateful that I got a chance to come here and experience everything I experienced.

Jamar Fletcher set the Wisconsin record for career interceptions with 21 in just three seasons. A consensus All-American in 2000 and the winner of the 2000 Jim Thorpe Award, Fletcher was a first-round draft choice of the Miami Dolphins in 2001 and played nine seasons with five different teams, most recently in Cincinnati.

The
NEW
MILLENNIUM

WENDELL BRYANT

DEFENSIVE LINE

1998–2001

I WAS BORN IN MINNEAPOLIS. My mom and my dad were together for a little while, but then they split up, and my mother ended up moving back home to St. Louis, where she raised me. I got a lot of help in life from my father figure, my grandfather Norman J. Wells. He's pretty much the one who introduced me to the game of football and pretty much put me on the path to a lifelong love of the sport. He was a brilliant person, which I didn't understand when I was a little kid. I just know that something Grandpa and I did was sit around on Sundays and Saturdays and watch football. I always knew he was excited about it, so I was really excited about it, too. He played some semipro football back when he was young and he played for his high school team. He had a lot of fun doing it and had a love for the game. It kind of rubbed off on me.

When I was around seven or eight years old, I started to understand what was going on and all the different nuances of the game—the different things people consider, like who plays on the defense? What does the defense do? What does the offense do? I learned those nuances and was able to keep up with the game. It's something that I fell in love with. My mother tried to get me into the peewee football league in St. Louis, but I guess at the time—I was about nine or 10 years old—I was bigger than most of the kids in my class. So they told me I'd have to play with 11- and 12-year-olds. My mother was a novice of the game, but she knew that she didn't want those big older kids hitting her 10-year-old. So the first time I was actually able to go out for the football team was in high school. I didn't play organized football until ninth grade of my high school. Before that, we just played around in the street, just running around with my friends, then we'd play tackle football in the fields when we had the chance. No organized football, no putting pads on, no putting a helmet on, no knowing where different stuff was supposed to go. I didn't know any of that until I got to high school. I remember I put on my pants for the first time and put on the helmet and everything, and I remember the first time I got hit. I didn't cry, I got up and just kind of kept doing it. It just kind of snowballed.

[Wisconsin assistant] Kevin Cosgrove recruited me. I never really worried about going to college to play football; it was one of those afterthoughts. I was pretty much a nerdy kid. I was a school-type kid, really had my head in the books. I was trying to be really intellectual in my younger years, I was a very bright kid. So I never worried about playing football, per se, or about making money, it was just something that was fun to do, something to be social, and something to kind of bring me out of my shell. I was a bigger kid than everybody else, so I was kind of shy. I just knew it was something to get me to interact with other kids, just to have a good time. My high school career with football was interesting. I went to Ritenour High School, and we were perennial losers, always had been that school that was the laughingstock of the league, and that kind of continued through my high school career. We'd always lose, or sometimes we'd step on the field and we'd just get blown out. The other teams were just better than we were, they were just stronger than we were. Playing on the freshman team, we won one game: we went 1–9. Playing on the sophomore team, we went 0–10. Then I finally got a chance to play varsity. I went up and asked the defensive coach if he thought there was a chance I'd get to play, because there was a guy ahead of me and he was older. They sent me in to play defensive tackle, and I had success. I was one of the bigger kids on the team, so I was a bigger body and took up space. I was actually pretty athletic for my size. At the time, when I first came in, I was about 6′2″ or 6′3″, 245 pounds, so I was pretty big. And I just kept getting bigger as time went along. So by the time my junior year rolled around and I was trying to get on the varsity, I was about 6′4″, 270 pounds. I used my size to physically dominate. As I got older, as Coach Cosgrove started recruiting me and as I got into college, I started to learn the game more, but at first we were just trying to overpower people. My junior and senior years we went 3–7.

173

Two-time Big Ten Defensive Lineman of the Year Wendell Bryant lists a sack of UCLA quarterback Cade McNown at the end of the 1999 Rose Bowl as a personal highlight. The Badgers beat the Bruins 38–31.

Around the end of my junior year is when I started to get letters from different schools. I think the first letter I ever got was from Cincinnati, and then I got another one from a junior college. So I didn't think anything about it.

But time went along and I started to get more and more letters. I think my turning point happened in my junior year when I went to Wisconsin's football camp in 1997, right before my senior year. Coach Palermo was running the camp, and he started calling me "Big Cat." That kind of stuck with me throughout the whole camp. I wasn't thinking that I had a chance to play Division I football. I knew there were kids who were really good in high school, but I didn't consider myself one of them. I was just playing because it was a fun thing to do. After my junior year, I started to get the accolades and was one of the only kids in my school to make first-team all-conference when I was a junior. So that kind of boosted me, brought me out of my shell a little bit, and allowed me to continue playing.

The funny thing is that I was still a novice to the whole recruiting situation, so I wasn't realizing the magnitude of college sports. I was kind of blown away. Wisconsin was, out of all my recruiting visits, probably the worst visit that I had as far as the standpoint of fun. Jamar Fletcher was my host, and I remember him taking me out, but I was still a wallflower and didn't really know how to interact with everybody. On all the other visits I went on, people, the recruiters kind of stayed with me and watched over me, and this was kind of a humdrum visit, and it's kind of weird, but that's the reason why I went there. That and the fact that, at the time, I really wanted to be a chemical engineer and Wisconsin had one of the best chemical engineering programs in the country. I figured I could actually become a chemical engineer and I could actually get a lot of work done [at Wisconsin] because it was boring. And that's what kind of really pulled me to Wisconsin. Obviously, my impressions ended up changing after the fact, but that was my first take. I really liked the people there, I already knew the coaches because I had come to the camp up there, so I decided to go there because I was really comfortable there.

My career highlights are easy to point out. My No. 1 highlight is the Rose Bowl with the sack at the end of the game in '99. I remember that there was an incomplete pass the play before. I was tired, I remember, and everything was just craziness. Everybody was screaming, and I was like, *Wow!* I was breathing hard and thinking, *Okay, we've got one more play.* UCLA had the ball, and Donnel Thompson was saying, "We got one more play, one more, we got one more play!" I mustered up everything I had and came off the ball. I really didn't know what I was doing and just made the same move that I'd always done when we were practicing. It was the same one-armed move where I lock my inside arm out and I just push. I kept pushing, and their guy fell down, and [UCLA quarterback] Cade McNown was right there, and I jumped and tackled him. Game over. Once I realized I sacked him, I looked down, looked up, and I just realized what happened and started jumping around. I remember Leonard Taylor came and jumped on my helmet and was hugging me, and I was jumping up and down and ran to the sideline and sat down. Game over.

My No. 2 highlight would be our game at Penn State in 2001. I always wanted to go to Penn State. I fell in love with it when I was 14. Penn State became one of my favorite teams, but they never recruited me, never tried to call me, never gave me the time of day. I had great motivation that day and I think I ended up with about five sacks. We won 18–6.

I first realized I was in the big time at Wisconsin when I ran out of the tunnel for the first time. I ran out of the tunnel and stopped and looked at all the people in the stands. I went to a high school where we had maybe a couple hundred people in the stands, and they were mostly the other team's fans, so now there's 70-something thousand people, and they're all behind you pretty much, rooting you on to victory. It was mind-blowing. I kind of stopped and turned around in a circle. That was a special moment.

I went to Wisconsin at a time when there was a lot of magic going on. I really was appreciative of everyone and everything that was going on because my high school was small and we used to lose all the time. So I really did appreciate it. I appreciated it that much more when I went to the NFL because I realized the people back at Wisconsin really cared about you. They wanted you to win, of course, but I felt they more generally cared about us not only as football players but as people. That, to me, was one of the best things about my experience at Wisconsin, that the people actually cared about you.

Playing in Camp Randall? There's nothing like it! I played in the Big House, Ohio Stadium, but nothing compares to Camp Randall. You run out to a sea of red, you've got Bucky doing pushups. Nobody out there, out of all the stadiums I've gone to, nobody has a beginning fourth quarter like we have. There isn't any place where they play a song and everybody in the stadium jumps around and it's continued for years now—about 15 years they've been doing this. I remember the night of the Drew Brees game in '98, it was nuts. The song came on, and everybody was jumping around, and you could feel sitting down the whole entire stadium moving. It's a pretty big stadium, it's pretty strong, but you can feel everyone in the stands jumping around, having a good time. It was an awesome time. I was so blessed and so appreciative to have been a part of that. I would never have known going to Wisconsin that I would have been able to be a part of two Big Ten championships and two Rose Bowls, back-to-back. You never know that you're going to be a part of history when you start out to do something. It means something to go to University of Wisconsin. There are people who went to the University of Wisconsin, wherever you go, and they're loyal to the university just like you're loyal to the university. They respect the red and white, and they respect the passion.

Wendell Bryant was a two-time Big Ten Defensive Lineman of the Year and a first-team All-American in 2001. He starred on two Big Ten championship and Rose Bowl championship teams. Bryant was a first-round selection of the Arizona Cardinals in the 2002 NFL Draft. He played three seasons in Arizona and played the 2010 campaign for Omaha in the United Football League.

BROOKS BOLLINGER

QUARTERBACK

1999–2002

I DON'T WANT TO MAKE HIM SOUND LIKE A CRAZY PERSON, but I'm pretty sure the story goes that, in the hospital, when my mom was holding me shortly after I was born, there's a picture of me with a football in my arms that my dad had stuck in there. My dad was a coach, and I was always around his teams. When he was coaching in central Missouri, my first memory is of being around football. He took the head coaching job at Northern State, in Aberdeen, South Dakota, but my family lived in Missouri. I had to start kindergarten, so I moved up to South Dakota with my dad, and my mom stayed with the rest of the kids. So it was him and me living in the dorm for two days in Aberdeen, South Dakota. I was too scared to stay in the room in the morning, so when he'd get up at whatever time he got up, I'd tag along. This was only for the week before school started—it seemed like forever for me, but I started to go down and go to practice. I got passed around from, who knows who they were, I'm sure my dad could tell you, but graduate assistant coaches or whoever else. I actually had my own desk in his office; I'm sure I ticked them all off. I was actually in the team picture that year—I was just around the game. There was never really a question of when it started or if I was going to play, it was just something I did.

Later, when my dad became a coach at the University of North Dakota, I was around the whole time. I'd always be around, I didn't have a ton of kids in my neighborhood, per se, who were my age. I don't think we had tackle football until seventh grade. I think in fourth or fifth grade I played flag football for my elementary school. That was really the first organized stuff I played.

Actually when I was in Grand Forks, there was junior high through ninth grade, then high school went 10th through 12th grade. In eighth grade they asked me to play on the ninth-grade team. They didn't have a quarterback, they were only junior high. And so I agreed and showed up for the first day of practice, and in the class ahead of me there were some pretty rough characters, one in particular, who had a reputation as a tough kid. So I walked into the locker room before practice, it was before school started—it was kind of nerve-racking—but I walked in and it was just quiet, there were all these ninth graders in there. The tough kid said, "What are you doing here?" I said I was there to play quarterback, and they kind of questioned me. I went out that first day and practiced, and I was so young and felt so overwhelmed. I remember sitting outside the coach's office to tell them I just wanted to play with the eighth graders. And I sat there and sat there, and he didn't come out, so I decided to go home. I went home and showed up the next day, and I think we went 9–0 and won a night game, which was a huge deal at the high school field. A lot of those guys on that team, I ended up being really close with in high school and had really good teams with and won a state championship in basketball, and lost in football their senior year. So it worked out. The next year as a freshman I played varsity with those same guys, they were all sophomores, so I made the transition with them in both basketball and football.

I started getting letters and stuff and just always assumed I'd go to North Dakota and play for my dad. Then he left there right before my senior year. I had a really good junior year. We lost in the state championship, and I started getting more and more interest from different teams. I decided that year I needed to go to a couple camps. I chose the University of Iowa camp, I don't really know how, except Bret Bielema was recruiting me. To be honest, I only talked to him a couple times. I can't remember if he called me beforehand. I kind of sat down with my dad and made a bunch of tapes. In the technology world, it was so long ago, you didn't just send out tapes. Most kids I knew weren't doing it. So I made up, like, 30 videos my junior year and sent them to all kinds of schools I thought I had no shot of ever going to. Anyway, somehow Bret was recruiting me at Iowa, and I decided to go to the Iowa camp. I went to the Iowa camp and remember talking to Bret

179

With 5,627 career passing yards, quarterback Brooks Bollinger ranks No. 3 in Wisconsin's records.

and met Coach Hayden Fry at the end of the week, but kind of left think-ing it wasn't for me and that I'd probably end up going to UND. But shortly after that I had an opportunity to go to Wisconsin's camp. I hadn't been planning on it, and I was playing baseball in Bismarck. I think we played three games and ended up winning the championship, and my mom had to pick me up, meet me in Fargo, and drive straight through the night to Madi-son. I slept the whole way. I got in and I hadn't showered or anything, I stunk, had all my baseball gear still on. We pulled into the hotel at 6:00 AM, I showered up, and we drove down to the stadium, and I was wondering what I was getting myself into. We parked up on Breese Terrace, walked down that little hill, and Coaches Hueber, Alvarez and, I think, Coach Wyatt were sitting out front, and that's where I first met those guys. I went to the camp for a day and a half and, at the end of the second day, Coach Alvarez came along, put his arm on my shoulder, and told me he was going to offer me a scholarship. I had still felt like my arm was dead from playing those baseball games. I felt like I was in over my head and that it had not gone that well. I remember Henry Mason was the receivers coach at that time, and during a couple drills I'd fill in and run some routes for him, just having fun with it. I was shocked at the end of the second half day, when I left, and Coach Alvarez had told me about the scholarship. So I went home and honestly didn't know anything about Wisconsin, but we talked it over. I don't remember much of the decision process, but it felt right.

I've been around football my whole life, and I think that the college foot-ball experience for just about anybody who really has a good experience or maybe even doesn't—I think the people are always what makes it special. That is to this day and will always continue to be the best thing about my experience. Everybody from coaches to players, right down the list, with my wife, my friends, equipment guys, trainers, SIDs, just the people and the rela-tionships that you make I think are the most important thing. We're so lucky, and we don't realize it until years after and people are writing books about it that we got to experience things that most people don't. I got to Wisconsin as an 18- or 19-year-old kid from North Dakota. The first year I redshirted, and we were having fun on the Sunset Strip and going to the Jay Leno show and playing in the Rose Bowl, and I was sitting on the sideline thinking, *Wow, this is pretty cool!* Then we did it again the next year. I just don't think at the time there's any way you can realize how unbelievable of an opportu-nity that is.

There are a few games that stand out to me. I always have to say the Rose Bowl that I played in is definitely one of them. Obviously, to be a part of the Rose Bowl is unbelievable. Just from my perspective, there were two games that I will never forget, that I think were just special. One was the Ohio State game in 1999, my first start at Ohio State. It's important for so many reasons—just to think where that team was, where I was, being the start of something special, and leading to the Rose Bowl. Just beating Ohio State that badly, and Coach Alvarez being up in the press box because he had a bum leg, it was just a really neat day. Also the Minnesota game in 2002, the last home game of my career. For most people, it's not going to go in the history books. The Minnesota game was special to me because we had, by our standards, a disappointing couple of years. We hadn't gone to a bowl game the year before, and we'd been up and down and just kind of fighting to get into a decent bowl game my senior year. If we'd lost that Minnesota game, I don't believe we would have gone to a bowl game. Obviously Senior Day we all remember, a lot of emotion, your last game in Camp Randall and at that point thinking it may be the last time I ever play football. And I just really kind of made up my mind that I wasn't going to—not that it was just me— but whether through motivating others, or just my play, but I wasn't going to walk off that field without winning the game. It all worked out, and we won and we went on to the Alamo Bowl, which is another one you can put on my list of memorable games. And the Iowa game in 1999, where Ron Dayne broke the rushing record. Maybe there are more than just a few memorable games for me.

I was so lucky to play for a number of years after college and become friends with a lot of guys who played at schools all over the country. And whether they were Division II schools or the University of Southern California or Miami, or wherever, I think if I could go back and do it all again, there's no place really like Wisconsin. And it's a combination of the town, the fans, the stadium, the tradition, the people I was able to play for. When we were in school in Madison, you just kind of assumed this is how it goes. You get to come here and get a scholarship and play on this team, and you win and get to go to a bowl game and get to meet all these cool people. Then you talk to people who went to these other schools who were home every Christmas and didn't get to have those experiences, and you realize how fortunate you are. I didn't know if Wisconsin was going to be good. I didn't know if I was going be able to start there. I didn't even think about all that. I thought,

Hey, it's a good fit for me, and they offered me a scholarship. I feel good about the coaches I spent two days with. But you see so many kids across the country who don't get to have all those experiences that we got to share, and it's pretty special.

When I think about what it means to be a Badger, I think about Coach Alvarez. I think about the things that he tried to instill in his teams and looking at the way he coached, not cutting any corners in discipline. "Don't Flinch" was one of his big things. We were a tough, hard-working group of guys who maybe didn't always have the flashiest or even the most talented team, but were tough and disciplined and found a way to win football games.

Brooks Bollinger ranks third on Wisconsin's career passing yards list (5,627) and, as a redshirt freshman, guided the Badgers to the 1999 Big Ten title and a Rose Bowl victory over Stanford on January 1, 2000. He went on to play six seasons in the NFL with the Jets, Vikings, and Cowboys before finishing his football career in 2010 after two seasons with Florida in the United Football League. He lives in Minneapolis.

183

LEE EVANS

WIDE RECEIVER

1999–2003

I THINK MY DAD WAS THE FIRST ONE to introduce me to the game. He's a huge football fanatic, so we'd always be in the house, and he'd always be watching the games and going crazy. That's how I got exposed to it. As I grew up, I just wanted to play—I loved the game, I loved watching it, and I loved playing it even more. I started off playing in the front yard with my friends, it was one of the things I wanted to do, and my friends pretty much knew I wanted to do it, even in the summer, guys wanted to play basketball, baseball. I would do that, but everybody pretty much knew that I wanted to play football all the time. And that's how we'd start, I was just playing in my front yard, my backyard. My parents would be mad because we tore the yard up, but it was something that happened pretty much every year.

My first recollection of organized ball was actually in a peewee league. My dad and one of his buddies had dropped me off, and at the time I wanted to play defensive end. I don't know why, but defensive end was what I wanted to play— I wanted to rush the passer. I remember I was standing on the sideline and had my helmet off, and a play was going on, and they ended up running me over— busted my lip. I had a big busted lip. And shortly thereafter my dad pulled up, and I was crying. He and his buddy were in the car, and he was looking at me like, *What's going on? What's wrong? Why are you crying?* and whatnot. So actually my first recollection of playing was me crying and my dad pulling up with—I wouldn't say a disappointed look, but it definitely wasn't a proud look.

High school was tough because we only ran a one-receiver set, a wing-T offense. Chris Chambers was there before me, coming into my junior year. He was the starting receiver on the varsity; we only ran one wide receiver, and he was the guy. So I really didn't get a chance to play. We had a couple packages in there when we'd both be on the field, but it really wasn't anything where I was on the field a lot my sophomore year, and then he ended up leaving and going to Wisconsin. I never really knew anything about Wisconsin, and as I progressed in my junior and senior year, Wisconsin was one of the schools that recruited me heavily. And so Coach Mason, the same one who recruited Chris, saw what I did on the football field and running track as well, and recruited me. They pursued me hard, and I took a couple visits, but once I visited Wisconsin, I pretty much had my mind set up.

I took visits to other schools, and when I came to Wisconsin, I just felt like this was the place where I understood the people, I understood what was going on. I had a good feel and a good vibe about the players who were there, the coaches who were there, and the students and the people who were there. So that was one of the things that gave me the most comfort in choosing that school. I think some of the other schools I visited were great, but just coming to Wisconsin and seeing the people and, at the time, they were going to the first of back-to-back Rose Bowls, so things were really, really exciting. But even outside of that, I felt I had something in common with the people, and that made the decision a lot easier.

185

The adjustment to college was tough. I'd be lying if I said there weren't many times when I felt like this wasn't for me and I wanted to go home. I had that thought many times, especially throughout training camp out at the seminary and being trapped there, trying to adjust to a completely different game than high school. You're not "the Man" as you were in high school; you've got to start over with a clean slate and really earn your stripes. Homesickness set in, and that first training camp was really tough.

But even though things were tough early, I still felt like I could play. That's one of the things that drove me, I felt I could play and was still very competitive. I wanted to play, I didn't want to fail, I wanted to try to elevate. As my freshman year went along, I got to play in some games early, and when I caught my first touchdown pass, that was really a big boost of confidence for me and really let me know the hard work was paying off. And hopefully with more hard work, more would come.

Wide receiver Lee Evans injured his knee in a spring game after his junior year. He rebounded the following season and caught the winning touchdown to end an Ohio State winning streak in 2003.

Each year took on its own identity, and that was something that was very special for me. Each year was different. You have guys come and go, so every year stood on its own. Freshman year was Ron Dayne and everything he did for Wisconsin and college football, the whole atmosphere when he broke the NCAA rushing record. The second year was the Shoe Box, that whole ordeal. [Several players were suspended for a variety of games early in the season due to an NCAA violation involving a store called the Shoe Box.] My third year was my breakout year, and I put myself on the map. The fourth year I got hurt, and the fifth year was the comeback. So they're all completely different years for different reasons.

My junior year was a sweet and sour season. I was able to put up some big numbers, and not just me, a number of different players put up big numbers that year. Wendell Bryant had a big year, Anthony Davis had a big year, so it wasn't just me, it was a lot of us putting the numbers up. But we didn't even get to a bowl game that year; that's why it was sweet and sour. It was fun putting up the numbers, having big games, but some of them were coming in losses, so that kind of made the taste in your mouth a little sour. Even doing so many good things, it made it tough. That year, you tried to enjoy things that you did, having personal success, but when you don't win the game, it makes things a little difficult.

I came back to school after my junior year for a number of reasons. One, at the time I felt as if there were some things I still needed to prove and I just didn't feel like I was all the way ready to be there completely. There were some things I still wanted to finish in school and come back and win. Coming from the Rose Bowl and things like that, I still felt like we could do that. And that was one of the things I wanted to do, so that was part of it as well. But more so, it was just me feeling that I needed to come back for another year to be all the way ready [for the next level].

Injuring my knee in the spring game between my junior and senior years and trying to come back was like running the Rocky Mountains, just up and down, up and down the whole time, just trying to get back. I didn't even want to miss the first game, but I had to go through two surgeries in that period. It was just as hilly and mountainous as you could have, from really high peaks to really low valleys. You try to figure it out, you want to have the certainty that you could do this, but you just have to work it out. And believe me, you can. Sometimes you lose belief. Sometimes you don't feel like you're getting better

187

and you just don't know what's going to happen. It was a tough year, it was a really tough year, especially when you're expecting to come back and play.

Jim Sorgi came in with me, so he and I have always been pretty tight. We knew what kind of quarterback he was—he had a really nice, soft-touch ball and could get it out there as well. We had a good relationship before I even caught a pass from him my senior year. We had a good relationship, just being in the program for the last four years together. So that was great in our last year, we were both captains, both trying to lead the team. It was a great relationship and a lot of fun to be able to share it with somebody whom I had come in with. There weren't very many people left from my recruiting class. Sorgi was one of them, so it was a lot of fun to be able to bounce back with him and have him lead us to everything that we did.

Our night game at home against Ohio State in 2003, when they came in with a 19-game winning streak, had an atmosphere like something I hadn't seen before. Being a part of that game was electric from the kickoff until the last whistle blew. That's the first thing that really jumps out at me— how electric the atmosphere was, how tense it was in the stadium. It really made for the best atmosphere I've ever played in. And I think the game really kind of summed up what I'd been going through for the whole year. When I say that, I think the biggest thing I learned from the injury was patience. And I think that game was a testament to that. I went through the entire game without even having a pass thrown to me, and then I made the winning touchdown catch late in the fourth quarter. I really had one opportunity and had to make the best of it, so that's pretty much what sums up the whole knee rehab and everything. I had a big opportunity there and made the best of it. It was such an electric atmosphere, and that really made it so much fun.

Coach Alvarez really brought toughness to the table. Barry is as tough as they come. And that's just football. Really, he just taught us about life in general—understanding how the things you do in football, or don't do in football, resonate in life. And I think that's one of the biggest things I take from Coach Alvarez, learning the little lessons of not only football, but of life. They're things I still live by now.

I just had a good vibe from the people at Wisconsin. The people really made my experience there as wonderful as it was. Without that, I think it would be a completely different everything. With that being said, Madison is a tremendous town, and you can have a lot of fun in it. And it's a town that not very many people know about. You tell people just how fun Madison is or what it was like going to school there, people don't believe. The people who do come to visit always have something great to say about Madison. Madison, I think, is a testament to the people.

What does it mean to be a Badger? Loyal. Tough. And Fun.

Lee Evans was a first-team All-American in 2001 and finished his career as the Badgers' career leader (No. 2 in the Big Ten) in receiving yards. Evans came back from a knee injury to enjoy a terrific senior year in 2003, including his legendary game-winning touchdown catch against Ohio State. He was a first-round selection of the Buffalo Bills in the 2004 NFL Draft and has played for the Bills his entire career.

ANTHONY DAVIS

RUNNING BACK

2001–2004

A FRIEND OF MINE GROWING UP—he was three or four years older than me—originally introduced me to the game of football, and we would play street ball all the time. We played tackle in the streets, two-hand touch, or 1-2-3 hold. I guess I found out I was good because we used to play this game called free-fall, which was like every man for himself. We usually played it with a tennis ball, and there were normally about 25 to 30 people playing. You threw the tennis ball up in the air and, when it came down, whoever picked it up became the ball carrier, and you'd have to run through everyone to the end zone. If you were tackled, you threw the ball back up. That's how I got introduced to the sport. My uncle thought I was fast enough to play organized football, so he signed me up for Pop Warner when I was around nine years old. I was a third-string left guard and was pretty bored. I didn't play much. They had a rule in Pop Warner where everyone had to play, and I was one of those guys who got just the bare minimum so that our team could be eligible. One day after practice, everybody on the team was racing, and I was winning a lot, and people started making bets, like, "I bet you can't beat him." The next year, the coach moved me to running back, and that was pretty much a done deal after that.

I went to a high school with not a lot of football tradition, but they were resurrecting the football program at our school. I came right around when they started getting back on their feet. I played a little bit as a sophomore but, by the time I was a junior, I was a starter on varsity and did really well. We ran a triple option attack. We went 10–0 and played in the state championship game, but lost. It was very controversial—I'll never forget that. I can't watch the game to this day. We were playing in Meadowlands Stadium, we lost 7–6, and there were two controversial plays. On one of them, I busted a run for something like 60-plus yards along the sideline, but the official said I stepped out of bounds. I don't feel like I stepped out of the bounds. There was another play where the other team scored a touchdown, but the replay showed they didn't. That was heartbreaking, but I guess that's just part of football and most sports.

I won the state track championship as a sophomore and was part of a national indoor championship team. I was pretty fast and started getting all these schools coming at me. ACC schools and SEC schools offered scholarships and looked at me and, before you knew it, that next fall I started getting football letters from schools like Nebraska, Boston College, Rutgers, Richmond, Northwestern, and eventually Wisconsin. I decided I didn't want to run track in college but would rather play football with the option of running track.

191

Football was my first love, and so when it came down to choosing a school, I started looking at the type of football each one played. I knew I wanted to go someplace where they ran the ball, so it really came down to Wisconsin and Boston College. At the time, they both ran a zone scheme, they both had really good tailbacks. Both schools' tailbacks were from New Jersey, so I felt like they were both schools that loved New Jersey players. I was really struggling to figure out which one between the two. I liked Wisconsin a little better, but Boston College was very aggressive, and I guess what it came down to was that I found out my best friend's sister was a professor at Wisconsin. I felt like if I went there, I'd have a little bit of support out there for me. Then I looked into the schools' student organizations, and UW actually had a chapter of the fraternity I wanted to join, and so that kind of took me up. So I left my recruiting trip to Wisconsin thinking I really liked the place. It was still a tough decision for me, but Coaches [Brian] White and [Joe] Baker came to the house and showed me some offensive clips. First they showed me some offensive clips of how to run a zone and what they look for out of their tailbacks. When I saw it, I felt like I could do it really well if I got the shot. Then they showed me a highlight tape of Ron Dayne, and it was amazing. That did it. I thought, *Wow, if he can do it—he's from Jersey and he could do it, I'm gonna try to do it, too.* That was all it took.

Making it through the first training camp at Wisconsin alone was an accomplishment for me. Not just because of football, but a week after I got to Madison—my second or maybe my third day after I got to training camp—I got a letter that one of my friends back home died. He was killed in a robbery. Two days after that, I got another letter in the mail saying that another friend of mine got shot and killed the day before he was supposed to leave to go play basketball at Kansas State, so it was a really rough training camp. That was right at the beginning of training camp, right around the time we finished our freshman camp, and it just really messed me up. It was hard enough making the adjustment from a very basic high school football offense to a more complicated college offense. The play calls went from toss right [in high school] to what sounded like dissertations the first time I heard them. That was challenging. Making it through the first training camp was an accomplishment.

Looking back, a few games really stand out to me. The 2001 Penn State game really stood out to me because it was right after the 9/11 attacks. Being from the East Coast, I remember the exact moment when I heard about the attacks and being scared and calling home and not being able to get a signal. I had a cousin who worked in the city and friends who worked in the city every day, and I didn't know what to expect or what happened. Coach Alvarez talked to us at practice and gave us some words of encouragement, and the whole team kind of just rallied around the guys from the East Coast. We all wore American flags on our helmets at that Penn State game, and it was my first 200-yard game and first time coming back home and getting to see my family that year. So it was huge for me. That was a big game. I also remember the Minnesota game the next year, needing to get a win to go to a bowl game. Coach was really putting a lot of faith in me all week, and that was really huge for me. So those two moments really stand out. In terms of my career, I definitely had a fast start. My first two years I felt like I had huge years, but then the next two years injuries hit me, and that was probably one of the more challenging things, dealing with some of the injuries. Trying to come back and not being ready and getting hurt again. It was just very frustrating. I broke my orbital bone in my senior year. It was crazy; it was the weirdest football injury ever. I had to sit out four games for that, and it was definitely tough.

Our running backs meetings, we probably had enough laughter in there for a lifetime. We were all pranksters and always used to play pranks on Coach

Though he faced injuries in his final two years with the Badgers, running back Anthony Davis, with 4,676 career yards, is Wisconsin's second-leading rusher.

White. He would use the mouse to work the computer to watch films, so we would put tape on the bottom of the mouse ball so the mouse couldn't move. This was where the old offices used to be in Camp Randall, and he would have to walk all the way over into the stadium side to go to the video services department and, as soon as he left, we would take the tape off the mouse. He would go over there and get the video guy and then would come back over, and the mouse would be working. He would curse the equipment, go get someone to fix it, and then it would be working fine. We had fun. We always had our own little language in the running backs meetings, and that always made me laugh.

I think when we were playing, there was a lot I didn't realize. Football is a sport where you have to be so focused on the task at hand, it was almost like having tunnel vision. You just have to be very focused. We would have veterans come talk to us. We were always taught to respect the veterans. We loved the "W" on our helmet, we would die for it. We were always focused on the task at hand. We're in winter conditioning, we're training to get ready for spring ball. It's spring ball, we're honing our football skills and making jumps to be better players and then there was summer conditioning. Now we're getting ourselves ready for training camp, now it's time to play football, it's time to win. We were so focused we didn't have much time to think about the fact that we were literally part of history being made. Looking back at it now, you gain so much from the experience. When we were playing, the atmosphere was just huge to us. It was like the arena. I looked at the football environment in Camp Randall and Madison like it was the Colosseum in *Gladiator*. The people came to see us. Every time we stepped on the field it was showtime. The locker room was like a sanctuary, we bonded there. That's where we got to know each other and where we gained each other's trust. That's where we bonded. It was a great experience.

Coach Alvarez used to work us hard and push us, but he treated us really well, first class, beef steak and lobster after the victories. When we traveled, we would travel with class all the time. We would do anything for him. Looking back at it, not being a player anymore, I think I just appreciate all the life lessons that I learned from Coach Alvarez and that I learned from playing at Wisconsin—how to deal with success, how to deal with failure, how to work relentlessly toward something that is months or possibly years away. How to be unselfish. How the little things can add up to big things in life. That's the Badger way. It was an amazing experience and was so much fun that I sometimes find myself referring back to times in football, saying, "Well, this was how I got through this situation. This is what Coach Alvarez would say, this is what Coach White would say, or this is what J.D. [then UW strength and conditioning coach John Dettmann] would say."

Anthony Davis remains the second-leading rusher (behind Ron Dayne) in Badgers football history with 4,676 yards from 2001 to 2004. He was a seventh-round draft pick of the Indianapolis Colts in 2005 and played two years in the Canadian Football League. Davis is currently an area coordinator and assistant football coach at Loras College in Dubuque, Iowa.

DAN BUENNING

OFFENSIVE LINE

2001–2004

My first experiences with the game were with my brother. We'd always throw a ball around in the yard and simulate all the aspects of the game. We had a pretty good time. As we got a little older we'd play with the neighborhood kids in organized games. We didn't have Pop Warner youth leagues when I was that age, so it was whatever we could organize, and we'd play football in the fall. I'd be with my brother. I didn't play any real organized football until middle school. I was probably one of the biggest guys on our team. It was a learning experience.

I actually started on the varsity for a while as a sophomore in high school, so I was pretty excited about all that. My brother was getting recruited by Wisconsin—he was two years older than me. I obviously wanted to do the same as him, so I went to a camp in Madison, I believe, the summer before my senior year. At camp I played both sides of the ball. I actually wanted to play defense, that's where all the glory was. When you're a kid, that's all you think about. When I was there, I was told that I was actually too small to play at Wisconsin, and I don't know if that was supposed to motivate me or what. So I was ready to go to Minnesota, but I wasn't really fond of their campus. Then in August, out of nowhere, [Wisconsin assistant] Coach Palermo got a hold of me and said they wanted to offer me a scholarship. So I said, "Coach, what's going on? I thought I was too small." And I told him I'd think about it, and I actually made him sweat it out for a week before I committed. I knew I wanted to go there. They just came off one Rose Bowl and came back and were ranked in the top of the polls the next year. That year, my senior year in high school, they went to the Rose Bowl again. So the team from my home state went to the Rose Bowl two years in a row and they want me to come play for them? Heck, yeah, I'm going to go there!

I ended up redshirting in 2000. It was my first year, but we had a number of suspensions the first week of the season. The day of the first game, I thought I was going to start—I didn't know who was going to be suspended. I was actually the second-team guard and was nervous. It worked out that I did not end up playing that season. I ended up redshirting and then had surgery that year on my shoulder. At the end of the year, the team went to Hawaii, but I didn't get to go, so that was the only bad experience I had. We didn't get to go again while I was there; that was my one chance to go to Hawaii!

I think some of the most rewarding things for me were bowl games. They stick out a little bit better than other games. The Alamo Bowl in 2002 was a great experience in Texas, and we ended up winning, beating Colorado, in a pretty tough game. Also, being able to be a part of running out of the tunnel at Camp Randall Stadium. The Fifth Quarter after my Senior Day game, the last game of my senior year, we ended up beating Minnesota and getting Paul Bunyan's Axe back. Our defense was on the field, so I didn't get to be out there to get the head start to run across the field and grab the axe from Minnesota's sideline, but there were, like, 30 seconds left, and they didn't set the ball for the final snap. The clock got to, like, :05, and they blew the whistle, and Minnesota was just standing around, just let the clock go, so I just took off. I was at the numbers before anybody else on the sideline had gotten going. It ended up that Scott Starks and somebody else with ungodly speed started running and, unimaginably, we got there at the same time and got to grab the axe and hold it up. That was something I remember.

197

In 2004, my senior year, I think we were No. 4 in the country with a 9–0 record. We were flying high but had a lot of guys who got beat up that year. On our defensive line, Erasmus James got clipped at Purdue, and after that he was half of what he was earlier in the season. Anthony Davis, I don't know if he even played the last four or five games. Our fullback, Matt Bernstein, had to play halfback sometimes and was trying to hurdle people—he did, but he didn't get going after he landed. I was proud of those guys, just being the captain of that team and making the run we did. Obviously, it could've turned out better, but we did what we could, most of it. The bowl games the

last

198

All-America defensive lineman Dan Buenning was an instrumental member of the 2002 Badgers team that beat Colorado 31–28 in the Alamo Bowl.

two years, I wish we could have won those. Those were obviously disappointing losses, but we still had a lot of fun.

Coach Alvarez was very consistent with everything he did. His body language was always the same, his temperament was pretty much level, and you could count on him to be there and just be the same guy every week. He was just a very good man to have as your head coach. He obviously had the ability to let his assistants, who were all very good assistants, do their jobs. He wasn't a micromanager. He had his hands in things, but he let those guys work their players. Jim Hueber, I can't say enough about him, teaching me techniques and skills and all that I needed to be a lineman in the Big Ten. And the rest of those guys, [assistant coach] John Palermo, bringing Bret Bielema in there as the defensive coordinator my senior year. Coach Alvarez had some great guys around him, and that allowed him to do things even better.

The atmosphere in Camp Randall Stadium is just electric. I come back for some games and get to see that from the stands. I can remember how it felt down there just to be a part of that, and it's just amazing to know that you had a piece of that; it's with you all the time. The teammates, the camaraderie, I still talk to these guys, we have a bond. We see each other in Heritage Hall or we meet up on the side before the game. It's just like you never left. So it's pretty cool.

Playing at Wisconsin means that you can't take anything for granted, that you're not going to have anything ever given to you. You have some schools, they're always going to be in the national championship talks, and that's not the way it is at Wisconsin. You're going to have to work, which is kind of the Wisconsin mentality, and bring your lunch pail, as Coach Alvarez always used to say. I think that's going to help you out later in your life. To be a Badger means that you worked hard to get there and you're going to get respect from everybody because you were a Badger. In the real world, as they say, I still use that mentality. When people say, "Of course you can play football, yeah, well how does that relate to this?" Well, I just tell them about the toughness and the hard work—about being a Badger—and once you tell them, they understand.

The O-linemen I got to play with, knowing they counted on me every play to be there—and I could count on them every play to be there—was a special thing. We all worked together very well as a unit. Without those guys there, I wouldn't have had the success that I had, and the team wouldn't have had the success that we had.

199

Dan Buenning was an All-America offensive lineman for the Badgers in 2004. He was a fourth-round draft choice of the Tampa Bay Buccaneers in 2005 and spent four seasons in the NFL. Buenning currently lives in Waupaca, Wisconsin, where he owns Uncle Dan's Guns and Gear.

JIM LEONHARD

DEFENSIVE BACK

2001—2004

GROWING UP PLAYING FOOTBALL in a small community, we didn't start organized football until seventh grade. That's a little bit later than a lot of people, especially in bigger cities kids get started a lot earlier, but ever since I can remember, growing up as a kid, we were playing in the backyard with brothers, cousins, friends. So I got started at a very young age. It's one of those things where you'd be watching football on the weekends and then very rarely did we ever make it through an entire game before we were outside playing ourselves. Even though I didn't start organized football until later, I had a lot of experiences just going in the backyard and playing football.

As a kid I played a little bit of everything. I loved basketball, loved baseball, and loved playing football. Those were the main three, but it didn't matter. As long as we were doing something, whether you were hitting balls or hitting rocks with a tennis racket, anything. As long as we were active, doing something, I didn't really care. But I would definitely have to say that basketball, baseball, and football stuck out above the others.

When I started playing football, I was a defensive back. Then offensively I played a lot of different positions—quarterback, receiver, running back. We had a number of kids who just played a little bit of everything. They didn't know where anyone was going to play or how much people were going to grow at that age, so they just kind of taught you football, and I think it ended up helping me down the road because I got to play a lot of different positions and got a good feel of how everything fit together and how the different positions work off of each other. Getting into high school, I played running back and quarterback on offense, but I always played safety on defense. I never played the corner very much, but I always played safety. And obviously, that was big, and I got a lot of experience, and it helped me out going into Madison.

I had a lot of success in high school as a sophomore and as a junior. I started getting a lot of attention in my community in northern Wisconsin, but really didn't get a whole lot of exposure outside of that. I didn't get a whole lot of looks as far as colleges outside of Division II, Division III schools in Minnesota and in Wisconsin. I think one of the biggest decisions I made was I decided to go down to the University of Wisconsin's camp the summer before my senior year. I received advice from a couple coaches, namely Coach O'Grady at River Falls, who had a lot of college experience. He said, "I think you can play down there, I think you can play at Madison. If you seriously want to give it a shot, you should go down to this camp and see what happens. The coaches run it, and you'd be able to get a pretty solid look." And I decided to do that before my senior season. It went great. Everything went well. I ran great times when they did their testing, looked good there, and once we got on the field doing drills, competitions, I performed very well. So coming out of that camp, the coaches basically said they were going to ask me to walk on. It gave me a lot of confidence going into my senior season, knowing that I had a lot of ability and even the University of Wisconsin was willing to take a chance on me. I had a big year, and I think that really is what led to being able to have success early at Wisconsin, as well.

First off, coming in as a walk-on at Wisconsin, not really knowing what to expect, my goal was to travel and to go to all the away games. I didn't know exactly what that meant. I knew you couldn't redshirt to do that. I wanted to play football right away. Once again, being a walk-on, I kind of put myself on a timetable of a year, two years, and if it didn't work out, I was going to go transfer or do whatever to try to play football. That's what I wanted to do. I'll never forget that first training camp because that is where I set myself up to get on the field as a freshman and to travel and do all those things that I set out to do. Everything went really well. I got my opportunities and made the most of them and was able to play a lot of special teams as a freshman and that gave me the confidence going into the next year. It really gave me that experience that I needed to be able to step out as a sophomore

Defensive back Jim Leonhard tied the school record for career interceptions, with 21, and set the Big Ten record for career punt return yardage (1,347).

and not be shell-shocked. It helped me to feel comfortable with the guys. Having limited snaps on defense, it really didn't affect me because I knew what the atmosphere was like and I knew what the coaches were like.

I guess the first game that really stands out would be Fresno State my sophomore season, which was the opening week. I found out during training camp that I was going to be the starter. From that point on, there was a lot of talk that we had a lot of players returning and safety was kind of a question mark because it looked like there was going to be a new starter with no experience playing defense. There were a lot of question marks going into that game. I didn't really get caught up in it. I was focused on what I had to do and ended up having a great game. I had a couple interceptions, returned punts, one of those magical kind of nights where everything came together. A lot of time and effort went into it, and we ended up getting a night win. Since it was a home game, it was a great atmosphere to start off a season and to play well— to have production and get interceptions and play well. That's a game I'm definitely not going to forget. One of the bigger ones later in my career was in my junior year against Ohio State the year after they won the national championship game. Obviously I remember a lot about that game with Matt Schabert to Lee Evans. It was just a huge game. There were so many highlights in that game, back and forth, playing one of the top teams in the country, once again at home at night. You can't beat the atmosphere, and you get a victory to end their 19-game winning streak. It was a huge night for the program, and it was a huge night for the players. Everything came together.

It was very humbling, the attention that I received, especially after having a couple successful seasons. Being a small-town kid, not getting a lot of attention coming out of high school, it seemed like everything fell in place at the right time. It was a little humbling because when you're going through something like that, you're not thinking, *I can't believe I'm doing this,* or, *I can't believe I've had the opportunity to do this or meet this person.* So it kind of shocks you. It doesn't seem like it's anything that crazy to you because it's just another day and you're getting these opportunities. But when you really have the time to sit back and think of a lot of the cool things that you've done or the experiences that you've had and the people you've met, it really is special. It's something that takes a few years to sink in. I've been very fortunate to meet a lot of great people who have helped me out in my career and to get me to where I am today. But it was a little strange at the time because I was getting a lot of attention for something that I didn't really think was that crazy. I was having fun playing a game, and I didn't quite realize the magnitude of what football meant and what Wisconsin football meant to so many fans. It took a little while for that to sink in.

The thing that's most special about playing at Wisconsin is the fans and how they interact with the players and team, and the support they give during good times and bad times. They're the true die-hard fans. I've never been to another university or heard of another university that has that quite the way that we do. Something's different about Wisconsin. And I'm very glad to have played there. The people I met along the way and the support that I got throughout the state of Wisconsin is unlike any other I've seen.

What made Coach Alvarez special is not only his football knowledge and coaching ability, but I think it's his ability to apply football to life. How he teaches you to mature and to grow up and become an adult. You get a bunch of 18-year-old kids as freshmen. A lot of them haven't been away from home very often and just haven't been exposed to a lot of different situations. I think he did such a great job of helping kids grow up. He's going to let you find your way, but he's also going to give you messages and give you advice on how to handle situations that apply not only on the football field but also later on when your career is over.

My parents instilled in me at a very young age the importance of academics. The longer you play this game—and I was very fortunate to end up at Wisconsin and to have the opportunity to get a scholarship after being a walk-on—you realize how valuable that is. So academics was huge in my career all the way through. You realize that even if you're fortunate enough to make it to the NFL or play professional sports that you're going to be done at an early age and academics has to be there; you have to have something to fall back on. You're never guaranteed anything in the sport of football, so if you put all your eggs in one basket and don't work on the academic side and don't set yourself up for life after football, you're going to struggle. You see it all the time. I credit my parents, my community, and family. They preached that to me at a very young age. It doesn't matter what you do on the field, it's what type of person you are, what type of character you have, and what values you have off the field that are going to make you successful.

To me, what it means to be a Badger is pride in not only your university but in the entire state, the community. The more places you go, you realize just how far the University of Wisconsin reaches and how many people it affects—there are Badgers everywhere. The passion that they have for the university, I just don't see that elsewhere. So I'm very proud to say that I'm a Badger and to have that group of people and that support behind you, just knowing that what you do in life, you'll always be a Badger and you'll always have that support group.

Jim Leonhard went from walk-on to three-time All-American at Wisconsin. He tied the school record for career interceptions with 21 and set the Big Ten record for career punt return yardage. A three-time first-team All–Big Ten selection, he was undrafted out of college but has played in the NFL for Buffalo, Baltimore, and the New York Jets since 2005.

BRANDON WILLIAMS
WIDE RECEIVER/ KICK RETURNER

2001–2005

I STARTED PLAYING FOOTBALL for the Mathews–Dickey Boys Club in St. Louis when I was six years old. It was a good Boys Club, having been around for 50-some years or so. They did a lot of sports and had a summer program. I was going to the summer program and ended up playing football in the fall. I was around football when I was young because both of my uncles played football in high school and college and played some semipro in St. Louis and were pretty successful. They both became coaches, so at a young age I was exposed to many different facets of football and track. It was always something I wanted to do.

The summer of my eighth grade year is when I first started lifting weights and started really working out and training for football in the off-season with my uncles. We would go to the local rec center and lift weights, go swimming, and go out on the field and run different routes. I was a running back, but my uncles told me I was too small and that I would have to transition to wide receiver if I wanted to play in high school. My uncles coached at Normandy High School, and that's where I went to school for my first two years. Laurence Maroney was there, too. Then I transferred to Hazelwood East. I lived in that school district, and that's where a lot of the friends I grew up with were going to school. I took pride in being an all-conference player all four years of high school.

We went on a miraculous run over two seasons. We were 10–1 my junior season and 14–1 the following season and finished as state runner-up my senior year. I was an all-state performer playing both offense and defense, quarterback and wide receiver, and doing returns, as well. My high school team had seven Division I players and three Division I-AA players go to the next level and play college football, including Tony Moss, Scott Starks, Jamal Cooper, and me. We were the best team in the St. Louis area for those two seasons.

Scott Starks and I were best friends in high school. We did everything together and at an early time decided we were going to go to college together. He was a year older than me so, really, wherever he went was where I was going to go. Scott had committed to Northwestern. Then he said he was going to Michigan State before he finally ended up going to Wisconsin. A lot of the times I would be at his house when recruiters would come over. I met [Wisconsin coach] Kevin Cosgrove officially my junior season when he came to visit Scott at his house, and I knew that if that's where Scott was going, then I'd see Coach Cosgrove at my house the next year.

My only official visit was to Wisconsin. That was the only visit I took because I felt like I didn't want any bad karma to come upon me by going to different places and knowing that I wasn't going to go to any of them. Coming out of high school, I thought I was going to go to Michigan State because Scott had committed to Michigan State. Bobby Williams was the Michigan State head coach and is from St. Louis, so he knew my family and everybody. But when it turned out Scott committed to Wisconsin, I started looking at some of the history of Wisconsin. The Fletchers, Terrell and Jamar, were from St. Louis and went to Wisconsin, and I just thought it was the place to be.

I had a great time at Wisconsin, on and off the field. I don't think there was much expectation of me playing and contributing as a freshman, but, in my mind, I always knew that I was going to play and that I wanted to play. Coach Cosgrove was at my house one time, and I told him, "I'm coming to Wisconsin and I want to play receiver, not quarterback." And I said, "I'm going to choose Wisconsin because you all are going to give me the opportunity to play receiver." I also said I was on the three-year plan, that I was only going to be there for three years, then I'd be out. You can ask him, I said that.

I broke the school freshman record for most receptions, and [fellow wide receiver] Jonathan Orr and I were both freshman All-Americans. I was a 5'10", 160-pound freshman playing in the Big Ten, trying to block guys and

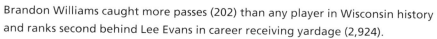

Brandon Williams caught more passes (202) than any player in Wisconsin history and ranks second behind Lee Evans in career receiving yardage (2,924).

taking hits. We played Arizona that year, and one of the hardest hits I ever took was from Lance Briggs. He hit me and, like, flipped me on a slant route, and I didn't even get the ball. My sophomore season was pretty good, too. That was the year [All-America receiver] Lee [Evans] came back [from a knee injury]. Playing alongside Lee, obviously, you don't get as much attention from the defense and you get to watch a great player do some of the things he did. I was honored to be on the same field with him. He was like a big brother to me, and we did so much stuff on and off the field, we had a lot of fun.

My sophomore year is really when I started getting injured, when I had my leg injuries. I played with a fractured tibia most of that year. A lot of people didn't really know that. I played pretty well that season, but really what hurt me was in that off-season I had to have surgery. I had to get a rod put in my leg, so they just drilled a hole in the middle of my shin. I never played in a spring game except for that first spring my freshman year. Those spring practices and spring games are really where you get better and stronger, but that whole time before my junior season I was doing a lot of rehabbing, trying to figure out how and if I was going to play. Coach Mason really thought I should redshirt, but, being naïve, I really didn't want to redshirt because I was still on my three-year plan, thinking I could still make it and still be good enough to go to the next level. Statistically, my junior year was the worst I ever had. I wasn't as explosive as I could have been and wasn't as strong as I should have been. So I think my junior year was probably my most challenging season, having that surgery and my leg not being fully healed and a lot of people not really knowing that. Going into my senior season, I was fully healthy again. I was back and ready to play and had the best season of my career.

Coach [Paul] Chryst came in [as offensive coordinator] and implemented some different things in the passing game to really open us up and spread us out a little bit and be more of a threat. I remember in that summer camp I had an interview with a reporter. I told him we were going to throw for 3,000 yards that season, and he looked at me like I had four heads. I said, "Trust me, we'll throw for 3,000 yards." And we threw for 2,969. So we came close to my prediction, but the guy who was interviewing me thought I was crazy for even saying it. One of my best moments was winning the Alamo Bowl in the fashion that we did. I made a fourth-down catch on the game-tying drive, and then Mike Allen kicked the winning field goal in overtime. That was one of the best times I ever had. Then my senior year, beating Auburn the way we did, going out, sending Coach Alvarez out the way we did, I was just ecstatic to be part of that. Being a part of Barry's legacy was very big for me. I looked at Coach Alvarez as one of my mentors and someone I looked at as a guide because he always had this cool, calm demeanor. It was like he always had a plan, he was on top of the plan and knew what we were going to do. To be a part of the legacy of him building the team from where it was to where he left it, I was just happy to be a part of that situation.

I'm honored that my class was the last class that Barry Alvarez coached, knowing that would happen, that feeling of being the omega of Coach Alvarez's career, it was just very special to all the guys on that team and in that senior class. We tried to uphold that as much as we could. We had a lot of roller coasters going from our junior year, when we were 9–0 and No. 4 in the country, to the depths of 2–6 or 4–4 in the Big Ten the year before that. We had our highs and we had our lows, but we always tried to work, to be the best, and I felt like we achieved college football greatness. During my time at Wisconsin, we went to four bowl games and won two of them. We won my freshman year, then lost two in the middle, then we won again my senior year.

Personally, I felt like I was an overachiever. Being one of just a few players in the history of the game to catch for 2,000 and return for 2,000 yards was something that I didn't even know until I got to the NFL, and I take a lot of pride in it. I owe a lot to Henry Mason, my positions coach at Wisconsin. He is much loved by his former players and, from a teaching standpoint, he was one of the best coaches I ever had.

Being a Badger was very special because playing at Wisconsin is history. Every time you play, it's really history. The atmosphere we played in at Camp Randall, there's nothing like it. You have some schools, they pack the stands with 100-some thousand and it's loud, but we pack the stands with 80-some thousand and it's just as loud. We draw just as much attention—our fan base and our students show up like no other. It's The Fifth Quarter with the band, something that you don't always get at every school or even at prestigious schools within the Big Ten like a Michigan or Ohio State. Playing at Wisconsin was different because there was just that feeling of family. Everybody knows that every football team in America right now has to have that feeling of family, but when you can literally go to Coach Alvarez's house or go to Coach Mason's house during the week, that's real family, that's real camaraderie, that's somebody who really cares about you. That's something that was very special. Being able to come back—a lot of guys say they want to get back to their roots, be back in school, where they made a name for themselves. It's an honor to be a part of the National W Club because a lot of people say they'll go back and say they'll have some roots at their college, but honestly when a lot of people leave, they're gone and forgotten. I honestly know I can go back to Wisconsin and hook up with people, and if I really needed help, someone would be there to provide whatever help they could. There are not a lot of schools out there that you can honestly say that about.

Brandon Williams caught more passes (202) than any player in Wisconsin history and ranks second behind Lee Evans in career receiving yardage (2,924) at Wisconsin. Williams was a third-round draft choice of the San Francisco 49ers in 2006 and played three seasons in the NFL. Williams currently lives in St. Louis and is breaking into radio and television sports broadcasting.

JOHN STOCCO

QUARTERBACK

2003–2006

I ACTUALLY FIRST STARTED PLAYING SOCCER, and I think that was just because soccer starts earlier than football does. I had three older brothers, and two of them played football. I started in probably fourth grade playing football and, whenever I think about that, I think about my dad because he put in a lot of time practicing with me. I'd pretty much beg him to go in the back-yard with me and play catch every day, whether it'd be football or baseball, and he was definitely a big help with that. I started right away playing quar-terback. My first year I only played quarterback, and then my second year I played just about everything—I played quarterback, running back, I think I played defensive tackle—I was one of the bigger guys at that time, so I was all over the place, but yeah, it all started with quarterback.

I was always playing other sports. I think I started in baseball first and then played soccer for a couple years and then switched to football. I played base-ball my whole life, even before I played football. Baseball was always there, then football kind of came in a couple years later, and then I actually started playing hockey, I think, in probably sixth or seventh grade, then switched to basketball when I was in junior high around seventh grade. I was playing everything. Football started getting really serious in junior high. My first couple years of football, we were one of the only teams to throw the ball, and right then I knew pretty quickly that I could have a shot to be pretty good. When I was in eighth grade, I played on the freshman team. Then, as

Quarterback John Stocco is Wisconsin's No. 2 career leader in passing yards, with 7,227. In 2006 he was a semifinalist for the Davey O'Brien Award.

a freshman, I was on the varsity, and the starting quarterback was a senior but he got hurt halfway through the year. So, halfway through my freshman season, I took over as the starter and started for the rest of my high school career. As far as being recruited, I think that started probably my sophomore year. Obviously it helped having Larry Fitzgerald as a wide receiver. People started noticing him and asked who was the guy throwing the ball after a while. That was definitely a big help for me.

Larry is a year older than me—he played his freshman year at a different high school and came to my school for his sophomore year—my freshman year—and he only played defense in his first year with us. But he actually was begging the coach to let him play receiver, too, so finally they gave in toward the end of the year. I just remember he made a one-handed touchdown catch toward the end of that year that was unbelievable. At that point we knew he had something special. I was throwing passes to him my sophomore and junior seasons. I can't even count the number of one-handed catches he made, diving catches he made. If we had a fade route called, I would just drop back and chuck it. It didn't matter where the defenders were, it didn't really matter where he was. Even now commentators talk about how his body control is unbelievable when he's in the air. I don't even know how to describe it. The guy can make catches in the air that are just amazing. He loves the game. We were always working out in summertime, always trying to get better. It was just a neat thing to be part of his career.

My high school coach actually knew [Wisconsin assistant coach Jim] Hueber pretty well, so that was kind of the connection there. Wisconsin was really one of the first schools that started to recruit me and far and away recruited me the hardest of anyone, so that was a big reason why I chose Wisconsin. The two schools recruiting me the most were Wisconsin and Minnesota, and Wisconsin was there from the start. Most of the other schools I'd just get letters from, but, really, Wisconsin and Minnesota were the schools that put in the most time, and Wisconsin was recruiting me a lot harder than Minnesota, so that went a long way with me. And the program, in general, that Coach Alvarez had going was just a very successful program. I remember my first time going to campus. I loved the campus and it was a great school, so it was a great fit for me. The only thing I was hesitant about was that Wisconsin didn't have a baseball program and, at that time, I was still considering both in college. So that's really the only reason I considered Minnesota as long as I did. But ultimately I decided that Wisconsin was a better place.

Obviously I grew up watching the Gophers because they were always on, but it didn't really become an issue since Wisconsin recruited me a lot harder than Minnesota did. And really, when Wisconsin started recruiting me, I started looking at Wisconsin more—the more I looked at it, the more I liked it, so it really wasn't that difficult for me to leave my home state. Wisconsin was just the better fit for me.

My first year at Wisconsin was Brooks Bollinger's senior year. So, talk about a great opportunity for me to learn from guys who obviously went on to become very successful in both Brooks and Jim Sorgi. It was just a perfect fit. I got to kind of sit behind those guys and watch how they were in the meeting rooms, what they were looking at film-wise, and I would watch them day in and day out at practice. That was huge for me. I got to see Brooks my first year and Sorgi my second year, and toward the end of the year I got in a little bit and then took over as the starter, so it was really a perfect situation.

There are a few games that definitely stick out—we beat Minnesota all three years that I started, so that was huge. The last game against Arkansas in the 2007 Capital One Bowl was a big one. The win at home against Michigan in 2005, at night, was another memorable game. The last play of that game, getting that one in for the touchdown, that was big, too. And Auburn my junior year in the bowl game—Coach Alvarez's last game—was a huge game for us, and we just came out and dominated. And I had a pretty good game, too. That was one that definitely sticks out. That's something that we talked about, it was a focus for us. We wanted to be on in that game, we wanted to be in the zone, play a clean game. Not only that but the fashion in which we did it, it was just classic Wisconsin Coach Alvarez football. We went out there from the first snap and dominated them, and you look at the last series we had, we took it 98 yards and took off seven or eight minutes, running the football, couple passes in there. Just overpowering them and then taking a knee at the end of the game—in my opinion you couldn't ask for a better way to send him out. That's something that I'm proud of, and I know a lot of other guys are too because he was a great coach and did a lot of great things for us and, I would say, for the whole football program at Wisconsin. It was a perfect way to send him out.

I think a big thing I'll always remember is the relationships I had at Wisconsin—the teammates, we had a great group of guys and the only people I really hung out with were football players. You really develop a great bond, you're working as hard as anybody else on campus, and you take pride in that. I'm biased, but I don't see how a potential recruit, a football player, could find a better place than Wisconsin. You look at everything, you look at Camp Randall with 80,000 fans, just renovated, giant scoreboard, got crazy fans, Jump Around—that whole deal—it's just a great experience. You couple that with the success they've been having in the program, the support from the fans is just unbelievable. It's all Badgers. You've got a couple pro sports teams in Milwaukee and Green Bay, obviously, but the Badgers are right up there. It's just fun to be in that type of environment where people want to see you play that much, they want to know how you're doing, they give you that much support. The whole football program is one of the best, I think. Then you look at the school, very good academics, and the campus. I don't know how you can find a better campus in the country.

Wisconsin is still part of my life. Even though I haven't played in a few years, you still see so many passionate Badgers fans around the country. It's a great network of people who come from Wisconsin and support Wisconsin, and that's one of the best things about it now at this point in my life. There are so many people who recognize you and want to know how you're doing and will support you still, and that's huge. Everyone who has been to Madison loves Madison, loves the Badgers. People you see throughout the country from Wisconsin, they're great people and they're great to talk to and will support you. I think that's the best thing about it.

The Badgers were 29–7 (.806) with John Stocco as their starting quarterback from 2004 to 2006. Stocco was a Davey O'Brien Award semifinalist as a senior and finished his career ranked No. 2 on UW's passing yards list. A native of Richfield, Minnesota, Stocco lives in Chicago.

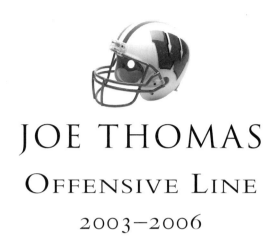

JOE THOMAS
OFFENSIVE LINE
2003–2006

ISTARTED PLAYING, LIKE MANY OTHER YOUNG KIDS, just kind of in the back parks and the neighborhoods, playing tackle football with a bunch of buddies, or throwing the football around with my dad. It wasn't until seventh grade that I actually started playing formal football in Brookfield, and then I played in middle school and went on to play on the varsity as a freshman in high school. When I started in seventh grade, I was about 6′2″ or 6′3″ and 140 pounds. I actually started out playing fullback because, like a lot of kids at that age, I wanted to carry the football as much as I could. I really didn't know a whole lot about defense, so defense took more time. As an eighth grader, I played tight end and outside linebacker, and that was kind of the position I stayed with through high school. Then, as a senior in high school, I started playing a little bit as a tackle and guard.

As a freshman in high school I played tight end and outside linebacker. I think I showed enough promise where the coaches were thinking they wanted me on the varsity to just get the experience and try to get a little bit of the flavor of the game with some of the older guys. When I was a sophomore, I took over as the starting outside linebacker and one of the starting tight ends. I was kind of an honorable mention all-conference type of player. I think it was my sophomore or junior year I started getting letters from colleges because I was a pretty good basketball player and was 6′7″ already as a freshman. I could move pretty well, pretty fast. I had pretty good ability. My football skills were still a long way from being polished or really impressing anybody, but I think I had enough talent, ability, and athleticism that coaches saw that a little bit. Going into my senior year, I was pretty highly recruited. I went to the Notre Dame football camp the summer before my senior year in high school and ran a 4.7 40. I think I was 6'7", 255 or 250. I wasn't really a heavy kid yet, but I think they saw that I was pretty strong, a skinny kid, and had some athleticism. I got letters from as far away as Miami and USC and scholarship offers from a lot of people.

When I started the process, I kind of had a grass-is-greener-on-the-other-side type of mentality. I wanted to get away a little bit, go to Colorado, USC, or Miami. Whatever the reason was, I had this thought in my head that things were better somewhere else. So I took all my trips, I took all five of my official visits. I visited Nebraska, Colorado, Virginia Tech, Kansas, Notre Dame, and Wisconsin—I went all over the place. And, of course, after all those visits, it became very clear to me that everything I really was looking for in a school was right in my backyard. I didn't have to go to Colorado or California or wherever to find what I was looking for; everything was right there in Madison. It had an excellent academic reputation, an excellent football program, great coaches. Jim Hueber, who was one of the best offensive line coaches in college football at the time, was there. I was really into track, really wanted to try doing track for a few years, and the Wisconsin track program was one of the top ones in the country, winning Big Ten titles every year. They had shown a really big commitment with Coach Alvarez and [track coach] Ed Nuttycombe, and the track program was really serious about letting me do track. It was just everything I was looking for and it was an hour down the street. And I just love the people in Wisconsin. I love the fans, the camaraderie that the team had, and there really wasn't anything I didn't like about the school. When I really was looking hard at it with my family, and I was rating all the schools and all the different things I was looking for, Wisconsin was No. 1 in every category.

There are too many highlights to mention, but the things that stand out are beating Ohio State my true freshman year in 2003, playing in that game against All-American Will Smith, and beating them coming off their national championship. They had not lost in 19 straight games and doing it at night, in the rain, in front of a Camp Randall atmosphere was amazing. The atmosphere is so much bigger and so much cooler than in high school that it was really hard to explain the emotions that take over your body when you're part of a game like that.

But probably the No. 1 thing that stands out when I look back on every-thing is the friendships I made. The guys I still keep in contact with today. I think I had five guys from the football team in my wedding party. The friendships that I made are something I'll never forget and something I'll cherish forever. There are guys in every class I played with, whether they were seniors when I was a freshman or whether they were freshmen when I was a senior. When we go to Buffalo and play the Bills and I see Lee Evans on the field, we go right up and give each other a hug because there's a really strong connection among Wisconsin football players. Even though he was a fifth-year senior when I was there and he was "the Man" and I was just a lit-tle true freshman, we still had a camaraderie about us. I still talk to Dan Buenning and Mike Lorenz and guys whom I played with on the offensive line. Jake Wood. These are all guys that I formed lasting friendships with.

When I got hurt filling in on the defensive line against Auburn in the 2006 Capital One Bowl, laying on the field, you immediately know what hap-pened because it's a feeling you never had before and you can't walk, so you really know it's bad. Laying there on the sideline, I just wanted to watch the game, just let the game consume me. I felt so bad because I felt like I was let-ting my team down. It was Barry's last game, playing a highly ranked Auburn team that nobody really gave us a chance to beat. We came out playing really well, had 200 yards rushing. Everything was going well for us. I felt like if we would've ended up losing that game and things had gone downhill after I'd gone out of there, I would've felt like it was my fault. That's probably not the right way to think about things, but I was just so worried about that. Winning made me so happy that it really didn't sink in that I was injured until I was lying in the doctor's office in the locker room after the game and was told I had a torn ACL. Of course, I knew that was a bad thing. In my mind I thought it was kind of like a death sentence because, growing up, you hear about people blowing their knee out and they've never been the same. You don't know if you're ever going to play again. You don't know what's going to happen, what the future holds. And, of course, all the worst-case scenar-ios always sneak in your head, so I was thinking, *Man, this may be it for me.* Those things kind of go through your head with an injury like that. I was kind of crying, my parents were crying. The defensive line coach, John Palermo, he's one of the toughest coaches I've ever been around, and he came in and, from what I remember, there were tears in his eyes. He just felt so bad that he'd put me out there and let me convince him to put me out there and help our team on defense and I tore my knee up. Obviously, people who know are aware that almost everybody comes back just as good as new, but when you're sitting there on the doctor's table, you don't know that.

Once I got home from the bowl game and settled down, let my emotions settle down, I really got a chance to research the knee injury and talk to doctors and find out more about things. People who know me know I'm a very optimistic person, I'm very good-natured, always got a smile on my face. Once I heard from the doctor that there was a very good chance that I'd be back to normal, back to new, better than ever, I took the mind-set that I was going to keep all the bad thoughts out of my head. I was only going to think positive things and attack this thing with optimism and vim and vigor. About a week after I got injured, I had a skip in my step again and I was ready to attack the surgery, the rehab, and I was going to take whatever this injury was that God had given me and was going to turn it into a positive because I knew there was a positive sitting in there somewhere. What the positive turned out to be for me was I was kind of a light player in my career, around 300 or 305 pounds, and I knew that I could play better if I was a little heavier, in the 310, 315 range. And I also knew that it would be better for my senior season and for my post-college career if I was stronger. So [then-UW strength and conditioning coach] John Dettmann and I sat down and came up with a plan to do everything we could to get my upper body super strong—I had a pretty strong lower body. I felt like if I could gain 10 or 15 pounds of upper body muscle in that off-season when I was rehabbing my knee and came back and my knee was healthy again, I would be a better player than the year before. And that's what we did. We just pounded those weights like nobody had ever done it before. I was able to gain about 12 pounds of muscle, my bench press went up probably 70 pounds, and I really became a strong player. I really think that carried over.

Once my senior season started, I still had a lot of thoughts in my head about, can I do this, going back out there, testing the knee, having somebody fall on it—those are all the things that are going through your head when you're coming off an injury. But I had that added confidence knowing that I gained all that strength in the weight room in my upper body, that I was stronger than anybody I was going to play. Having that extra confidence really helped me play that senior year. I played really well that whole year and then, of course, it culminated in being a first-team All-American, winning the Outland Trophy, the first in the school's history. It was really just a special moment

In 2006 offensive lineman Joe Thomas became the Badgers' first recipient of the Outland Trophy.

and made everything I went through feel like it was worth it. And everything that happened just felt like it happened for a reason. Things fell into the right place, and of course it carried over being the No. 3 pick in the draft the following spring.

I look back on my time and feel like I'm one of the luckiest players, or athletes, to go through the UW athletic department because I won multiple Big Ten championships in track, set a school record in the shot put in the indoor, was runner-up in the outdoor shot put, set the school record for wins my senior year, won the Outland Trophy, was a two-time All-American, was on teams that won 10 games my junior year and my senior year, was named the captain, and was able to play for Barry Alvarez and then Bret Bielema. The only thing I feel like I didn't accomplish was obviously win a Rose Bowl, which was something that anybody who goes to Wisconsin dreams of doing. That was something that all of Barry's classes had done. And you know what? I still feel a little bit of emptiness, just a small part of me, that I never got to play in the Rose Bowl because I think it's such a special thing for players who play in the Big Ten and guys who go to Wisconsin. But outside of that, the longer I'm away from the university and from Barry and from Bret now, the more I realize what great coaches and outstanding individuals they are. When you're in the NFL and you get a chance to talk to players from other colleges and universities, and you get to talk about their experience and their coaching staff and how they handled things, you really start to understand, first of all, the first-class environment that the student-athletes get to operate in at Wisconsin. But also the way that the coaching staffs treat their players is better than anyplace else in the country. Hands down. I don't care what anybody else says. The way they treat the players is like nothing else. I was only with Bret for one year, and it was his first year, and he had great success. But the longer I'm away and I start to reflect on the things that Barry did with the team, the way he treated us and how he operated and how he treated his assistant coaches and stuff, you start to understand why he did everything he did. And you start to realize what an exceptional coach he was. I think those same things can be said about Bret. I can see now how he's pulled a lot of the things that made Barry such a great, successful coach, and he's starting to do those things, too. And that's what really makes me excited about the program in the future because, in my opinion, Barry's one of the greatest college coaches, one of the greatest football coaches ever. I think Bret is really falling in the same mold.

What it means to be a Badger is more than athletic accomplishments, it's more than individual or team accomplishments. To me, it's who I am. It's who my family is. It's about the type of person that the university and the football program send out into the world. There were guys who came from total opposite ends of the country; totally different economic backgrounds; totally different social statuses; people from Greenwich, Connecticut; kids from Florida; kids from Cleveland, Ohio; Milwaukee, Wisconsin; Brookfield, Wisconsin; farm boys from northern Wisconsin; southern boys from Texas, Florida, and Georgia; guys from the East Coast; tough kids from New Jersey; surfers from California. And everybody came together as a big family. I think what it means to be a Badger is family. The guys I see to this day are still guys I would give a big hug to. I think that camaraderie and that sense of family and that bond that we had every single year I was there was something that was unique to the University of Wisconsin. I don't think you can find that in any other college.

Joe Thomas, a native of Brookfield, Wisconsin, was a two-time All-America offensive lineman for the Badgers and became the school's first Outland Trophy winner in 2006. He was the third player chosen (Cleveland Browns) overall in the 2007 NFL Draft and appeared in the Pro Bowl each of his first four seasons as a pro.

TAYLOR MEHLHAFF
KICKER
2004–2007

Growing up, I played a little bit of everything, football, baseball, video games, whatever. I was always staying busy. I was a four-sport athlete and played football in the fall, hockey in winter, track in the spring, and baseball in the summer. I actually wanted to play quarterback and baseball in college and attend a smaller university to do that as a quarterback or attend a bigger school on a kicking scholarship. I was fortunate enough to have a number of different options from around the country as a kicker, so that's basically how I got started with football.

I was in the biggest conference in high school, and we played 11AA. In South Dakota, it was a bigger school, we had 1,400 people, so it was a pretty good-sized school. Just being from a smaller state, my senior year of high school was something I'll never forget. Our team was 12–0 heading to the state championship, and we actually got beat in the state championship game. We just weren't quite able to finish it off, but it was an awesome ride. The recruiting process was, at times, pretty confusing, but at times I actually enjoyed it. You have the Big Ten coaches calling your house at night, and it was probably just as cool for me as it was for my dad going through that stuff. I attended a national kicking combine, and after the combine I ended up being ranked the top kicker my senior season. Up to that point, other than just area schools, nobody really knew anything about me. I wanted to play quarterback or baseball, and it's very tough to get recruited from a smaller town. People came out there, and scholarship opportunities began to come in from schools around the country at the Division I level. I remember my dad used to always take me to Nebraska football games growing up, and I thought it was the coolest thing, the atmosphere there. I just wanted to be part of big-time college football like that. After taking my visit to Madison, I just fell in love with the place and knew it was a great school academically as well as athletically. I wanted to be somewhat close to home so my family would still be able to come to the games, although it was still a nine-hour trip for them every single weekend. But I think the only game my dad ended up missing was the game we played at Arizona my freshman year. It was pretty cool to have my parents come over for all the games like that.

During the recruiting process, late in December, I'd made my choice soon after Coach Alvarez flew into my hometown. I had a great amount of respect for him at that time and even more today after seeing, over the years, the type of person he is. I ended up verbally committing to Wisconsin and then a couple weeks later, right before the national signing day, the University of Nebraska ended up making an offer to pull me away from Wisconsin. For a couple days, I was back at square one looking at my options all over again. Deciding where to get your education and spend the next four or five years is a pretty big decision, and Nebraska had been my dream school all along, so I thought it was worth reevaluating the situation. When it was all said and done, I decided to stick with my gut feeling of becoming a Badger. And I had verbally given my word, and I believe you should stick to that. It was one of the best decisions of my life.

I'm really big on the atmosphere of college football and don't think there's anything better than Camp Randall. The thing I'll remember most is the game days in Madison. The walk from the locker room in the stadium, all the fans going absolutely crazy, running out onto the field, the stadium being jam-packed, it's just an unbelievable feeling. I still get goose bumps thinking about it. I just think we have some of the best fans in college football— they're what make Camp Randall a special place. There's Jump Around—I remember every game during Jump Around I looked over at the other team, and they were just looking up in awe at the fans, our student section.

The challenging part was probably the time and effort of being a Division I student athlete. Being successful was basically a full-time job, but one that I actually loved. Coach Alvarez always preached paying attention to detail and doing all the little things because the little things are the difference between

225

being a good football player or being great. I just took pride in that. And I was training in the weight room all the time, in the off-season being in there kicking, honing my craft and working on kicking. I worked so hard at that and just felt like I owed it to the university on a full-ride scholarship to do whatever possible to be the best football player I could be for them. Overall, it was a challenge just juggling being a student-athlete at that level. I think a lot of people don't understand how much time and effort goes into that.

The game that really sticks out in my mind was my sophomore year when we beat Michigan at home on that last-second touchdown by John Stocco. It was my first Big Ten game as a field-goal kicker because, as a freshman, I just handled kickoffs. My sophomore year, I took over all the kicking duties, and it was kind of my first big game. I had three field goals in the game, and it ended up being a pretty close game. I just remember that game being unreal. It was a night game and just electric in that place.

We had a big group of specialists. As a kicker or punter or snapper, by nature you just spend a lot of time with those guys during practice, but you're kind of doing your own thing. You're not as much with the team. The group of guys we had there, I don't think I could've asked for a better group of guys. Some of those guys are my best friends today.

For me, we had those first two years when I was with Coach Alvarez, then the change was made. Coach Bielema came in, and it was really nice to have that kind of a change of pace. It was a nice transition, just change things up a little bit. I had so much respect for Coach Alvarez, what he did and the kind of person he was, the things that he'd done with that program, turning things around. It's pretty awesome.

Coach Bielema is obviously a younger guy coming in, he'd just come in the locker room and you could have a conversation about anything with us and he could really relate to the players. When he talked, or when he would speak to the team in a team meeting or wherever it is, he had a passion about him, and I absolutely loved listening to him in team meetings. You never knew what kind of story he was going to tell, and he'd always give an analogy about football—he'd stir up some crazy story that related to something in life. I feel like I learned so much outside of football from Coach Bielema and am really excited for him and his future, as well as the football program after what Coach Alvarez started.

I feel so blessed to be part of such an awesome football program at that level. I tell all the guys when I come back to Madison how fortunate they are and

Kicker Taylor Mehlhaff currently ranks third on Wisconsin's all-time scoring list (295 points), and second in career extra point percentage (.979).

how good they have it at UW and to not take it for granted. Everyone wants to play in the NFL and go on to the next level, and they think they're going to be treated so well. Once you do leave Madison, you realize how good you really did have it and how it's really just a special place. As a Badgers football player, people look up to you, and you represent a great program at the university. When you put on that uniform, you're instantly a hero and a role model to some of the young kids. So I tell them don't take it for granted. When you're out of school, you really sense the pride that all the Badgers alumni across the country have for their school. You don't fully understand the importance and significance of being an alum until you actually are one. I just love being able to tell people I attended the University of Wisconsin and was part of the football program there. I just really feel like I grew up and learned a lot about myself in those four years in Madison and was able to do it in one of the best college atmospheres in the country.

Just to be given an opportunity like that, I feel so blessed and so fortunate because there aren't a lot of people who get that opportunity to play at that level and be part of something like that. I just feel so lucky that I could do that. It's something I'll never forget, from this day on. If I'm not in Madison, I'll always be coming back for games and will always be back for the bowl games.

228

One of the best moments I remember is the first game that I came back to when I was in New Orleans with the Saints. After I was released, I came back to Madison, and we played Penn State at home. That was the first time that I attended a game as a fan and not as a player. I remember walking up Breese Terrace right before kickoff and just seeing the madness and seeing wall-to-wall people covering the entire street. It was just unreal. And walking into the stadium for kickoff and seeing everything—it was really cool just to see that and to see how important it was to all the people in the stands, knowing that I was a part of playing out there for a few years. That was pretty cool for me to see that from that point of view.

Taylor Mehlhaff was a first-team All-American in 2007 and a two-time semifinalist for the Lou Groza Award. Mehlhaff left UW ranked No. 2 on the school's career scoring list. He was a sixth-round selection of the New Orleans Saints in the 2008 NFL Draft and has seen parts of two seasons of action in the NFL. Mehlhaff continues to train and also runs Taylor Mehlhaff Kicking LLC, in addition to pursuing other teaching opportunities.

TRAVIS BECKUM
TIGHT END
2005–2008

MY INTRODUCTION TO FOOTBALL was watching the games on TV. I've been a Packers fan all my life. I'd watch the Packers on TV and then go out and try to do what they did. That's kind of how it started. It was just me playing with the kids around the neighborhood. I was always taught to play with people older than me because that made me play harder. The first time I played any kind of organized football had to have been my fifth- or sixth-grade year, and I mostly played tight end and defensive end. I usually just played football but also ended up having a love for basketball—I started to really get interested in basketball my freshman year in high school.

When I was younger, I just wanted to go right from high school to the NFL, but then I realized that I needed to go to college. I played JV my freshman year, played linebacker and defensive end, which wasn't too difficult for me because my eighth-grade year I played quarterback, defensive end, and linebacker. Then toward the end of the season they moved me up to varsity to play a couple snaps in a game. It was very nerve-racking to be a freshman in high school playing with these older guys. So I played a couple games as a freshman. My sophomore year I actually didn't think I was going to be playing, starting on varsity, but I ended up being a starting linebacker as a sophomore on varsity. It kind of just went from there. I continued at linebacker and then, my senior year, I played wide receiver probably about four games and only a couple plays, just trying to go out there and have them throw me the ball. My sophomore year was the first time I actually heard anything from a school. The University of Miami was the first school to express interest in me playing ball for them.

I took visits to Oklahoma and Tennessee, and was planning to go to Miami, Florida State, and Ohio State. But it just came late during the season when I figured out that I wanted to be close to home so my family could watch me play. I was kind of a home person and really didn't want to travel too far. Coach [Brian] Murphy was the outside linebackers and special teams coach at Wisconsin. He and Coach Bielema recruited me. They did a great job and really made me feel welcome at Wisconsin. I was a linebacker at the time and just felt at home at Wisconsin. Coach Murphy and I developed a good relationship, and we still have that today. He was one of the reasons I attended the University of Wisconsin.

I'd been a linebacker, but my freshman year as a linebacker at Wisconsin, I found the playbook was tough and felt I didn't have much time to study it. I was kind of thrown into the fire, you either get it or you don't. Probably the toughest thing for me was that more toward the end of my freshman season I was playing defensive end as opposed to linebacker and, I kind of figured my freshman year wasn't what I expected it to be. I hadn't played a lot. I was a star in high school, and not playing much as a freshman in college kind of threw me off a little bit. So I reevaluated myself and decided I wanted to play another position. I looked at a couple different positions and realized that tight end was something that I wanted to try out. I ended up telling Coach Bielema that I wanted to try out tight end in the spring. He laughed, and I said, "No, Coach I'm being serious." I ended up trying to play tight end the spring before my sophomore season, and I've played tight end ever since. My breakout game was my sophomore year against Michigan. I had a couple catches in the first half, and we were down, I want to say by a touchdown or two. It was one of our last drives, and they went to me on two passes, one going across the middle and the other one on the far sideline. My numbers went up from there. I always got a kick out of playing the good teams, and I think if you look back at my numbers, you'll see that a lot of times they went up against the tougher teams—the Ohio States, Penn States, and Michigans. I tried to rise to the occasion. I expected to play well in big games, and I think it all worked out.

Both Coach Alvarez and Coach Bielema were very close with the players, and that's what coaches need to do, have a good relationship with the

Travis Beckum is the third-leading receiver in Badgers history, with 2,149 yards, making him one of five Badgers to have more than 2,000 career receiving yards.

players. I met with both of them several times, both of them met my parents several times, and once a coach shows some interest, it makes you feel more comfortable. It's one thing to meet with a coach in person and another to talk to a coach when you're halfway across the world. It's just a different feeling. It's good to know that the coach is taking time and coming to meet the player and the player's family, you can see the interest in the players.

It felt great being a finalist for the Mackey Award. Knowing the fact that I'd only played the position for two years, it was a great experience to go down to Florida for that awards show and be with the other guys and to now be playing with them in the NFL. We were babies back then. And to look at it now, it's crazy to kind of compare the two. To play in the NFL now, it's kind of funny to look back and laugh at the kinds of things we thought in college.

Wisconsin was great. They took care of the student-athletes not only on the field but in the classroom, as well. I think they do a great job of combining the two. And the relationship with my coaches; it's always great to have coaches be close to players.

Our teams at Wisconsin are tough, but I think sometimes other teams underestimated our speed, too. One thing we sure have is power, and I think that can get you so much more. They say speed kills, but when you're also a powerful team, then you're tough to beat. We had smart teams. We didn't always have the No. 1 player or the top recruits, but we played together as a team, and that's one thing that was always unique about being a Badger. Whether or not it was going to the Rose Bowl, like the team did in 2010, or going to the Capital One Bowl or the Outback Bowl, we beat some top teams where, talent-wise, we might not have looked like the better team on paper, but we were always the team that was going to play you tough and smart. Being a Badger is being powerful and strong, mentally and physically.

Travis Beckum was a first-team All-America tight end in 2007 after becoming a finalist for the Mackey Award, given to the nation's top tight end. Beckum is still the third-leading receiver in Badgers history and one of just five with more than 2,000 career receiving yards. Beckum was a third-round pick of the Giants in the 2009 NFL Draft and has played two seasons in New York.

LANCE KENDRICKS
TIGHT END
2007–2010

Istarted out with flag football because in Milwaukee we didn't have Pop Warner. The earliest thing we could possibly do at the age of nine or 10 was flag football, so we all did it. My first organized football was through a recreational center up the street from my house. We spread the word around school, and everyone said, "Yeah, let's do it." Soccer was my other sport; everyone played soccer in Milwaukee. It was either soccer or flag football, or some kids played hockey, but mostly soccer. In eighth grade, we actually played through a firefighter league. We were sponsored by the Salvation Army. I played on a team with Josh Ogelsby—he was in the seventh grade, and I was in eighth grade—and we won a championship that year, too, so it was pretty cool. That was my first experience playing contact football.

Growing up, I always knew I was going to play college football. I think that was my mentality all the way through it, even as a freshman in high school. As a freshman, I came in and, since I played soccer, I was a kicker. I was a kicker on the varsity, JV, and freshman team, and we had some pretty good receivers at the time, so all I did was kick for the varsity team. I was actually kind of better than a lot of the receivers we had, but they were seniors and I was a freshman and I had to wait my turn, so that's what I did. I think my junior year was my best year, and that's when I started to become noticeable throughout the state and a little bit throughout the country, mostly in the Midwest. I went to a Nike camp at the end of the season my junior year and ended up doing really well. I think I placed third out of about 300 guys. I actually did the Nike camp at USC, so it was kind of a big deal. A lot of the letters came rolling in my senior year. I was offered by Wisconsin at the end of my junior year, so that's pretty much how it went.

One of the main things is I came to camp in Madison three years in a row—at end of freshman year, sophomore year, and junior year. That got me familiar with a lot of the coaches and helped build relationships. I built a good relationship with Coach [Henry] Mason—he was coach when I played receiver. I think it was the winning tradition for me. It's your hometown, you see them win a lot, and it's fun to watch them play. The other school that was really high on my list was LSU, but they didn't offer me until after the Nike camp. I went down there and visited and saw some nice things. It was a really cool school and everything, but I think overall for academics and football-wise, Wisconsin was just a better place for me.

In my childhood my brothers and I loved cartoons. What my brothers would do is watch a cartoon and then go off and try to draw what they saw on TV, without actually looking at another picture on TV. They'd just draw from memory. And I'd try to do the same thing. The older brother closest to me was six years older. I'd try to do the same thing as them, but I wasn't as good as them. I practiced more and more and more and eventually got a little bit better. By the time I got to elementary and middle school, I took art as much as they offered it and developed a good relationship with my art teacher in middle school—she definitely encouraged me to continue it. I didn't think I'd be able to, just because of sports, going into high school. But my dad always told me to take advantage of everything—whatever is offered, take advantage of it, do whatever you can. So in high school I continued art, and I think my sophomore year I won my first competition. It was through the art museum, and they placed all your artwork throughout the city and the suburbs of Milwaukee, and you either got a gold key or a silver key, depending on how it's ranked. I got a few silver keys and a few gold keys as I got older, so that was good for me. My senior year I actually placed an oil pastel medium in a competition, I think it was called the Fourth Congressional District Art Competition, and the winner from each district in the United States—I'm not sure how many districts there are—but each district winner got a painting put in the U.S. Capitol building for a year, and I ended up winning the district. So that was my big claim to fame, that was the biggest thing for me. Outside of football, I would come home and work on

Tight end Lance Kendricks was a Wisconsin team captain and the team's leading receiver, helping the Badgers claim the 2010 Big Ten title.

a project. Art in my high school was really competitive, just as competitive as sports was, so it was like I was dealing with two different competitive things.

Socially, my transition to Wisconsin was fine because a lot of guys from my high school came to Madison. On the field, everything was so much faster. We never actually had complex play like they had at Wisconsin. I was never taught to play wide receiver, I just played it. So coming to UW, I was way behind, although athletically I was similar to a lot of guys who were here. I ended up redshirting because I just couldn't keep up with the pace and everything. After the end of the season my freshman year, I ended up moving to tight end. They had moved Travis Beckum to tight end the year before, so they felt like it was a good fit for me, as well. I had Coach [Bob] Bostad for my first and second years, I think, and it was rough. It was really rough. There were all these different blocking schemes, and I didn't even know what I was doing. At that point, I was wondering whether or not I could do it. But somehow I stuck with it. I think my parents encouraged me just to stick with it and see what happens. I stuck with it, and it definitely paid off. My parents and my brothers, they definitely helped me throughout the process of just being in college, to be successful throughout college. I think one of the main things is to have a strong support system. You always have to have a strong family, and they've helped me out a ton.

I remember my redshirt sophomore year we played Marshall, and I think I had three catches for 94 yards. It's funny because when the ball used to come to me, it was like a rocket was coming at me. I barely caught the ball, it was ridiculous, I was so nervous. As time went on, though, the game began to slow down, I began to study a little bit more and understand what was going on and be able to understand the whole play as opposed to just knowing my route and what I was supposed to do. I think that helped a lot. So my junior year, I was a little bit more comfortable going to a bowl game. I think between the last game and the bowl game, that's when I did a lot more studying film and everything. By the bowl game, I was a little more comfortable and ready to go.

The 2009 Champs Bowl against Miami was definitely a big game for me. I think I had seven catches and 128 yards, so that was kind of like finally getting my foot out the door and being able to let loose and play like I played in high school.

My senior year, guys were just being themselves. [John] Moffitt's always going to be Moff, I'm always going to be me, Gabe [Carimi] is always Gabe, Jay Valai is always Jay Valai. It was like nobody stepped out of his element to try to be somebody he wasn't in order to be a captain. I think that was the main thing—guys were just themselves. For me, it was leading by example, for Moff he was a more vocal leader, for Jay Valai more so vocal. I think that's what it was. The younger guys took notice of that and said, *These guys are just being themselves, and as long as we respect that, we can play hard.* I think that's what happened.

I remember the 2010 Ohio State game being one of those picture perfect games. I was actually out there on the first kickoff return, so it seemed like everything was just perfect, like it was meant to be. It was just a great feeling. I had never played in a game or even watched a game like that before. Just to be able to take part in something like that was amazing. I think for the Northwestern game, when we clinched the Big Ten title, guys were just hungry. I really think that game we imposed our will on Northwestern. We really built an identity my senior year. We always talked about building an identity, and I think we did it. Without even mentioning an identity, we built one. That's great to be able to do.

I appreciate the tradition at Wisconsin. It's not like any other team. You come in, you redshirt, you grow as a person, as a player, as a knowledgeable football player, and you graduate and have an opportunity to play in the NFL. That seems to be the tradition. Everywhere else you play, if you're good enough, you play three years and you leave. I think here it's just all about getting the degree and all about developing as a human, as a football player, developing your body for your position—I think that's what I mostly appreciate. Coach [Joe] Rudolph definitely helped me a lot. He gave me a lot of advice about life and, having a daughter at a young age, he was able to just let me know what my priorities should be and what I should do to stay on track. He helped me identify what I needed to do to help the football team, which was playing special teams, being an H-back on offense my junior year, or whatever the case may be. I think I was definitely ready to have him as a coach. Guys around you are just like you, they think the same way, they act the same way. I think that's why the team is so successful, just because every guy has the same mentality.

Coach Bielema demanded a lot from us. He was able to make us go the extra mile for ourselves and as a team. I think it represents being in the fourth quarter. The game seems over but maybe the other team is catching up to you. The game isn't over, and you still have that extra push to finish it off. He uses the word "finish" a lot, and that's what it's all about, just finishing strong and being able to get that victory at the last minute or however long it takes.

Our program is about hard work, the physical nature, being relentless, strong-minded, just outworking and out-toughing our opponents—that's what you keep hearing and that's true. No matter what it is, like Coach Rudolph always says, it's all a race, everything's a race. You're racing against your competition, but by doing that you're only making yourself better, and I think that's what it is. You work hard to achieve as much as you can, but in the end, you're just making yourself the best person you can be.

Lance Kendricks was Wisconsin's leading receiver as a senior in 2010, earning first-team All-America honors and serving as a team captain as the Badgers won the Big Ten title and appeared in the Rose Bowl. A native of Milwaukee, Wisconsin, Kendricks was also a finalist for the John Mackey Award as the nation's top tight end.

JOHN MOFFITT
OFFENSIVE LINE
2007–2010

I STARTED PLAYING YOUTH FOOTBALL when I was about eight years old. My dad asked me if I wanted to play. Actually, he more than just asked. It was "You're going to play football," or, "You're going to try it." Probably the first thing was I was such a big kid and it just made sense. On top of that, my dad is a huge football fan and would've played football himself if his high school had offered it, so it kind of was like both ends of the spectrum. It seemed like the right decision.

I never played anything before organized football. I played full pads youth football but never played flag football or anything before that. I might have messed around in my backyard, throwing the football with my dad and stuff, but I always played a lot of other sports like basketball and baseball, lacrosse, and stuff like that.

I gave it a try and have been playing ever since. I played all through youth football, then started playing high school football and on throughout college. I was always one of the bigger kids until I started playing at Wisconsin. In high school, you don't run into many guys who are 6′4″, 270, which is what I was. I was always an offensive or defensive lineman. It's been a lot of fun. There have been a lot of times I wanted to quit, though. I almost quit football three times in high school. I think that's part of the game.

I went to two high schools. My first high school was a public school, and I always joked that I'm like Billy Madison because I did two years then

Offensive lineman John Moffitt was a two-time, first-team All–Big Ten choice and a first-team All-American as a senior in 2010.

transferred and did three years at the next high school. I repeated my sopho–more year. So my first year I was a freshman, I played a little bit of varsity, I was a long snapper. The first year went really quick. The second year I played my sophomore year, I got injured late in the end of the season; I had a knee injury. After that I transferred to Notre Dame West Haven, which is where Tarek Saleh went. We had great coaches there, coaches who had ties to Wisconsin because of Tarek. I played well my junior year and then played really well my senior year. I really came out of my shell my senior year. I think it kind of all clicked that I would have an opportunity to play at a Division I school then. I had offers going into my senior year, but midway through that year I was heating up a little bit. I was never a huge recruit, but I was getting to the point where I had the idea that I could play at the next level.

The ties with Tarek, along with the fact my coach knew Coach John Palermo, who was the Wisconsin D-Line coach at the time, helped a lot. I went out to Wisconsin and visited. I always wanted to play in the Big Ten, anyway. I always knew if you wanted to be an O-lineman, play in the Big Ten. I always had respect for the conference, I loved the kind of football that the Big Ten plays. So I went out on a visit and really fell in love with Madison. I felt Madison was a place I could easily live for five years. I think that was a big thing in my decision. I wanted somewhere I could be comfortable living along with having a great football program and being a great school. I think those were the top three things I wanted in a school. I really loved Madison and I liked Coach Bielema and what I knew of the coaching staff that he had. So it really was an easy decision. I committed two days after I left the official visit.

I did a lot of growing up at Wisconsin. Maybe not even right off the bat when I got there, but I have patience with playing and I can let things develop, so I was fine. I knew redshirting would be the smart thing, so I redshirted and just developed and tried to become better on the field with that. Maturity-wise, between my junior year and senior year is probably when I grew the most, just taking care of my responsibilities and things like that. I think that's something that was forced upon me with the responsibility I was given with being a team leader. Right off the bat, redshirt year was a lot of fun. We had a great team with guys like Joe Thomas around. We were 12–1, and things were really good. I started playing the next year, halfway through the season. My first start was at Indiana, then I basically played ever since. I dealt with injuries at certain times—I pretty much experienced the whole college football deal with injuries and losing and winning. I faced team issues and my own personal off-the-field issues like academics and being a captain, which is really a great honor. So I feel like I ran the whole gamut being a student-athlete at the university.

I'll always remember the Ohio State and Iowa back-to-back wins our senior year. Ohio State was special because we had never beaten them during my career, and I wanted to beat them before I got out of college. They were the No. 1 team. The stadium was the most electric I had ever seen Camp Randall in my five years there. It was just like a destiny game, it was meant to be that we were going to win, and I think everybody just knew it. So that was really special; I had never experienced anything like that. Then the following week going to Iowa and beating them with that last drive. I think those two games were the greatest experiences of my life on the football field, hands down.

Outside of the Xs and Os stuff, which is the preparation we put in—we all understood what it took to win and we all respected winning and how much goes into winning at the Big Ten level. I think everybody understood that. But outside of that, everybody genuinely cared about each other on our team my senior year, mostly senior year—I noticed it a little bit junior year. We were all brothers and all loved each other and were happy to be in each other's company. I still step back and look around at guys and see how well we knew each other on the team and how well we bonded. I've been on teams where it wasn't like that and we weren't successful; that makes a difference.

242

Coach Bielema really does a good job of knowing his team, knowing the morale of the team, and adjusting things to help with that when he feels it's needed. If we're not very motivated or we're kind of worn down, I think he always has his ear to the ground with that, then adjusts it to give us that breath of fresh air. As a head coach, I think that's a key thing, knowing your team. I think he definitely knew us.

I don't know if I've ever enjoyed playing with a guy as much as Gabe Carimi. We have a lot of history; I've never played with anybody as long as I played with Gabe. It was a total of four years, and I was next to him on the line for three of those years. We knew each other so well and communicated very well with each other. It was just a very smooth thing that we came to develop, which made it easier and made us successful. And on top of that, the rest of the offensive line guys were just such hard-working, selfless guys and really good guys and guys you could call for anything. They'd be there in a second. That's just the kind of character guys that we had, and it's not even just because we went through a lot together, which we did, it's just because they were a group of really good guys.

Some of the best times of my life—or *the* best times of my life—were the five years I spent at Wisconsin. There's nothing like playing on a team at that level. Obviously the next level, the NFL, is something else, but I don't think they have that same kind of brotherhood and bond that you have in college. It's not about money in college, it's about playing for the love of the game. And just having the opportunity to play on that stage—in Camp Randall in front of 80,000 people, and then after the game, meeting people from Wisconsin and meeting great fans and people who really love us and respect us and it's mutual—is terrific. And then doing the academic side, going to a major university gives you a great advantage. I think on all levels it was a really great experience, not only playing on Saturdays but also doing the college thing and meeting all kinds of new people who have really affected my life in a great way.

I try to embody what is preached at the University of Wisconsin, or what was preached on our football team, and I think it means I try to be someone who is hard-working, who is blue-collar, not the flashiest, but understands what it takes and does what it takes to be successful, with a lot of work and preparation. And then on top of that, the Wisconsin side of people—what I've seen of people from Wisconsin, just humble, caring, great people. If you blend that together, that's what it means to be a Badger.

John Moffitt, who started 42 games during his UW career, was a key element in Wisconsin's outstanding offensive line as the Badgers won the 2010 Big Ten title. He was a two-time, first-team All–Big Ten choice and a first-team All-American as a senior. Moffitt was selected in the third round of the 2011 NFL Draft by the Seattle Seahawks.

SCOTT TOLZIEN

QUARTERBACK

2007–2010

I WAS SIX YEARS OLD WHEN I STARTED to play football, and that was tackle. I was playing against guys who were three years older than me because I was on my older brother's team, so I was basically the runt. I played the whole season just scared all the time—the difference between six years old and nine years old is incredible. Then, the year after that, my dad began coaching, and I was No. 61, our right guard on offense. After that, in baseball my dad was always telling me I had to extend my arm when I threw; I had this shortened delivery. I'd just basically take the ball from my ear and fire it. He finally said that that was a pretty good quarterback motion. So my third year in football I started playing quarterback and have been playing quarterback ever since.

We didn't have JV at my high school. It's freshman, then sophomore, then varsity. So freshman year I played freshman, and sophomore year I played sophomore, and then junior year and senior year I was fortunate enough to be the starting quarterback. The one thing that was nice is I've seen a lot of high school games now, and I was lucky that we actually threw the ball quite a bit my freshman and sophomore years. I think that helped prepare me well. It wasn't just one of those fake to dive, dump it five yards, and then you do that five times a game and that was your passing game. It was actually a fairly complex passing game and was a lot of fun—it made me really love football that much more. My junior year, I distinctly remember the second start of my career I threw seven interceptions in a game. It was my birthday, and my dad was out of town, and he'd been to every game since I was seven years old, and I threw seven picks. That was probably, knock on wood, the low point of my entire football career. It was one of those learning experiences and, looking back, I wouldn't have it any other way. The summer after my junior year is when the recruiting picked up. My only offers at that point—everyone was late—were from Northern Illinois, Western Michigan, and Toledo. I got a late offer from Kentucky midway through my senior season. Then I took some visits. The day after I came back from Kentucky, they signed their second quarterback, so they were out of the picture. Western Michigan signed a quarterback, they were out of the picture. Toledo signed a quarterback two days after I got back from their visit, so I basically lost all my offers. I had one from Northern Illinois. I told the coaches all along that I wasn't going to make my decision until after my senior season, that I was going to focus on that and focus on my teammates and that whole journey I've been on with those guys. Then about two weeks before signing day, Wisconsin offered me a scholarship, so I took it.

I was recruited by Coach [Paul] Chryst—they were fair with me, they said there were other quarterbacks they were looking at. That's how recruiting is—it's a big draft board, and they have their favorites. As time went on, those guys committed to other schools, and I started to, I guess, move up the board, and two weeks before signing day I got the call and committed on the spot.

245

I think everyone talks about the speed of the game—that was the biggest adjustment for me coming to Wisconsin. It was a huge adjustment. Then people will say the playbook is not a high school playbook and rightfully so; the playbook's intense. So that's a process in itself. The one thing in my case that stuck out is I wasn't able to reach my potential as a player until I had full confidence in myself and full confidence in the guys around me. I nailed this playbook; I learned it like that. I spent a lot of time, worked my tail off to learn it, but that wasn't enough. I think it was because I didn't have the confidence in myself at that point. I was still doubting myself and, when I'd make a bad play, it would bug me and it would affect my next play. Like they say, at quarterback, you have to have a short memory, but I didn't. It wasn't until I finally had that complete confidence in myself that I was able to say, *I can do this.*

I guess I didn't put it all together until fall camp before my junior season. Dustin Sherer was set to come back as the senior quarterback. The spring game came around, and I took one series with two minutes to go with the

Scott Tolzien set the school pass completion percentage record (.681) in 2010. He ranks fourth in career passing yards at Wisconsin, with 5,271.

No. 1 offense; I was No. 3 on the depth chart finishing spring ball going into my junior year. I'd shown glimpses but the coaches were looking for the most consistent guy, and I wasn't consistent. And I knew at that point I had spring ball and the summer and fall camps to win the job. Otherwise, Curt Phillips was going to be there, and they were going to go with him over me—that's just the way it was and the way it should be. If two guys are even, you go with the younger guy because he has the time window. So it was that summer when I knew that was it. I had to get better and there was no one to blame but myself. I had to be accountable to myself and I said, *Hey, you have to find a way to play better, no matter what it is, you've got to find it from within and put it together.* Because fall camp is typically three weeks long, I knew I had two weeks to try to separate myself. It was going to be make or break.

I had so many great players around me, and that made it that much easier. You look around the country, and there's so many quarterbacks that I think very highly of, and I think they just have so much talent, but yet they don't have the pieces around them to really showcase their talents. I think it's probably the other way around with me. I was nothing special, I'm not flashy, but all these guys around me made me look good because they're making the plays. That made it that much easier for me. What I'll remember is the camaraderie with them. There's something to be said for putting together a list of goals, and a hundred-something guys working toward the same goals. The thing that I think gets lost for the outsiders is just how much time is really put into this. There are so many hours where you're grinding, you're up at 5:00 AM working out or running. Guys are throwing up in workouts before the sun's even up. Film sessions are just long, long, long. What you appreciate is when you put in all that work, you all have the same vision. It's not just talk, you're actually doing that. And to be able to reach a goal like going to the Rose Bowl, it means something. There are times in life where you feel like you got the short end of things, but there are also times where you realize all the work is worth it.

We've been lucky. In 2009 against Miami, it was special because I don't think anyone picked us to win that game, and we did. In 2010, the first one obviously that comes to mind is the No. 1 team comes to town, ESPN's *College GameDay* is in town, Camp Randall is just electric, and David Gilreath takes that opening kickoff back. I've never been in a stadium louder than that in my life. That was special. Then, a week later, Iowa. That's arguably the toughest place to play in the Big Ten, the crowd's right on top of you. Their

247

program is a mirror image of ours, and to be able to come back like that was special. I know we were down and had some key plays down the stretch, but to do it—there's something gratifying about it. There's 70,000 in Kinnick—everyone decked out in the yellow—and there's basically 70 of us and our parents. You feel it's you against the world, so it's really gratifying to come out with a win on that. Then to beat Northwestern to clinch the Big Ten title; there's only a handful of teams that can say they did that.

My relationship with Coach Chryst was very tight. I spent hours and hours and hours with him. You see why he gets all the accolades and the positive talk. When people talk about Coach Chryst, it's nothing but positives, and I was able to live that, fortunately, and he really is the same guy throughout, from start to finish. I loved him just as much when I was third-string, thinking I'd never play as I did when I became the starting quarterback. He treated me the exact same way, which is as a competitor. But he also believes there's more important things than football. He helped me put things into perspective. You go on the road to Iowa or Ohio State and just see him before a game, he's laughing and he's loose because he knows how much preparation he put in that week. The other thing is just that he's not a talker, he's a doer. He doesn't preach about all the good things. There's so many different things that he's done behind the scenes that no one ever realizes, and that's just the way he wants it. I think that's a special quality in someone. You don't want any of the attention, you just do it and you do it because that's who you are and that's what you stand for. I really appreciate what he did for me in my five years. Other than my immediate family, he's probably the most influential person in my life, and I say that with the utmost respect and humility.

Coach Bielema—the thing that everyone talks about is he relates well to his players because of his age, and I agree with that. The other thing is, everyone says people make a place, and he has brought good people into the program from top to bottom. Whether it's assistant coaches, medical staff, or just players. He's done an awesome job in creating this family environment by bringing good people to Wisconsin.

When I was a youngster, I was a wide-eyed kid who viewed athletes with awe. I remember going to a high school football game and being the ball boy, and when the quarterback walked by, I'd just think, *Wow!* That was just me as a kid. So having that platform was awesome, where you could be the guy who makes it a big deal for someone else. Obviously, my parents raised me the right way, and I give thanks to them. It was just fun to have been given a platform like that.

I think knowing who I am and knowing what I've heard from other players, what I'll miss most is the competition. Whether it's playing in front of 80,000 in Camp Randall or playing on the road in the Big Ten or even just a Tuesday practice and a two-minute drill where the defense is the enemy, that's what I'll miss the most. Whether I go into coaching or the business world, there's always that competitive aspect where you're trying to beat the competition. To be actually physically on the field as a player, I think I'll miss that. What I thought the university was going to give me, it's given me tenfold, football-wise, academically, and socially. I remember when I came to Madison my first year, it was a struggle, and I was like, *Man, people say college is the best years of your life, but this ain't it; this isn't fun!* But as the years went by, I've loved it more and more. It was the best five years of my life so far. Hopefully, it gets better.

What does it mean to be a Badger football player? I'd say it means you're disciplined, you're doing the right things on and off the field. Then just as an alumnus, it means good people. People like to have a good time, obviously. Everyone thinks Wisconsin and they think beer, brats, and cheese. I've learned that that's the truth during my five years. People have a good time, and they are just hard-working, blue-collar people.

249

Scott Tolzien quarterbacked the Badgers to the 2010 Big Ten championship and an appearance in the 2011 Rose Bowl. Tolzien won the 2010 Johnny Unitas Golden Arm award after setting the school pass completion percentage record. Wisconsin was 21–5 during Tolzien's two seasons as the starting quarterback.

BRET BIELEMA
HEAD COACH
2006–Present

Ι GREW UP IN A FAMILY OF FIVE with two older brothers, and they both played football. When they started getting involved heavily in the sport, I remember watching them and getting a chance to play in the backyard. Ironically, one of the first competitive environments I was ever in was the punt, pass, and kick competition that was held in our hometown. I usually fared pretty well in the pass and the punt, but not so well in the kick; that might have been a sign of future things to come! But it was always a yearly thing that I looked forward to, and I trained for it. I'd go out in the front yard and do as much as I could to get better every year.

My first organized football experience was as a quarterback in seventh grade. My coach was, I believe, my fourth- or fifth-grade science teacher and the guy who is now teaching my godchild and my nephew back in my hometown. They signed us up for basically a day of camp where you were going to do every position and work every drill. Because I was bigger, they were going to put me on the line or at tight end, but I went out for a pass and they overthew me, so I ran after the ball and threw it back in like I knew how to do it. So they grabbed me and moved me to quarterback, and I did that my first couple years. They let me play defense a little bit, but not a lot. Then one game my freshman year there was a toss play to my right, so I tossed it, turned around, and airlifted the defensive end on the right side with a little cross-body block and got a personal foul. My coach started yelling at me and said,

"So you want to hit somebody?" I said "Yes!" He asked if I wanted to play defense. I said "Yes!" so they moved me to defense, and I started playing linebacker and quarterback. It stayed that way until my junior year, when we had a quarterback who was pretty good, so they switched me to tight end and middle linebacker.

My brothers both played and were very good players. My second-oldest brother, Barry, was involved in a car accident and had football taken away from him. It was something that made a huge impact on me because he was a very good player, a very good athlete, and it was taken away from him in the blink of an eye in a car accident. Luckily, he survived, keeping his life, but didn't get to keep football. That made a huge impact on me at a very young age—I was in eighth grade—about how fast something can be taken away from you. So I went into my high school years and had visions and dreams of playing at the varsity level my first year, but that didn't get accomplished. The interesting spin is that during the halftime of the varsity games I went and played in the band, so it was a full night of work for me. I eventually became a two-year starter beginning with my junior year. We were a pretty good football team. I played tight end and was the second-string quarterback, but my true love was middle linebacker. I had gone to camp at several high school camps, including one that led me ultimately to the University of Iowa, where they let me walk on. I had opportunities to go to Division III, Division II, and Division I-AA schools. One quote that my father gave me when I was trying to decide whether to go to a smaller school and play or go to a larger institution and walk on was, "It's better to play in excellence than excel in mediocrity." It wasn't a knock on all the other schools, but I'm so glad now that I chose to shoot high and dream big because I would never be where I am today.

My redshirt freshman year at Iowa, Coach [Hayden] Fry prepared us to play at Wisconsin by telling us, "They're going to yell at you and they're going to call you all kinds of names. They're going to throw pennies and marshmallows at you, and they're going to dump beer on you and walk away." And they didn't disappoint us! They did all those things, and we won that game. I distinctly remember my father had gone to the game and was sitting in the stands with Tom Kujawa—one of my college roommates, Paul Kujawa, was from Cudahy, Wisconsin—so they were very well entrenched with the histories and traditions of Wisconsin football. After the game was over, they usually came over and met us at the bus before we

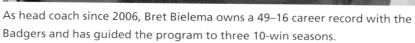

As head coach since 2006, Bret Bielema owns a 49–16 career record with the Badgers and has guided the program to three 10-win seasons.

left, and Tom grabbed my dad's arm and said, "Hey, sit down, we've got this thing called the Fifth Quarter." So my dad began to watch the Fifth Quarter. My dad asked Tom what Wisconsin fans did when they won a game, and Tom said they did the exact same thing, win or lose! I think that made a lasting impression on my dad.

When we came back to Madison in my junior year, Coach Alvarez was in Madison, and it was a nip-and-tuck ballgame. Wisconsin actually scored a touchdown, but it was called back—a penalty called on Joe Panos for holding me—and so, ironically, I've now come full circle; Joe's one of my closest friends here in Wisconsin, and we were very, very fortunate to win that game. I think that's when I began to realize how dominant a turnaround Coach Alvarez was beginning to make at Wisconsin. My next memorable stop at Wisconsin was as assistant coach at Iowa when Ron Dayne was on his way to the rushing title, the NCAA record, and the Heisman Trophy in the '99 season. I remember hearing the chant, "Ron Dayne!" in my head for the next three weeks after I left. I remember Kirk Ferentz, when we came into the office the day after the game and Wisconsin had handled us pretty well and they won a Big Ten championship and Ron had set the NCAA rushing record, said if we could capture what Wisconsin has in their stadium, we'll have a pretty good thing going forward. And now I get to live it on a daily basis.

253

I was a defensive coordinator at Kansas State; we were very, very good. We had been a top-five defense both years that I was there, and I actually had an opportunity to go to the Pac-10 as a co-coordinator and really a new opportunity that I was excited about. I really felt my time at Kansas State had come full circle, and I wanted to call my own shots and be my own defensive coordinator. When Coach Alvarez called me and asked if I had any interest in coming to Wisconsin as defensive coordinator to replace Kevin Cosgrove, I was very excited. In Coach Alvarez fashion, he met with me a few times, and we discussed Wisconsin. When I agreed to come for a visit, I told him I needed to go back home before I decided. I'll never forget at the end of the day I just thought I was going to be able to go back to Manhattan [Kansas] that night. Well, I walked into his office, and he had three reporters sitting there waiting to interview me about taking the new job as the defensive coordinator. He didn't give me a chance not to accept it, so I thought that was a pretty big statement by him. I'd told him I'd take the job, but I hadn't told my current boss at Kansas State, Bill Snyder. Back then, the speed of the

Internet was starting to spread like wildfire and, by the time I'd gotten out of the offices that day and got to my hotel, I already had a contact from Coach Snyder asking me what the deal was. It was a very, very strong move by Coach Alvarez that worked out very well.

I think the part that excited me about coming to Wisconsin was that Barry was the athletics director. I didn't have any grand dreams or aspirations of becoming a head coach at Wisconsin. I did, in the future, want to become a head coach, and I expressed that to him. He told me that, as an athletics director, he could help me get to that point. This was during my interview process to become the defensive coordinator. I was thinking more along the lines of helping me get a job somewhere else if I did a good job for him. I didn't really think he was in the mind-set of retiring. The season before he stepped down, he came to me and asked me if I could handle the job. He said he was going to step down and name me the head coach to be, and that it would give me the chance to observe things for a season. I think a lot of people have tried to copy what we've done here, the head coach–in–waiting thing, but no one did it like we did it. He did it in a way that I was tagged as a head coach and could evaluate everybody for a year, but I wasn't recruited under the plan to become the head coach. I didn't come in new; I had already been here a year, the people were familiar with me. I got to evaluate everybody and draw my own conclusions, not knowing I'd ever become the head coach. That's invaluable. I think when people try to hire guys now and plug them in and say, "You're going to be the guy in a year," everybody's on edge. So I think the way we did it was truly a blueprint for success.

First of all, I didn't know if he was joking or not. He was feeling me out, and I could tell very quickly that he was sincere about it. He named off two or three things that he'd witnessed during the time he'd known me that showed I could become this guy. He didn't want me to have success here and then go build a program somewhere else, he wanted to maintain here. That was a big statement to make to me. It was overwhelming. I think the bad part was I needed to keep it a secret for a very long time; I didn't tell anybody, not one person, not one soul, not one relative; that was a very difficult thing to keep to myself, but I'm glad I did because it allowed me to be true to what I believe in and really watch and observe every aspect of our program, and that was a very key point for me.

Two things make my job at Wisconsin special. First of all, it's the people I'm around on a daily basis—players and coaches. To be able to take a player

I meet when he's 17 years old and see him leave our program as a Big Ten champion means a lot to me, and that's a part of my job, that's very reward-ing. But then also all the effect you have on this community, this university, the state, I get so much positive feedback from people that we bring a special light to their life, and that's very rewarding for me. I think all coaches enjoy wins. I remember my first win in Cleveland against Bowling Green as much as I remember the win in 2010 against No. 1 Ohio State. They all have a spe-cial place in my mind. I think fans tend to remember the big ones more than the other ones, but as a coach you appreciate winning so much; you remem-ber all those other ones in a very special way. And I think that's what makes my job so rewarding.

I go back to my first experience in Camp Randall as a player when I real-ized how passionate the fans were in supporting their team. Obviously, things weren't going well back then. But now I've come full circle as the head coach at the University of Wisconsin, a school that represents all that's right in col-lege football. We don't have kids who have put themselves in a negative light; we have kids who have just won a Big Ten championship, but also had the highest grade-point average in the fall of any team ever to come through the University of Wisconsin. I think those two things together give an indica-tion of what kind of kids we have here. And then to be able to work daily with people in our athletic department, people in the university, people within our community, and the people of this state, and any UW alumni, it's just a great way to represent something that's really, really good.

255

I think what it means to be a Badger is you're living a dream. You're part of something that has been very successful in the past. As a head coach, you get to move that forward in your own way. You have to react to certain situ-ations on a daily basis that are really uncharted waters, and you have to rely on the faith of what you know and believe in and what you've seen have suc-cess here at Wisconsin and move forward. Ultimately, what it means to be a Badger is you've proven to a lot of people in this world that you know how to win, and you know how to win in the right way.

I think because of the way we transitioned in this program from Coach Alvarez to myself, and him becoming the A.D., I'm like nobody else in this profession. I was able to follow a man who had been so successful here, who wanted me to take the head coaching job but did not want to give me advice on how it needed to be run. He wanted it to be independent of the way he ran it because of the way I thought. He gives me great advice. A lot of times it's more community-media-alumni-related—not so much Xs and Os—but to have someone in the position he's in, overseeing what I have to do on a daily basis, is priceless. He's given me so many good examples and advice and helped guide things in a way that has resulted in us having success here.

Bret Bielema has been the head football coach at Wisconsin since 2006. A native of Prophetstown, Illinois, Bielema was named the 2006 Big Ten Coach of the Year after leading the Badgers to a 12–1 record in his first season. Bielema, who owns a 49–16 career record with the Badgers, has guided the program to three 10-win seasons, including an 11–2 mark in 2010 that included a Big Ten title and trip to the Rose Bowl.

NEY WILLIAMS · DALE HACKBART · DAN LANPHEAR · JIM

DEN   K · DAVE CROSSEN · DAVID

MEN   R · DON DAVEY · TROY VINCE

CIL MARTIN · MIKE SAMUEL · RON DAYNE · CHRIS MCI

LLINGER · LEE EVANS · ANTHONY DAVIS · DAN BUENNIN

YLOR MEHLHAFF · TRAVIS BECKUM · LANCE KENDRICKS ·

CKBART · DAN LANPHEAR · JIM BAKKEN · PAT RICHTER

REK · DAVE CROSSEN · DAVID GREENWOOD · MATT VAN

N DAVEY · TROY VINCENT · JOE PANOS · LAMARK SHAC

N DAYNE · CHRIS MCINTOSH · KEVIN STEMKE · JAMAR F

VIS · DAN BUENNING · JIM LEONHARD · BRANDON WILL

ANCE KENDRICKS · JOHN MOFFITT · SCOTT TOLZIEN · B

KKEN · PAT RICHTER · RON VANDER KELEN · STU VOIG

EENWOOD · MATT VANDENBOOM · DARRYL SIMS · AL TO

NOS · LAMARK SHACKERFORD · JOE RUDOLPH · TAREK S

VIN STEMKE · JAMAR FLETCHER · WENDELL BRYANT · BI

ONHARD · BRANDON WILLIAMS · JOHN STOCCO · JOE T

FFITT · SCOTT TOLZIEN · BRET BIELEMA · SIDNEY WILLIA

NDER KELEN · STU VOIGT · LARRY MIALIK · DENNIS LICK